THE
LOST
MAJORITY

THE
LOST
MAJORITY

WHY THE FUTURE OF GOVERNMENT
IS UP FOR GRABS—AND
WHO WILL TAKE IT

SEAN TRENDE

palgrave
macmillan

THE LOST MAJORITY
Copyright © Sean Trende, 2012.

All rights reserved.

First published in 2012 by
PALGRAVE MACMILLAN®
in the United States—a division of St. Martin's Press LLC,
175 Fifth Avenue, New York, NY 10010.

Where this book is distributed in the UK, Europe and the rest of the world,
this is by Palgrave Macmillan, a division of Macmillan Publishers Limited,
registered in England, company number 785998, of Houndmills,
Basingstoke, Hampshire RG21 6XS.

Palgrave Macmillan is the global academic imprint of the above companies
and has companies and representatives throughout the world.

Palgrave® and Macmillan® are registered trademarks in the United States,
the United Kingdom, Europe and other countries.

ISBN 978–0–230–11646–7

Library of Congress Cataloging-in-Publication Data

Trende, Sean.
    The lost majority : why the future of government is up for grabs—
and who will take it / Sean Trende.
        p. cm.
    Includes index.
    ISBN 978–0–230–11646–7
        1.Political parties—United States—History—20th century. 2.
Political parties—United States—History—21st century. 3. Two party
systems—United States. 4. United States—Politics and government—
20th century 5. United States—Politics and government—21st century.
    I. Title.

JK2261.T74 2011
324.0973—dc23   2011021698

A catalogue record of the book is available from the British Library.

Design by Newgen Imaging Systems (P) Ltd., Chennai, India.

First edition: January 2012

10 9 8 7 6 5 4 3 2 1

Printed in the United States of America.

To Emy. 1 Cor. 13:8-10

CONTENTS

ACKNOWLEDGMENTS

GETTING THIS BOOK TOGETHER in a relatively short period of time was a truly Herculean effort, one that would not have been possible without the contribution of more people than I could possibly ever list here. Nevertheless, I would like to give my thanks to:

Emily Carleton and Laura Lancaster, backed by their wonderful team at Palgrave Macmillan, for patiently working with me to make this book infinitely better than the first draft that I turned in;

Byrd Leavell, for patiently standing by this book in all its variants since I first suggested it to him years ago;

John McIntyre and Tom Bevan, my employers at RealClearPolitics, both for giving me the opportunity to work for them and tolerating my frequent absences while I completed my manuscript;

Jay Cost, for listening to my ideas and helping me flesh out the themes of the book;

The Honorable John Charles Thomas, for teaching me how to edit, and therefore how to write, and for believing in me when few others did;

Dave Leip, for creating a truly outstanding database of election results, available at www.uselectionatlas.org;

Dr. John Aldrich, for dedicating far more time than he needed to in order to serve as the thesis advisor to a young J.D./M.A. student, and for successfully predicting that my innate geekiness would draw me back into the world of political science sooner or later;

The staff at the University of Richmond library, especially Laura Horne-Popp, for patiently taking a researcher who foolishly asked, on his first day of research, where the periodicals were kept and teaching him the wonders of the college's online databases;

Kevin Driscoll and Melissa Davis, for reviewing early versions of the draft and providing useful commentary;

Tucker, for urging me to do the right thing in my life in October 2009;

A horde of teachers, coaches, and professors, far too numerous to list here, but whom it would be a crime not to at least mention;

My mother, father, and sister, the shoulders on which I stand;

My son Judd, who inspires me in ways I can't describe here without risking shorting out my computer keyboard;

My son Will, who was born two weeks before I started work on this book, and who thankfully won't be able to remember the hours spent in a "Baby Bjorn" while I typed away. . . . I promise you slept for most of them;

And finally my wife, who stood by me and loved me even when I was cranky, lost in my thoughts, engrossed with a book on party coalitions in the 1910s, or just generally being a pain to live with. Which, I'm ashamed to say, was most of the time while I was working on this project. I love you more than words can possibly say, and I'll always work to guard your dreams and visions.

INTRODUCTION

ON NOVEMBER 4, 2008, Barack Obama strode across a brightly lit stage in Grant Park, Chicago, turned to a massive, multiracial crowd, and delivered his first speech as president-elect. It was an eloquent call to America to unite, to "bend the arc of history," and to move forward together on an ambitious agenda. Few who saw that crowd and followed the election returns that night would have believed that this agenda could end up in critical condition less than a year later. Except, perhaps, someone who studied the fragile forces that set Obama's path toward that stage, decades before the president was ever born.

To many, Obama's coalition seemed invincible—a solid wall of minorities, liberals, youths, independents, and more than a few Republicans. They had converged to give Obama 53 percent of the vote, the largest share of the popular vote received by any Democrat since Lyndon Baines Johnson in 1964. The Democrats won over 250 seats in the House, and it looked like they would fall just short of a filibuster-proof Senate majority.

The win awed pundits, who declared that Republicans were being reduced to regional party status, and that an extended period of Democratic dominance was forthcoming.[1] Susan Page of *USA Today* characterized it as a "decisive" victory that "reshaped the electoral map that has defined American politics for a generation."[2] The *New Republic*'s John Judis celebrated the vindication of the "emerging Democratic majority" theory that he and Ruy Teixeira had pioneered in their 2002 book of the same name. Some Democrats talked of a "permanent progressive majority" and the "end of the conservative era" that had begun in 1980.[3] Michael Lind of *Salon* even went so far as to declare the wholesale rebirth of the nation and the dawn of what he termed a "Fourth American Republic," where the debates over the New Deal and Great Society would fade away and Barack Obama, like George Washington, Abraham Lincoln, and Franklin Roosevelt before him, would oversee the beginning of a new era of progress.[4]

Needless to say, liberal Democrats didn't expect a return to the gradualism that characterized the Clinton presidency and that they had come to loathe. Obama had promised to "fundamentally transform America" and had assured reporters that he "actually believe[d] my own bullsh*t" about remaking the country during his presidency.[5] The left urged him to follow through. Harold Meyerson exhorted the president-elect to "Bring on the New New Deal," while Paul Krugman said it all with the title of his postelection column: "Franklin Delano Obama?"[6] Some even speculated (or hoped) that the Republicans were facing a Whig-like extinction.[7] Conservatives did little to counteract the fanfare, meekly urging the president to chart the moderate course at which his campaign had sometimes hinted.

But two years later, Obama's majority appeared to be in shambles. The Democrats lost more House seats than either party had lost in a midterm election in 72 years. The net shift in the percentage of total votes cast for congressional candidates from 2008 to 2010 was 18.2 points in the Republicans' favor. Another point, and congressional Republicans would have achieved the largest improvement for a party over the course of a single election cycle in history, edging out the Democrats' 19-point gain from 1930 to 1932. Republicans picked up six Senate seats, added six governors to their ranks, and flipped an astounding seven hundred state legislative seats, giving them their largest share of the state legislatures since 1928. Obama's "New New Deal" coalition had lasted less than two years.

■ ■ ■

The United States has been through six freakish elections in a row. In 2000, we endured the extended Florida recount. In 2002, Republicans shocked the political establishment—which had predicted big Democratic gains as late as August—by gaining House seats. In 2004, America elected a Republican president in a high-turnout election—something many thought was impossible—leading some to claim that Democrats had become a regional party and that a Republican majority was forthcoming.[8] Democrats dashed these Republican dreams in 2006 and 2008 by seizing Congress and the presidency. Two years later, Republicans came roaring back. It is the most difficult political landscape to try to make sense of in decades.

This book aims to provide a sense of order to our current politics, by fundamentally reevaluating the way that political majorities are made. It makes three interrelated claims. First, that the 2010 midterm elections were a result of Barack Obama and the Democrats misreading both their mandate and how they had been brought to power, imagining a realignment in 2008 when, in fact, none had occurred. Second, that the emerging partisan majorities described by theorists from both parties are mirages. Third, that the entire concept of realignments/permanent alignments, which underlies much of the misbegotten analysis of the 2008 elections, is bankrupt and should be abandoned.

The first claim is explored largely in parts I and II. Here, the book explores the sudden demise of Obama's seemingly impregnable coalition. Too much analysis has focused on short-term explanations for the downfall such as the economy, the health-care bill, and the tea parties. These explanations dodge the more fundamental question: If Obama had really assembled an FDR-like coalition on the basis of a campaign promise for an aggressive, activist government, why was he unable to overcome these forces, especially the latter two? Analysts have struggled to answer this question because they fail to question their ingrained assumptions about how Obama's political coalition came to be in the first place. Press hype aside, Obama's winning coalition was not something that sprung Athena-like from David Axelrod's brow. Rather, it was a descendant of Bill Clinton's successful coalition, a coalition premised on moderate progressivism and fiscal rectitude. Obama's failure to continue that centrist tradition, combined with some bad luck, brought about the Democrats' defeat.

But the problems with the dominant narrative go deeper than a failure to understand the nature of Obama's majority. When discussing Obama's win in 2008, analysts frequently threw about the terms "Reagan majority" or "New Deal coalition" in ways that evinced a very shallow understanding of how those coalitions came about and how they ended. In order to give a proper context for the politics of the last decade, the book therefore begins by urging us to unlearn much of our understanding of the politics of the last hundred years. Part I begins by exploring the early seeds of the New Deal coalition, which were sown in 1920. In that year, Republicans brought together an incredibly broad winning coalition. But as we'll see again and again in this book, these "coalitions of everyone" that form from time to time are unstable and tend to break down quickly. Over the course of the 1920s, various components of that Republican coalition became dissatisfied with the GOP and flirted with the Party of Jackson. FDR emerged as the one politician, possibly in all of America, who could fully take advantage of the missteps made by Republicans throughout the 1920s and create a broad coalition based upon these disenchanted Republican groups.

Far from creating an enduring, dominant coalition, however, FDR's choices sparked the exit of the South, the oldest component of the Democratic Party, beginning in the mid-1930s and continuing throughout the mid- to late twentieth century. Other actions by Roosevelt and his successors alienated the white working class and the West. In other words, the Roosevelt coalition did not dominate American politics into the 1960s, as many claim. It ceased functioning in 1938 and fell apart during the 1940s. America entered a period of unsettled politics, with congressional majorities swinging wildly and with both parties capable of winning the White House.

The Reagan coalition *did* arise from the ashes of the New Deal coalition, but it formed much earlier than most realize. It was the election of Dwight Eisenhower in 1952 that helped stabilize the unsettled politics that arose in the wake of the New Deal's demise, creating a coalition that was probably the most successful in American history. From 1952 through 1988, the Eisenhower coalition lost only three presidential elections, two by the narrowest of margins. While Democrats held Congress for most of this time, Republicans effectively controlled that body through a coalition with Southern Democrats. As the Democrats continued their leftward shift, and as the country chafed under a prolonged existential threat from the Soviet Union, the Eisenhower coalition enjoyed an extended lifespan unequalled in American history.

In other words, the "Reagan coalition" is better understood as the "Eisenhower coalition," and Reagan's presidency marked the end of a period of Republican dominance, not the beginning. The Republican Party's rightward shift came just as the issues that had perpetuated the Eisenhower coalition were losing salience and at the same time that Bill Clinton was pulling the Democratic Party back toward the center. These dual shifts formed the basis for a new coalition, which was actually beginning to form in the Reagan years. The "Clinton coalition" took the existing Democratic base of minorities, liberals, and the remaining Southern Democrats, reestablished the Democratic Party's connection to working-class Americans, and pulled suburbanites loose from their Republican moorings. After a rocky start that gave Republicans complete control of Congress for the first time in 40 years, Clinton righted the ship. By emphasizing minimalist programs like school uniforms and health-insurance portability, he became an avatar of gradualism against the onslaught of increasingly radicalized Republicans. In a sense, he fractured the Eisenhower coalition precisely because he governed like an Eisenhower Republican and because the Republican Party seemed determined to reject its moderate past as vigorously as possible.

We end part I with Bill Clinton having bequeathed to his successors a Democratic Party rebranded as the party of balanced budgets and fiscal rectitude. In part II we explore the swift breakdown of this coalition and the onset of our increasingly unstable politics. Clinton's efforts to rebrand the party set the stage for the Democratic takeover of Congress in 2006, as well as the election of Barack Obama. This point is critical: Barack Obama's coalition was not novel. It wasn't even that broad. It was a *narrower* version of Clinton's. Obama's election saw the final collapse of Democratic voting strength among Democrats in Appalachia and in those states settled by Appalachian Scots-Irish, areas that had been voting Democratic since Andrew Jackson. He was the first Democrat since Lewis Cass in 1848 not to carry Floyd County, Kentucky, and the first *ever* to lose Knott County. For perspective, in 1996 Clinton carried Floyd County by 45 points and Knott County by 55 points. Even George McGovern carried these counties by double digits.

Of course, there was a positive side to the 2008 ledger as well. Obama ran stronger among liberals, the young, minorities, and suburbanites than did Clinton, and he brought more of these individuals out to vote. As a result, while Obama lost ground by building a coalition that was narrower than Clinton's, he made up for this narrowing by creating a coalition that went much deeper among certain demographics. This had two great implications for 2010. First, with fewer groups in his coalition, Obama had little room for error. If suburbanites or the white working class tired of him—and the latter group was brought fully on board only after a horrifying economic collapse that occurred shortly before the election—the party would be in deep trouble. Second, the narrower Democratic coalition was problematic in the context of congressional politics, where parties need to appeal to a wide geographic swath of voters in a variety of districts in order to win. Almost two dozen Democrats held onto seats that were located in "Greater Appalachia" (which we'll describe more fully below), where loyalty to the national Democratic Party had only recently begun to break down. If this breakdown began to extend downticket, the Republicans would be well on their way to big gains in Congress. Moreover, if some other portion of the narrowed coalition moved toward the exit door, the Republican gains would be historic.

This failure to appreciate the true nature of the FDR, Reagan, and Obama coalitions had real-world consequences. Pundits and the president-elect should have focused on how tenuous all three majorities were and, most important, how dependent on unique historical circumstances they were. Instead, the pundits imagined the first two presidents creating new, long-lasting majorities by force of personality and urged President Obama to do the same. The end of part II describes the Obama administration's attempt to construct a new majority by pushing for an activist, aggressive federal government, embracing deficit spending to combat the economic downturn, while suffering from a slow recovery. It shows how the result of this effort was to tarnish the Democratic brand that Bill Clinton had built, resulting in heavy losses in congressional districts where Bill Clinton had either stanched Democratic bleeding or outright swung the area toward the Democrats.

This historical narrative provides a launching pad for the broader claims, which are explored in part III. *The Lost Majority* is intended as a corrective to those analysts who believe that Democratic or Republican dominance is about to be written into the demographic stars. In 2000 and 2004, both Republicans and Democrats popularized variants of this "permanent majority" idea. Karl Rove famously attempted to construct a durable Republican coalition, comparable to the Republican coalition that (supposedly) dominated from 1896 through 1932. Some thought it had arrived in 2004, as authors like John Micklethwait and Adrian Wooldridge argued that 2004 represented an important step in the development of a Republican majority in America.[9] This belief in a permanent Republican majority drove the choices made by the Bush Republicans in the mid-2000s. But the permanent majority was not forthcoming, and these choices resulted instead in a transfer of power to the Democrats.

At the same time, Democrats argued that *they* were set to become the dominant party. John Judis and Ruy Teixeira's seminal work, *The Emerging Democratic Majority*, first made the case for durable Democratic dominance in 2002. After the Democratic victories in 2006 and 2008, this narrative was perpetuated and broadened in scores of papers and journal articles. It became an article of faith among many Democratic strategists that this theory, or one of its variants, represented the future of American politics. Republicans now respond to this argument by pointing out that they have won three of the five elections since *The Emerging Democratic Majority* was published. Democrats retort that Republican wins have been the result of fluke-ish environmental factors, such as the response to 9/11 and the poor economy. But Republicans could say the same of the 2006 and 2008 elections. So which elections represent the future of American politics: the ones in which the Republicans enjoyed the big wins, or the ones in which the Democrats came out on top?

The answer is, "both." Most modern pundits' understandings of politics were shaped during a time of Republican dominance of presidential elections and Democratic dominance of Congress. Those who took political science classes had this view reinforced when their professors taught them that American politics are driven by periodic "realignments," in which one party becomes the dominant "sun," while the other becomes the pale "moon." In other words, we're conditioned by experience and education to look for dominant parties. But the experience of growing up in the 1952-to-1988 era was an anomalous one. Party coalitions typically have relatively short lifespans, more like the Roosevelt and Clinton coalitions. So the type of instability we've witnessed recently is really the rule in American politics, whereas extended dominance of either the presidency or the House is the exception.

In other words, the idea that the Republican or Democratic Party is heading for permanent minority status is as absurd as the idea that the Democrats were heading for electoral extinction in the early 1990s, or that the Republicans were doomed in the 1960s, or that the Democrats would disappear in the 1890s. In fact, virtually every election gives rise to some analysis of why the football game is now over and how the losing team should simply pack up its bags and go home. To drive this point home fully, we'll begin each chapter with a quote from some unfortunate prognosticator forecasting electoral doom that never occurs. For the political game is never over; there is always another major election two years away, and if the American people are unhappy with the course of the previous two years, they will give the other side a shot.

For now, let's just put it this way: If the Republicans were able to win the popular vote for Congress six years after the 1936 debacle, and if Democrats were able to win the popular vote for the presidency four years after failing to field their own candidate in 1872, we can safely assume that we will be hearing plenty from both parties over the course of the next few decades. Because we tend to hear more about an incipient "Democratic majority" today than a dominant Republican majority, and because the recent collapse of President Obama's coalition was so spectacular, we'll focus on that party. But just to be clear: *neither* party is heading for extinction or "rump" status in the near future. Instead, we're at a time of near parity between the parties, when either party can enjoy a win, only to see it slip away quickly. During such times we can't really call a win for either party an outlier.

At their core, the "emerging Democratic majority" and "emerging Republican majority" arguments share two basic flaws. First, they rely far too heavily on linear projections of demographic and political trends and therefore underestimate the delicacy of any emerging coalition. As noted above, Judis and Teixeira were absolutely correct to dismiss those who wrote off 1992 and 1996 as outlying elections. They trenchantly observed that a new Democratic coalition was emerging in 1992 and gaining strength in the late 1990s. The problem with the broader thesis, especially as fleshed out further by subsequent analysts, is that it assumed that we could project what politics would look like 30 years out based upon such a brief window.

In other words, emerging Democratic-majority theorists tend to look at the competitive Democratic coalition, note that the Latino vote is growing, and conclude that the Democratic coalition is therefore set to grow. The obvious problem is that this does not take into account the potential Republican response to that coalition and the internal frictions that these changes will bring about within the Democratic Party. For example, Latinos do typically vote heavily Democratic, and they are a fast-growing share of the population. But what if that changes? In fact, Latinos have gradually trended toward the Republicans over the past several decades, and there is substantial evidence that as these voters move out of heavily Latino areas and become more integrated into Anglo culture, they vote more like non-Hispanic whites. Moreover, what if the Democrats' increased reliance on Latino votes forces them to take positions on issues, such as immigration, that will push moderate white voters out of the coalition? In states like Arizona, this is part of what occurred in 2010.

As we go through these arguments in part III, just remember that a political commentator in 1924 could be absolutely sure of three things: African Americans would never join up with a party that had just deadlocked its convention over whether to condemn the Ku Klux Klan, the Democrats would always have a base in the "Solid South," and the party was absolutely doomed because New York alone gave Republicans one-third of the electoral votes of the entire combined South. Yet within ten years African Americans would give 70 percent of their vote to a Democratic nominee who would not even back an anti-lynching bill. Within 30 years, the Solid South would be irreversibly split. Within 50 years the South would have some of the fastest-growing states in the nation, with two states preparing to surpass New York's population. Not all linear projections will meet with such fates, but most will. In the medium to long term, demographic trends are simply too unpredictable to serve as the basis for accurate projections.

The second flaw in "permanent majority" theories is that they tend to assume that parties will behave in ways that please all the factions in their coalitions. But "coalitions of everyone" have always proved unstable in the past, and we should expect that they will be unstable in the future. In a diverse country, you cannot appeal to everyone over an extended period of time. As an example, Judis and Teixeira's emerging-Democratic-majority theory was written in the immediate aftermath of the Clinton presidency and was expressly dependent— although many chose to overlook this—on the Democrats remaining only a moderately progressive party. Few seemed to question what moving away from this "progressive centrism" would mean for this coalition.

The answer was embedded in a careful examination of the 2008 returns. Democrats who celebrated electing arguably the most liberal president in American history in 2008 frequently overlooked that Barack Obama was running amid two unpopular wars, a nasty recession, and a full-blown financial panic that was consuming 401(k)s and housing equity—not to mention that his opponent was a disorganized, gaffe-prone candidate. In a year when political science models suggested double-digit Democratic wins, and when every conceivable intangible suggested that the Democratic wins should be on the high side of those models' error margins, Obama won by only seven points and was actually trailing in the polls after the convention season closed. As the Democratic Party enjoyed more success, its elites had pulled it leftward, and in doing so had exposed their right flank. The leftward shift didn't exact immediately obvious costs in 2008, but the price was steep in 2010.

This leads to the book's third major claim: analysts who have looked for realignments over the past decade have been consistently disappointed because they are searching for a chimera. Realignments simply do not exist, at least in any meaningful sense of the term. This is examined toward the end of part III. The term "party realignment" dates back at least to the 1930s, but it was brought into mainstream political science literature in the 1950s with the work of famed political scientist V. O. Key. It was greatly expanded in the 1960s, most notably by Walter Dean Burnham. The theory has since been tested, reexamined, and revised, but the basic assertion, examined in the first few weeks of almost any American politics class offered at a university, is that American politics experience a major political shift, or realignment, every 32 to 36 years.[10] In 1800, the Democratic-Republicans supplanted the Federalists. In 1832, the Jacksonian Democrats rose to power. A period of moderate Republican strength began in 1860 and lasted until 1896, when McKinley Republicans became dominant. In 1932, the New Deal Democrats came to power. And in 1968, the country began shifting toward the Republicans.

Permanent-majority theorists on both sides almost universally work within this framework, which suggests that a realignment is now overdue. The problem is that realignment theory has not aged well. Yale professor David Mayhew has argued, devastatingly, that 50 years after entering mainstream political science discussion, it is time for it to exit. Almost none of the theories propounded by realignment theorists has endured the test of time; instead, after decades of both quantitative and qualitative analyses, we are left with nothing more than a series of ad hoc judgments about "critical," "maintaining," and "deviating" elections.[11]

It turns out that finding a "realigning" election is a lot like finding an image of Jesus in a grilled-cheese sandwich—if you stare long enough and hard enough, you will eventually find what you are looking for. People looking for 32-year cycles cram 1896 into the "critical" definition, even though the 1908 election looks a lot like the 1888 election. The election of 1920 is apparently not considered "critical," even though it marks the ascendancy of the conservative wing of the Republican Party, and the Republican Party was able to win at least one state from the Old Confederacy in two of the three elections from 1920 to 1928. The election of 1952 has many of the hallmarks of a realignment, but it does not fit neatly into the 32-year cycle, so it is considered "deviating."

This is not to say that American politics are either random or static. Even if you do not accept that American politics run in 32-year cycles, it is impossible to argue that American politics in 1936 were not fundamentally different from those in 1924. But it does not require an embrace of historicism to explain these shifts. Instead electoral history is best understood as being filled with forks in the road.

Sometimes the parties and its leaders choose wisely, and sometimes we are left wondering what might have been.

In 1916, Woodrow Wilson had a coalition that looked like it might breathe life back into a moribund Democratic Party, but he chose poorly in his method and style of governance, and the coalition quickly fell apart. In 1932, Democrats had a choice between John Garner, who favored a national sales tax (a deflationary policy that would have had disastrous consequences if enacted in the midst of a severe recessionary period); Al Smith, a Catholic who might not have been able to carry the South, even in 1932; and Franklin Roosevelt. Obviously, they chose wisely, and FDR was able to put together a successful coalition, although it did not last as long as many believe. But the reason for the Democrats' success in 1932 wasn't that we were 36 years beyond the last "realignment," nor was the reason for their failure in 1920 because only 24 years had passed. They made good choices and had good luck in 1932, while the Republicans made poor choices, both in the years leading up to 1932 and during Hoover's presidency. The opposite was true in the 1920 elections. This made the difference.

Taken together, these claims form the overarching thesis of the book. "The" lost majority isn't just "Obama's" majority, or the "Nancy Pelosi" majority, or George W. Bush's "William McKinley Part Deux" majority. When we clear out the muck dredged up by realignment theorists and reexamine electoral history in a fresh light, we see scores of "lost majorities" littering the electoral landscape. Some flourished, while others never made it past the embryonic stage. The truth is that voter coalitions in a broad, diverse country are inherently fragile. Issues that cause disparate groups to band together tend to fade quickly, while new issues arise that can put these groups at loggerheads. The other party is usually more than willing to work to appease the losing side in these new battles. Parties tend to overinterpret their mandate and overreach. And above all else, wars, recessions, domestic unrest, and other contingencies will inevitably intrude, throwing coalitions into disarray, shifting loyalties, and making long-term forecasts about the future impossible. At a time when both parties have been pushed toward their extremes, it is very difficult to lay claim to the center, and violent shifts in elections, like those we've seen over the past decade, become the norm.

But before we really dig into this argument, there are a few background matters that demand some attention.

"THE SOUTH" (AND ITS VARIANTS)

Some question whether "the South" exists in any meaningful sense today. In one sense, it is inarguable that the poor, uneducated, agricultural South of the early 1900s has been fundamentally remade; this economic transformation plays a crucial role in the transformation of that region from Democratic bastion to Republican stronghold. Today, even rural Southern counties tend to have paved roads, electricity, a crop base other than cotton, and schools that are in session more than four months out of the year. None of this was true one hundred years ago. Southern cities now sport suburbs crammed with gated communities and food chains that are indistinguishable from those in the North. Even the difference between Northern and Southern accents is not as severe as it was only a few decades ago.

But this book also shares the assessment of historians like William E. Leuchtenburg that "place" is still important in understanding this country's politics. The accoutrements of "Northern-ness" described above have been laid over a landscape and culture that are still distinctively "Southern," if only in diluted form. Entire books could be written about this.[12] For now I'll just observe that when I departed from Oklahoma (admittedly a borderline Southern state) to Connecticut for college in 1991, I was honestly shocked to learn that there existed a place where Dr. Pepper was not readily available in every restaurant, where my Catholic upbringing was not an oddity, and where some high schools had thriving lacrosse teams, played something called "field hockey," and yet (most shockingly) had no football teams. And while accents have become more muted, a college friend from Long Island who tried to get my phone number over one summer break claims to have called directory assistance three times before he found an operator he could understand. Certainly even a cursory look at electoral maps demonstrates the continued salience of "place": since the end of Reconstruction, Vermont and Georgia have cast their electoral ballots for the same presidential candidate only four times.[13]

Because people disagree on whether "the South" really exists, it should be unsurprising that they also disagree on what exactly counts as Southern. Everyone agrees that the 11 states that seceded in the 1860s should be included (although Virginia and Florida are increasingly suspect). But the South is both broader and narrower than this. It is broader because large portions of the "non-South" were settled first by Southerners—especially Virginians—and retain what is clearly a Southern culture and an affinity for conservative Democrats. The U.S. Census Bureau actually includes Delaware, Maryland, Kentucky, Oklahoma, and West Virginia in its definition of the South for this reason. Leuchtenburg argues for including Kentucky.[14] As for this book, I will keep it simple. When I refer to the South, I am referring to the Old Confederacy. The border areas described above are still important for their leanings toward Southern culture; I will discuss these areas in the context of what I call "Greater Appalachia."

At the same time, the "Old Confederacy" definition of the South is overinclusive because even if there is a distinct culture that can broadly be considered "Southern," the South is nevertheless far from homogenous. This is important because there wasn't really *a* party switch in the South in the 1900s. Rather, there were a *series* of switches tied to geographic and cultural stratifications within the broader South. To understand this, we don't need to go *quite* as deep as V. O. Key's classic *Southern Politics*, which found unique political cultures in each Southern state.[15] But when looking at an electoral map, we should be able to distinguish, as do most historians and political scientists, between the "Deep South," usually defined as Alabama, Arkansas, Georgia, Louisiana, Mississippi, and the Carolinas, and the "Peripheral South," which had fewer African American residents than the Deep South, less of a stake in the maintenance of Jim Crow, and stronger cultural and economic ties to the North and West. Digging a bit deeper, we can identify four key political subregions that we'll refer to over and over again.

The Republican Mountains: The GOP actually dominated the politics of the Appalachian Mountain regions of Virginia, Tennessee, and North Carolina long before Al Smith stepped onto the political scene; the Knoxville-based Second District in Tennessee has not elected a Democrat since 1852. These "Mountain Republicans" had little use for slavery or secession and were favorably inclined toward the Whig/Republican agenda of internal improvements; indeed, these improvements were critical to their economic development and integration with the rest of the country. These states thus always maintained what one observer called "the rudiments of a two-party system," and they gave the GOP a base from which to build.[16] GOP roots also ran deep in the Hill Country of central Texas, where Germans and Czechs brought a rare dose of European immigration to the South, as well as in the

Ozark region of northwest Arkansas (this spilled over into the southwest portion of otherwise-Democratic Missouri).

The Jeffersonian Lowland South: The remainder of the South was solidly Democratic after African Americans were disenfranchised in the late 1800s. But these state parties were far from uniform. Most had disparate factions that were held together at the national level by little more than a desire to support Jim Crow.[17] Many of these intraparty divisions were personal and revolved around a system of "friends and families," where candidates counted on winning strong support in their home counties and neighboring counties. But some divisions were ideological and traced back to the settlement patterns of a particular area.

In particular, the plains that are wedged between the Atlantic Ocean or the Gulf of Mexico on one side, and the foothills of the Appalachian Mountains on the other, were largely settled by English aristocrats from southern England, who moved westward across Virginia, North Carolina, and South Carolina until they hit the Blue Ridge, then swung southward across Georgia, Alabama, Mississippi, and into Louisiana and Texas. The rich, black soil in the areas they settled gave much of this land the nickname "the black belt." Later, the massive amounts of cotton this fertile earth was able to produce came to require large numbers of slaves to maintain, and the region's nickname took on a second connotation. This was the land with the most to fear from slave uprisings and, after the Civil War, from enfranchised blacks. The voters in these areas tended to favor minimal government, an aristocratic, top-down society, and, above all, the maintenance of racial segregation and disenfranchisement. After all, once African Americans were enfranchised, white voters in many of these areas would be in the minority, as they were after Reconstruction.

The Jacksonian Upland South[18]*:* The upland areas in the western Carolinas, northern Georgia, Alabama, Mississippi, and most of Tennessee had a very different flavor to their politics and culture. This hilly backcountry was settled by the first real immigrant wave to America: those from the Scottish-English border and northern Ireland.[19] Finding much of the farmland east of the Blue Ridge occupied, the Scots-Irish slipped down the Shenandoah Valley into western Virginia and North Carolina, across the Cumberland Gap into Kentucky and then Tennessee, and from there into southern Ohio, Indiana, and Illinois.[20] Later, they surged into Arkansas, Missouri, northern

Texas, and eventually southern Oklahoma. They transported their unique politics, worldview, religion, and even accent across this broad swath of America, creating what I call "Greater Appalachia."

Greater Appalachia dominates most of the Peripheral South and touches the fringes of Deep Southern states. On the Northern side, it extends roughly to that famous latitude first surveyed by Charles Mason and Jeremiah Dixon, which extends roughly from just south of Philadelphia, across to Springfield, Illinois, and through northern Missouri.[21] The demarcations between the areas north and south of the Mason-Dixon aren't as sharp as the famous depictions in Bugs Bunny cartoons like "Southern Fried Rabbit" (Bugs crosses the line and is immediately shot at by a Confederate uniform–clad Yosemite Sam); even before the Civil War a massive wave of German immigrants had diluted the Southern culture of southern Ohio, Indiana, Illinois, and central Missouri. But these demarcations are still apparent if you look closely enough.

Unlike their mountainous kinfolk, these voters did not favor the Northern Republican Party, whose puritanical ways, taste for progressive governmental regulation, and isolationist, dovish approach to politics were antithetical to their individualistic, hawkish views. At the same time, they did not tend to crops that required slaves, and African Americans played a smaller role in their communities than in the Lowland South. Racism still ran deep, but the "Negro Question" was not of paramount importance to them.

These Scots-Irish brought with them to the New World a deeply personalized religious faith based upon an intense distrust of organized religion, reverence toward familial bonds, and an equally irreverent attitude toward high society.[22] They developed what one prominent historian describes as the "Jacksonian strain" in American politics: hawkish on foreign policy, antipathetic toward both big business and big government, skeptical of "strange, European ideas" such as labor unions, and near fanatical in their devotion to a personal relationship with Jesus and evangelical religious gatherings.[23] This individualistic worldview resulted in a political outlook that was distinct from that of the more aristocratic Lowland South. These small farmers and craftsmen formed the geographic backbone of the Southern Greenbacker and populist uprisings in the 1880s and 1890s.[24]

The Cities: It is important to understand that when our story begins in 1920, the South was overwhelmingly rural, with an economy dependent upon one crop: cotton. In 1900, the South had really only one major city of note: New Orleans, which boasted a population of around 300,000. The rest of what we think of today as major Southern cities were minor cities at best. Richmond's population in 1900 was 85,000, Charlotte's was 18,000, while Raleigh had 13,000 residents. Atlanta was a veritable boomtown, with almost 90,000 inhabitants, especially compared to Dallas's and Houston's populations of roughly 45,000 apiece. Miami had attracted only 1,700 inhabitants by this point. But these cities were growing quickly, becoming cultural, political, and financial hubs for what was already being called the "New South." And as the residents became wealthier, they flirted with Republicanism.

We can see how these divisions played out in the South by fast-forwarding briefly to the 1968 elections (see figures 0.1 and 0.2). Republican Richard Nixon received 35.2 percent of the Southern vote, Democrat Hubert Humphrey received 30.1 percent, and American Independent George Wallace received

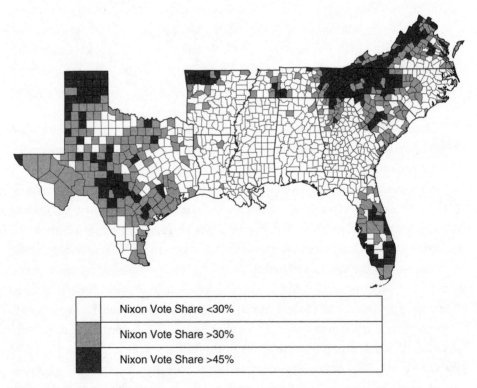

	Nixon Vote Share <30%
	Nixon Vote Share >30%
	Nixon Vote Share >45%

Figure 0.1   1968 Nixon Vote

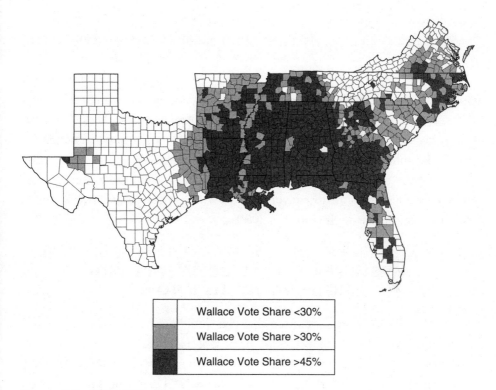

Figure 0.2 1968 Wallace Vote

34.1 percent.[25] But the votes were very unevenly spread. In only about 200 of the roughly 1,100 Southern counties did all three candidates receive more than one-quarter of the vote.

Nixon's vote was concentrated in historic Republican areas in the mountains, in the hills of central Texas (and in the Texas panhandle), and, although it is harder to see, in urban areas like Dallas, Tampa, Miami, Charleston, Atlanta, Richmond, and Charlotte. The Wallace vote was more concentrated in the Jeffersonian Lowlands and the black belt. Humphrey's vote is harder to map, as he ran reasonably well across the entire South, providing the opposition to Nixon and Wallace, whose votes barely overlapped. He dominated in south Texas and in the counties with the heaviest African American populations across the black belt, where even marginal African American enfranchisement provided him with a solid showing. He also provided the alternative to Nixon in the cities, where the relatively few liberal white Democrats were clustered, and where a substantial African American population had accrued during the "Second Great Migration" of African Americans off the farms and into the cities in the 1930s.

But most important, Humphrey still ran well in the traditional Jacksonian Upland areas of central Tennessee and Arkansas, and down into north-central Texas. If we were to examine the rest of Greater Appalachia, in West Virginia, Kentucky, Missouri, and Oklahoma, we would see a larger band of unusually strong Humphrey support running across the center of the country. Even while the rest of the South was abandoning the party of Jackson, these border areas proved the most difficult to convert. As we will see, they would not begin to favor Republicans strongly until the 2000s.

A FEW TECHNICAL CONCEPTS YOU MIGHT WANT TO KNOW

I wrote this book with the intention that you would not need a political science degree to understand or enjoy it. A lot of the tables and graphs are moved to the endnotes to avoid cluttering the narrative. The book also tries to avoid heavy statistical analyses, and I think it largely succeeds. There's nothing that you wouldn't encounter on popular statistics-based websites like Fivethirtyeight. com; in fact, most of the concepts in this book are pretty rudimentary by that site's standards. When the book does use these concepts, it is almost always only to provide supplementary data. You can usually just smile, nod, and move on without really missing the main points in the book.

But for those who would like to read the book and understand everything, a brief primer on some of its more high-level concepts follows.

Two-Party Vote: This is a calculation of what the vote would be in an election year if you remove the third parties. As an example of how this calculation is useful, consider that in 1960, Richard Nixon and John Kennedy both received 50 percent of the popular vote (after rounding). Eight years later, both Richard Nixon and Hubert Humphrey received 43 percent of the popular vote, with the remaining 14 percent largely going to American Independent candidate George Wallace. If we were to track the performance of the Democratic Party over the years, we would look at these numbers and conclude that the party performed terribly in 1968, especially compared to

1960. By removing the third-party vote in 1968, we can compare the two elections more directly and view them both as 50/50 elections. This works well when dealing with minor candidates, but it is sometimes problematic for successful third-party candidates. In reality, it is unlikely that Wallace's vote would actually have been split evenly between the parties had he not been running, but absent exit polls that asked the right questions (like we have for 1992, 1996, and 2000), it is the best that we can do.

There are also times when it is appropriate to use the parties' absolute vote shares, even when a third-party candidate is present. For example, it is significant that Nixon was able to retain 30 percent of the vote in Georgia in 1968, even with a neo-Dixiecrat on the ballot. The previous time there had been a Southern/Northern Democratic split, in 1948, the Republican had received 18 percent of the vote in Georgia, suggesting that the base Republican vote in the state had increased greatly in the intervening years.

Partisan Voting Index (PVI): This is a state (or county's) vote for a candidate, as compared to the national vote for the candidate. It gives us a measure of the state's "base partisanship." As an example of why we might want to use this, consider Massachusetts. As Table 0.1 shows, in presidential elections from 1976 to 1988, it gave the Democratic candidate 58 percent, 50 percent, 49 percent, and 54 percent of the two-party vote. Looking at these numbers at face value, one might conclude that Massachusetts was trending heavily Republican and was a swing state in the 1980s.

Of course, we know that this isn't the case. The Democrats were faring poorly on the national level at the time; in these circumstances, a state that barely leaned toward the Democrats was likely to be pretty heavily Democratic at its core and likely to return to Democratic strength at the national level when the party nominated a stronger candidate. The best way to deal with this is to use the PVI popularized by elections prognosticator Charlie Cook. By subtracting the Democratic share of the vote in the state from the national Democratic share of the vote, you see that Massachusetts was actually pretty stable during these years, voting five to eight points more Democratic than the country as a whole in all four elections (see table 0.1).

When the book refers to the "lean" of a state, county, or demographic group, it is referring to the PVI. In other words, a state or county that is said to "regularly lean Democrat" in a given set of years is one that regularly has a Democratic PVI.

Table 0.1 Democratic Vote Performance and PVI in Massachusetts: 1976–1988

Year	Dem Share in MA	Dem Share Nationally	PVI
1976	58.1 percent	51.4 percent	D+6.7
1980	49.9 percent	44.7 percent	D+5.2
1984	48.6 percent	40.8 percent	D+7.8
1988	54.0 percent	46.1 percent	D+7.9

DW-NOMINATE: Elections analyst Jay Cost describes it best: "DW-Nominate is a very complex methodology that produces a very simple result. Legislators are given an ideological score that ranges from -1.0 to 1.0—with -1.0 being extremely liberal, 0.0 being moderate, and 1.0 being extremely conservative."[26]

That is probably all that you really *need* to know, but there are three other important considerations that can be helpful. First, in practice, very few members score beyond 0.5 or -0.5. In other words, a score of .3 is still generally quite conservative. Second, DW-NOMINATE can't really be used to compare legislators' ideology over extended time periods. DW-NOMINATE scores are derived by looking at legislators' votes and proceeding under the basic assumption that the most liberal legislator will vote most frequently with the second-most-liberal legislator, with the third-most-liberal legislator the second most frequently, and so forth. Using a complex algorithm driven by this assumption, DW-NOMINATE does a pretty good job of assigning liberal and conservative scores for any given Congress.

But because it looks only at "yea/nay" vote outcomes, its calculations do not account for any shifting agenda from Congress to Congress. In other words, a congressman who voted with Republicans against the relatively liberal agenda of the 103rd Congress (1993–1994), and then with Democrats against the fairly conservative agenda of the 104th Congress (1995–1996), would appear to have moved leftward, even though his basic ideology might have remained the same.[27] This has several important implications, but for now, just bear in mind that "conservative" and "liberal" scores derived by DW-NOMINATE are relative only to the other members of Congress and can actually mask a shift in agenda.

Finally, for extremely complex methodological reasons, DW-NOMINATE filters out votes from roughly 1930 to 1970 that were primarily motivated by race and creates a separate score for those votes. This is especially useful to know when examining the voting patterns of the South. By filtering out the racial issues, it allows us to focus better on where the South stood on economic issues during various time periods.

With that, we're done with our housekeeping tasks and can finally begin understanding why Obama's coalition *was* in many ways similar to FDR's—and why that wasn't necessarily a good thing.

PART I

HOW WE GOT HERE

CHAPTER 1

THE EMERGING DEMOCRATIC MAJORITY

1920–1936

The "solid south"—Long the fetich [*sic*] of one section of the country and the bugaboo of the other—has at last been shattered to such a degree that all the king's horses and men of the nursery rhyme could not put it together again, and with its destruction there vanishes from the field of American politics the long and bitter struggle over the slavery question.

Burr J. Ramage, 1896[1]

1920: THE SPLINTERING OF THE DEMOCRATIC PARTY

As Franklin Delano Roosevelt prepared to deliver his Second Inaugural Address in January 1937, he was surely aware of the historic nature of the occasion. The Twentieth Amendment, ratified in 1933, had moved up the date of his inauguration by two months, so the mere fact that he was delivering the address in January was novel. But as he read the famous words off the rain-spattered pages—"I see one-third of a nation ill-housed, ill-clad, ill-nourished"—the deeper significance of the event must have dawned on him. He was, after all, the first Democrat in over one hundred years to win back-to-back popular vote majorities. In fact, he had just received 60.8 percent of the popular vote, the largest total received by any president up to that point. His Electoral College win eclipsed even that of James Monroe in 1820, when the opposition had effectively conceded the election to the Democratic-Republicans.

Roosevelt had won an unprecedented victory with an unprecedented coalition. Yet this coalition—which would shatter in less than two years—was several decades in the making and came to be in the 1930s mainly as a result of choices made by the Republicans during the 1920s. As FDR was keenly aware, the Democratic Party had historically been little more than an awkward group of sectional interests. One prominent historian aptly describes the arrangement this way: "In the early nineteenth century, northern Democrats and southern Democrats had made a pragmatic deal, joining forces in a marriage of convenience and mutual empowerment, not a marriage of love."[2] Northern Democrats received the party's nominations for the presidency, but they agreed not to interfere with Southern institutions, particularly slavery and, later, Jim Crow. Southern Democrats then provided the major electoral muscle for the Democrats. The big-city machines—increasingly dominated by Irish and other immigrant voters as the nineteenth century rolled on—provided just enough votes to keep a handful of Northern states competitive, receiving patronage in return when the Democrats controlled the presidency. H. L. Mencken aptly called the pre–New Deal Democrats "two gangs of natural enemies in a precarious state of symbiosis."[3]

The Republican Party was different. Before 1860, strategists believed that a party needed both a vibrant Northern and Southern wing to win the presidency. But as slavery came to dominate the political debate in the 1850s, that was no longer possible. The Whig Party collapsed because its Northern and Southern constituencies could not agree on the issue, and the Republican Party arose in its place. It was the party of the North, founded on an audacious gamble that it was possible to win the presidency while writing off an entire section of the country.[4] The Republicans were competitive in the South in the decades immediately following the Civil War, but the end of Reconstruction in 1876 and the final disenfranchisement of African Americans toward the end of the nineteenth century drove the Southern Republican to near extinction.

Republicans responded by reconsolidating their power in the North. In 1896, the Democrats nominated former Nebraska representative William Jennings Bryan, whose campaign terrified sometimes-Democratic Northern industrialists. When Bryan famously swore that he would not be crucified on a cross of gold, he was essentially insisting that the government create inflation by abandoning the gold standard, which would help farmers who had increasingly had difficulty paying their debts due to the gradual deflation of the 1880s and 1890s.

Inflation makes debts worth less, which would certainly have helped farmers in the South and West. But it threatened to wipe out the Northeasterners who owned that debt. Industrialists promised their white working-class employees of layoffs should Bryan win and spent roughly the equivalent of $1 billion (in today's money) on William McKinley's campaign. All this, on top of Bryan's evangelistic rhetoric, turned white working-class Catholics from a 25 to 30 percent Republican group into a 40 to 45 percent Republican group,[5] enabling McKinley to become the first Republican ever to carry Manhattan.[6] Northern Democrats were still more commonplace than Southern Republicans, but they had definitely become the minority party. The Democratic congressional caucus became, in one historian's memorable words, a "hopelessly outnumbered confederate alumni society."[7]

These developments brought about one very odd consequence: both parties maintained what would today be considered conservative and liberal wings. Conservative Republicans and Democrats alike promoted the interests of businesses in their states. The liberal wing of the Republican Party called themselves "Progressives." Progressives tended to oppose international alliances and foreign wars, supported regulation of businesses, and pushed to break the back of what they saw as control of government by corrupt big-city (usually Democratic) machines and moneyed interests.

Republican Progressivism came in several varieties. In eastern cities, it tended to be elitist and concerned with regulating industrial capitalism. In the Great Plains and Rocky Mountains, it was sometimes nearly socialist; North Dakota's state-owned bank and grain silos were established under Progressive Republican governments. On the West Coast, Progressives were reformist, pushing through good-government measures like the initiative and referendum.

"Liberal" Democrats, on the other hand, tended to be populists. Populism grew out of the Greenbacker and Populist movements of the 1880s and 1890s. It was angry (its leaders had nicknames like James "Cyclone" Davis and Davis "Bloody Bridles" Waite), anti-industrial, and agrarian. It concentrated its fire on railroads, corporations, and, above all else, Wall Street.[8] Populists toyed with backing both parties before finally becoming subsumed within the Democratic Party in 1896. Obviously, the philosophy expounded by Southern Populist tenant farmers and that of New England patrician Progressives had important differences in tone, reasoning, and motive, but they nevertheless espoused programs that were similar, although not identical. This bipartisan center-left vote became the swing vote in the country, moving between two parties that would both be considered center-right today.

Things had gotten bad for the Democrats in 1896, but the darkest days for the party came after Woodrow Wilson's disastrous second term. Progressive Republicans, especially those in the Mountain West, had generally supported Wilson in 1916 over the relatively pro-business Charles Evans Hughes, but the United States' entry into World War I in early 1917 severed that support.[9] The war also enraged the major Northern ethnic groups, who had swung back toward the Democrats in the 1910s: the Germans loathed the decision to go to war with Germany, while the Irish balked at fighting alongside Great Britain. The peace was no less damaging than the war. The League of Nations was perhaps even more anathema to Progressives than the entry into World War I. German Americans were angered further by the punitive measures taken against Germany in the Treaty of Versailles, while the Irish were outraged by the treaty's failure to address the question of Irish independence. Italian Americans, Polish Americans, Czech Americans, and just about every other ethnic group bore some grievance against the state boundaries set by the treaty.

As November 1920 approached, things only seemed to get worse. Postwar inflation reached almost 15 percent in 1919, and unemployment hit double digits.[10] An influenza outbreak claimed the lives of over a half-million Americans. Labor unrest and strikes swept the country. Radicals began a string of terrorist bomb attacks; Attorney General A. Mitchell Palmer barely escaped death when his brownstone in Washington, DC, was destroyed by a bomb. Numerous other officials were wounded or killed, and over 30 bombs were intercepted en route to various destinations.[11] In perhaps the most dramatic attack, anarchists sent a horse-drawn wagon loaded with sash weights and dynamite into Wall Street at lunchtime. The ensuing explosion killed 38 people, seriously wounded 143, and vaporized the horse.[12]

The Democrats had sailed into a perfect storm. The result was a disaster that makes the recent elections of 2006, 2008, and 2010 look like modest affairs. The Republican ticket of Ohio senator Warren G. Harding and Massachusetts governor Calvin Coolidge swamped the Democrats, who were led by Ohio governor James Cox and 38-year-old Franklin Roosevelt, then Assistant Secretary of the Navy. Harding won by what is still the largest popular vote margin in American history—26.2 points. He carried Michigan by 50 points, Illinois by

42 points, Massachusetts by 41 points, and both New York and Pennsylvania by 38 points.

If 1896 had weakened the Democrats' coalition, 1920 sliced it open from stem to stern. Outside the South, Democrats won only 35 of 330 House seats and lost every non-Southern Senate seat up for election that year. In the state legislatures, Democrats won only 911 of 6,262 seats nationwide.[13] They were shut out of the Maine and Nebraska state senates and sent nary a soul to the entire Michigan legislature. White ethnics swung hard against the Democrats. Harding carried all but one district in Irish Boston and became only the second Republican to carry Manhattan.[14] He did so by a spectacular 59 percent to 29 percent margin, carrying heavily German, Italian, and, amazingly, Irish precincts.[15]

Even the South looked a touch shaky for the Democrats. Harding carried Tennessee, the first Southern state to vote Republican since the end of Reconstruction. The Democrats lost three House seats in Tennessee, while the German-Catholic hill country of central Texas sent Republican Harry Wurzbach to the House. House Democrats had close calls across the South, and had Republicans not left one-third of the Southern House seats uncontested, they might have fared even better.[16]

Harding went to bed on election night with his mistress, Nan Britton. Democrats went to bed wondering whether their party was still viable. But even in these extreme circumstances, no Whig-like extinction occurred. By tearing up the electoral map and weakening the sectional divisions between the parties, the election of 1920 actually made the New Deal possible. The breadth of the Republican coalition made it unwieldy; the Republican pursuit of a "coalition of everyone" ended up alienating key Republican constituencies throughout the 1920s. The next time Franklin Roosevelt strode across the national stage, he would lead a Democratic coalition that was broader, deeper, and stronger than any other the country had seen.

1924 AND THE PROGRESSIVE/ REPUBLICAN SPLIT

The Democrats didn't just lose the next two presidential elections—they lost them by landslides. Political scientists tend to lump the Republican wins from 1896 to 1908 together with the elections from 1920 through 1928. But the wins could not be more different. The most obvious difference is size: only Teddy Roosevelt's 19-point drubbing of the hapless Alton Parker in 1904 approached the margins from 1920 to 1928. More important, the Republican presidents in the 1920s were mildly to staunchly conservative, a sharp contrast from the more progressive candidates who generally stood in the early part of the twentieth century.

Even lumping together the three elections from 1920 to 1928 is difficult to justify. The 1924 and 1928 Republicans actually relied upon substantially different coalitions. These differences were critical and (at least in retrospect) provided glimmers of hope for the Democrats. Progressive Republicans, so crucial to Democratic wins in 1912 and 1916, had swallowed the Harding nomination in 1920 because he was considered mildly progressive. But in 1924, they could not swallow Calvin Coolidge. Coolidge was as stingy with the public fisc as he was with his verbiage—a woman once told him that she had bet her husband that she could get Coolidge to say more than three words; Coolidge quipped, "You lose." He slashed income taxes, refused to increase spending, and famously declared that "[t]he business of America is business." Horrified Progressive Republicans bolted and formed their own party, just as they had in 1912. Their nominee, Wisconsin senator Robert LaFollette, Sr., won only 17 percent of the vote. But his run highlighted the tenuous relationship between the Progressives and the increasingly conservative Republican Party.

The breakdown in the relationship between conservatives and Progressives was especially pronounced in the Mountain West. Progressives in the Northeast and on the West Coast had tentatively rejoined the Republican Party after Teddy Roosevelt's failed run as a Progressive candidate in 1912 mainly because their only alternative was to find common cause with the reactionary urban machines that dominated the Northern wing of the Democratic Party. But there were few cities, let alone machines, in the Mountain West and on the Great Plains.[17] Progressives there actually found that they frequently had more in common with their Populist counterparts in the Democratic Party than with the mine owners and businessmen who commanded the local Republican parties. Progressive Republicans in the Mountain West backed Wilson in 1916. Even after they turned on Wilson during World War I, they kept pulling the lever for Democrats for Congress, Senate, and governorships.

Democratic nominee John W. Davis ran behind Democratic congressional candidates in every region of the country in 1924, suggesting that most of the

LaFollette voters were voting for Democrats in the congressional elections.[18] After the 1924 elections, Coolidge did little to mollify the Progressives. He signed the Revenue Act of 1926, which Progressives castigated as a sop to the rich. He vetoed the McNary-Haugen farm bill, intended to assist farmers on the Great Plains, who were suffering the earliest symptoms of what was to become the Great Depression.[19] From 1924 through 1928, Democrats saw a spike in their performance in the Mountain West in House, Senate, and gubernatorial races, while third-party movements gained strength on the Great Plains. With the right candidate and the right platform, the Democrats might have been able to nudge these voters into their fold at the presidential level as well, just as Wilson had in 1916. Given that Progressives had mounted third-party runs in two of the four elections from 1912 to 1924, there was even a chance that they could be brought permanently into the Democratic coalition. This possibility was fraught with significance, as Davis and LaFollette had combined for a majority of the vote in 26 states worth 235 electoral votes—almost enough votes to win.

1928: THE NEW WHITE WORKING CLASS

The Republicans' nomination of Herbert Hoover in 1928 temporarily mollified the Progressives. At the time, Hoover was considered a Progressive; he had supported Teddy Roosevelt's bolt from the Republican fold in 1912 and had even been encouraged to run with Roosevelt as the Democrats' nominee in 1920.[20] But if 1928 brought the Progressives back into the Republican fold, it revealed a much greater problem for the GOP.

In the late nineteenth and early twentieth centuries, America received a massive influx of immigrants from around the world. From 1900 to 1925, a stunning 17.3 million immigrants arrived, almost as many as had come from 1840 to 1900 combined.[21] By 1910, a majority of children in the nation's 37 largest cities had foreign-born fathers.[22] These immigrants clustered in the nation's cities, remaking the demography of much of New England and the Midwest. Seventy-nine percent of Milwaukee was foreign born by 1910, as was 76 percent of Cleveland and 75 percent of Detroit.[23] There were religious implications to this immigration as well: by the 1930s, Rhode Island was 60 percent Catholic, Massachusetts was 50 percent Catholic, and Connecticut was 49 percent Catholic.[24]

Presidents Harding and Coolidge were sufficiently worried by the surge in immigration that they decided to sign the Emergency Quota Act of 1921 and the Immigration Act of 1924, largely shutting off the immigration spigot.[25] The flow of immigration slowed to a trickle, but not before it altered the trajectory of the country's politics irreversibly. The leading edge of the massive immigrant wave was, from 1900 to 1925, completing the onerous naturalization process, while their children were beginning to approach the age of majority as well.[26] As newcomers to the political process, they had not yet adopted any strong political leanings. All they needed was a candidate to bind them to a party and encourage them to vote.

Enter Al Smith. Smith had narrowly won election as New York's governor in 1918 but lost in the Harding landslide. Undeterred, he bounced back and scored a huge win in 1922 and defeated Theodore Roosevelt, Jr., two years later.[27] Although Smith identified with the Irish community, he was actually a combination of Irish, English, German, and Italian. He was a "wet"—the term for an opponent of Prohibition—who flouted Prohibition publicly, a boisterous speaker with a sharp Lower East Side accent, and a devout Catholic. In other words, he epitomized the twentieth-century American immigrant experience.

Smith had run for the Democratic presidential nomination in 1924, but the year when the Democrats would narrowly refuse to condemn the Ku Klux Klan was, unsurprisingly, not the year they would nominate a Catholic. By 1928 it was a different world, and Smith was nominated on the first ballot. He chose Senator Joseph Robinson of Arkansas as his running mate, the first Southerner on a presidential ticket since the Civil War, and the "happy warrior" marched out to do battle. The results looked, at first blush, to be the same as those of 1920 and 1924: the Democrats lost in an Electoral College and popular-vote landslide.

A peek beneath the surface, however, reveals a *very* different election from 1920 and 1924. In 1920, the heavily Irish and Italian precincts in New York City had given Governor Cox only 47 percent of their vote, while the Germans had awarded him a paltry 28 percent. Davis had improved only modestly on this showing in 1924. With Al Smith as the nominee, however, the immigrant vote gelled. Eighty-two percent of the Irish vote went to the Democrat, along with 77 percent of the Italian vote and 73 percent of the German vote.[28] That vote also swelled. In Massachusetts, Hoover improved upon Coolidge's showing by about 70,000 votes. But Smith ran an astounding 500,000 votes ahead of Davis, largely concentrated in counties with large working-class populations like Suffolk (Boston), Bristol (Fall River), and Hampden (Springfield). Smith became the first Democratic presidential candidate to win over a majority of Massachusetts voters—ever. Perhaps the most astounding result came from New York, where Hoover added a respectable 373,286 votes to Coolidge's total. But Smith improved upon Davis's showing by an eye-popping 1,139,067 votes.

Smith had tapped into a new well of votes for the Democrats. But it came with a price. Even with Joe Robinson on the ticket, Smith lost a good portion of the Solid South. Smith's Catholicism was obviously a major liability in the heavily Protestant South. But Smith's errors worsened the problem. In 1927, Virginia senator Carter Glass had warned that Smith could carry the South as a Catholic but not as both a Catholic and a wet. Yet Smith's telegram to the Democratic Convention accepting his nomination prominently argued for the repeal of Prohibition. His ties to Tammany Hall (the New York City Democratic machine), his thick accent, and his appointment of a Republican Catholic to head the Democratic National Committee were too much for the South to accept.[29]

Smith held on in the so-called black belt counties, whose voters were unwilling to abandon the party of Jim Crow even when it nominated a liberal urban Catholic. Everywhere else in the South, including many of the major Southern cities, Smith lost.[30] He failed to carry Virginia, North Carolina, Tennessee, Florida, or Texas, and he very nearly lost Alabama. Republicans picked up congressional seats in the Peripheral South, and a few congressmen in Deep Southern states found themselves facing unexpectedly close calls.[31] Republicans even went from 3 seats to 12 in the North Carolina state Senate and from 16 to 36 in the state House.[32] The South had sent an important message: it was still solid, but that would change if the Democratic Party became too urban, too liberal, and too ethnic.

Taken together, the elections of 1924 and 1928 showed that the Republican coalition was shaky. Without Progressives, Republicans won 54 percent of the vote in 1924. Without white ethnics in 1928, they won 58 percent of the vote and did so only because of historic wins in the South. Absent that vote, they would once again have been held to around 55 percent. If Democrats could figure out a way to win over the dissident Republican groups without causing a revolt in their own ranks, the Republicans would have a hard time winning an election. Events made that possible for a short while, but in the long run that task proved impossible.

1932: THE NEW DEAL COALITION

When Wall Street crashed in October 1929, people initially assumed that good times would soon return, as they had after the sharp recession of 1921–1922. The 1930 midterm elections were not so bad for the Republicans, as they maintained control of both the House and Senate and even won the popular vote for the House by six points. Democratic gains were smaller than they had been in 1922. Michael Barone, the founder and editor of the *Almanac of American Politics*, has calculated that nearly half of the 52 seats Democrats picked up were seats they had held going into the 1928 elections, while another 8 to 10 were from districts along the North–South boundary that had historically swung between the parties.[33]

As the 1930s wore on, however, it became clear that prosperity would not return quickly. The Republicans' fortunes began to crumble, even in their longtime strongholds. On November 3, 1931, a Democrat won a special election to Congress in working-class Saginaw, Michigan; the district had voted for its Republican congressman by 35 points a year earlier.[34] The Republican candidates to replace Harry Wurzbach in Texas combined for a paltry 18 percent of the vote.[35] Democrats picked up seats in central New Jersey and southeast New Hampshire that had been heavily Republican and narrowly missed picking up a Republican Pennsylvania district.[36] By the time the 1932 elections arrived, Democrats had already won control of the House. Winning the presidency looked inevitable given the right candidate.

Finding "the right candidate" proved easier said than done. Most of the Democratic candidates were either too Catholic, urban, and liberal to win the South (Smith), too Southern to win over the cities (House Speaker John Garner of Texas), or too reactionary to appeal to Progressives (Governor "Alfalfa Bill" Murray of Oklahoma). But there was one potential nominee who was acceptable to all these groups: Franklin Roosevelt.[37] Roosevelt's availability as a nominee was serendipitous. He had survived a bout with polio in the 1920s, a miracle in and of itself. Even more miraculously, he had rehabilitated himself to the point where he could walk, with braces. He won election as governor of New York by only six-tenths of a point in the Republican landslide of 1928, before winning a solid reelection in 1930.[38] And he had built a profile that was perfect for the 1932 race. He was viewed as a mild Progressive, was a Protestant, had no ties to Tammany Hall, and yet knew how to appeal to voters in big cities. He even had a "second home" in Warm Springs, Georgia, where he rehabilitated his polio-stricken legs. His rural, patrician background resonated with voters in the Deep South, while his wife's Southern roots made for good copy in the newspapers. He even spoke the Southern language, calling the Civil War the "war between the states," and referring to Reconstruction as "America's Dark Ages."[39] He was also fluent in the seamier side of Southern dialect as well, referring to "the Negro" as a "semi-beast"; his notes and anecdotal evidence passed along by colleagues suggest that "darky" and "n*gg*r" sometimes replaced the term "Negro" in his speeches, jokes, and thoughts.[40] In 1932, Al Smith was the candidate of New England, while Roosevelt owed his nomination to support from the South after its true favorite sons, such as Garner, faded.

Roosevelt fared poorly in the primaries, much to Herbert Hoover's dismay. Hoover thought that with Roosevelt as the nominee he could turn the election into a liberal-versus-conservative referendum and emerge victorious by holding the South and chipping off conservative Northeastern Democrats. He even worked behind the scenes to manipulate William Randolph Hearst into ensuring Roosevelt's nomination at the Democratic convention.[41] This was one of the last in a long series of misjudgments by the onetime "boy wonder."

Roosevelt defeated Hoover 57.4 percent to 39.7 percent in the popular vote. Democrats gained almost one hundred seats in the House and took control of the Senate. Across the country, Republicans lost governorships, state House seats, and downticket races. In the Northern cities, Roosevelt retained the advances pioneered by Smith.[42] In New York and Chicago, he received around three-fourths of the vote in heavily German, Jewish, Polish, Irish, and Italian precincts.[43] The Progressives in the Mountain West and on both coasts swung heavily to Roosevelt, and at the same time he crushed Hoover in the South. It was a rout, but there was an order to it: Roosevelt had held together the traditional Democratic coalition while peeling away groups that had already suggested they were unhappy with Republicans.

A party many had left for dead had suddenly sprung, phoenix-like, from the ashes of the Wilson coalition. Republicans were left with little more than their historic base among Protestants of Anglo-Saxon descent, a shrinking portion of the population, and African Americans. But once again, despite appearances, rehabilitation was less than a decade away.

1936: THE LAST PIECES OF
THE NEW DEAL PUZZLE

Republicans entered the 1936 elections fully confident that they would win. True, they had suffered a setback in 1934, when the Democrats became the first party since the Civil War to hold the presidency and still gain seats in a midterm election. Republicans wrote this off as a temporary surge due to the "relief vote"[44] and noted that their base of donors had temporarily deserted them: the Republicans ended 1934 with only $352 in liquid assets.[45] The next year was better for them, as they won back the New York Assembly, made major gains in Massachusetts and Ohio, and won the Philadelphia mayoral race. At the 1936 convention, Republicans nominated Kansas governor Alf Landon, the only Republican governor to survive the 1934 drubbing.

Most observers assumed that the Progressive Landon could bring back the West, forcing a close election. Donations came pouring in. In 1932, Republicans and Democrats had shared contributions in excess of $1,000 roughly evenly, with $1.2 million going to the Democrats and $1.6 million going to the Republicans. In 1936, Democrats again received $1.3 million in these large donations, but Republican donations swelled to $3.9 million.[46] The *Literary Digest* poll, which had accurately predicted the elections of 1924, 1928, and 1932, anticipated that Roosevelt would receive only 42 percent of the vote.[47]

Of course, nothing like this happened. Alf Landon received only 37 percent of the popular vote, losing badly in the West and taking only 43 percent of the vote in historically Republican New England. Even the vaunted Republican machine in Philadelphia collapsed under the weight of the Democratic onslaught, as Roosevelt became the first Democrat to carry the state since James Buchanan in 1856. Republicans won one North Chicago House district and a few on the outskirts of Boston, but otherwise they were almost completely eradicated from the country's major urban areas.

Republicans who thought that their party was strengthening were correct in a sense: Landon had actually received almost a million more votes nationwide than Hoover had in 1932. In major Northern cities like Chicago, Detroit, New York, Cleveland, Pittsburgh, and Philadelphia, the Republicans won roughly the same number of votes as they had in previous elections.[48] Indeed, had the size of the overall electorate remained unchanged from 1932 to 1936, Roosevelt's win would have been much more modest. But Democratic participation in the electorate had once again exploded. Roosevelt eclipsed his 1932 total by almost five million votes.

Republican registration had remained stable from 1922 through 1938 in Manhattan and the Bronx, at about 100,000 and 50,000 registrants, respectively. During that same time, the number of Democratic registrants increased from about 200,000 to 500,000 in Manhattan and from 90,000 to 500,000 in the Bronx.[49] These voters, many of whom were helped by New Deal programs, chose overwhelmingly to throw their lot in with the Democrats. The story was the same in cities throughout the nation. In the old-line Yankee counties, which had seen few immigrants in recent decades, the Republicans maintained a stable registration advantage over Democrats. But in places like Pittsburgh, Albany, Philadelphia, and other urban centers with high concentrations of immigrant voters, the number of Democratic registrants exploded, while the number of Republican registrants stayed constant.[50] The experience of the Democratic and Republican parties during the New Deal period is best summed up in Figure 1.1:

In 1932, Roosevelt had mostly relied upon vague promises of relief, railed against budget deficits, and waited out Election Day. In the words of biographer William Leuchtenburg, "Roosevelt presented himself not as the paladin of liberalism but as father to all the people, not as the representative of a single class but as the coordinator of a series of interests."[51] In 1936, however, Roosevelt emerged as a neo-Populist class warrior, one who famously told a campaign crowd at Madison Square Garden that he hoped his second term would be the one where the "forces of selfishness and of lust for power…met their master."[52] It had won him the election. It also won the Democrats some new followers. Not everyone was excited about this last development.

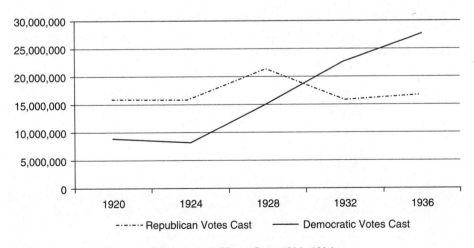

Figure 1.1 Republican and Democratic Votes Cast, 1920–1936

FAREWELL TO THE PARTY OF LINCOLN: AFRICAN AMERICANS AND THE NEW DEAL

If the introduction of class consciousness to American electoral politics would have seemed unlikely in 1928, the addition of African Americans to the Democratic coalition would have seemed impossible. But like Progressives and white ethnics, African Americans had been tiring of GOP neglect. Whether it was Teddy Roosevelt dishonorably discharging a regiment of African American soldiers who had been accused (on scant evidence) of firing shots into the streets of Brownsville or purging black delegates from the Progressive convention in 1912 in an attempt to sell that party in the South,[53] Harding and Coolidge failing to reverse fully the Wilson administration's efforts at segregating the government, or the Republicans segregating African American delegates at the 1928 convention, the list of slights was long. African Americans nevertheless stayed with the Party of Lincoln because, even in 1928, many remembered which party had passed the Reconstruction Amendments, and because, however bad the Republicans were, the Democrats were worse (Democrats placed African Americans behind chicken wire at their 1928 convention). Hoover won African Americans overwhelmingly in both 1928 and 1932, despite spending much of his administration trying to build on his 1928 successes in the South by taking such steps as supporting lily-white Southern Republican parties and attempting to appoint a (former, so he claimed) segregationist to the Supreme Court.

But four years later, African Americans were one of the Democrats' strongest groups, even as Southern Democratic senators continued to fight the most basic civil rights legislation. Table 1.1 shows the steep decline in the Republican share of the vote in heavily African American precincts in major U.S. cities from 1928 to 1936.

Table 1.1   Republican Share of Presidential Vote in Heavily African American Precincts, 1928–1936[i]

	1928	1932	1936
Chicago	72%	75%	51%
Cleveland	72%	82%	38%
Knoxville	56%	70%	44%
New York	66%	46%	17%
Philadelphia	82%	71%	30%

[i] Nancy J. Weiss, *Farewell to the Party of Lincoln: Black Politics in the Age of FDR* (Princeton: Princeton University Press, 1983), 206.

It was certainly not FDR's civil rights record that had brought African Americans into the fold. While he did insist on desegregating some New Deal programs, he left others alone and could not even be persuaded to support basic civil rights programs, such as an anti-lynching bill.[54] While his wife, Eleanor, became a prominent supporter of African American equality, Roosevelt remained in the background and refused even to denounce the violent Detroit race riots of 1943.[55]

But the number of African Americans who remembered Abraham Lincoln was shrinking. The younger generation—two to three generations removed from slavery—did not share their elders' reverence for his party. Nancy Weiss has painstakingly reconstructed the generational gap among African Americans by examining the political affiliations of participants in *Who's Who in Colored America* by decade of birth. Older African Americans largely retained their GOP allegiances, but younger African Americans were willing to consider the Democrats.[56]

More important, even if African Americans held segregated jobs in the WPA, at least they had jobs. For the first time, a rising tide was lifting their boat as well. Democratic advertisements in African American newspapers made much of this: "Distress Knows No Color Line" was the slogan.[57] Alfred Edgar Smith, an African American who worked for the WPA, created a movie to be shown in African American film houses called *We Work Again*. Leading African American newspapers noted that Abraham Lincoln was not on the ballot and argued that the election was about "the present economic adjustment, social justice, labor equality, better housing, and meat and bread and education."[58] Weiss concludes, in her seminal study of African American political behavior in the 1930s, that

Table 1.2 African Americans Self-Describing As Republican by Decade of Birth[i]

	1933	1937	1942
1850	91.9%	88.9%	87.5%
1860	82.6%	80.2%	80.2%
1870	78.3%	77.2%	75.8%
1880	76.1%	72.4%	74.4%
1890	65.6%	62.3%	60.6%
1900	65.6%	59.5%	56.8%
1910	—	—	28.6%

[i] *Id.*, 230–31. The typical decade in this sample included 300 observations.

while black political leaders focused on a civil rights agenda, "the racial expectations of most blacks fell considerably short of the protest voiced by black spokesmen.... [T]he key to black electoral behavior lay in economics rather than race." This is evident in the class breakdown of the African American vote—in 1936, blacks in largely lower-middle-class precincts voted substantially more Republican than blacks in largely lower-class precincts; the same class cleavage that had emerged in white politics was emerging in black politics.

■　■　■

FDR's persona and choices were important, but he did not single-handedly transform American politics. He exploited preexisting fissures in the opposition party that began during the supposedly "normal" elections of 1920 through 1928. His coalition was by no means inevitable, and it was certainly not foreseeable. There were simply too many contingencies at work here. What if Republicans had been more solicitous of African Americans or of Progressives? What if Al Smith hadn't sought the nomination in 1928, mobilizing white ethnics and binding them to the Democratic Party? What if FDR had been unable to secure the nomination, which seemed likely at times? For that matter, what if FDR hadn't survived polio, hadn't won in 1928, and hadn't survived the assassination attempt that occurred just before his inauguration? Had any of these contingencies come to pass, the arc of history would have been shaped very differently.

FDR initially seemed to appreciate the underlying fragility of his coalition. He carefully worked not to scare any portion off. While his "100 days" is remembered as a series of historic experiments today, at the time it was carefully calibrated to placate different wings of his party. The Agricultural Adjustment Act appealed to Western Progressives, the Rural Electrification Administration and regulation of Wall Street appealed to Populists in the South, and the Works Progress Administration and repeal of Prohibition appealed to the white working class.

But the unintended consequence was that African Americans were now a core portion of the same coalition that included Northern liberals, Western Progressives, socially conservative white ethnic voters, and reactionary Southerners. It was a truly innovative coalition, and it was broad. This breadth made it powerful but also unstable. It would crack sooner than anyone had anticipated.

CHAPTER 2

THREE WEDDINGS AND
A WAKE

BUILDING THE EISENHOWER
COALITION: 1938–1988

How to revitalize the Republican party under such conditions
looks almost impossible.

Ogden Mills to Herbert Hoover, November 16, 1936[1]

SHORTLY AFTER ROOSEVELT'S ELECTION, his massive coalition began to crumble. This was to some degree inevitable, as "southern conservatives, New York liberals, and African-American autoworkers in Detroit could not continue indefinitely to cohabit the same political party."[2] By the mid-1940s, the New Deal was a spent force, both legislatively and electorally. This is not to say that Democrats could not win elections—they obviously posted presidential wins in 1948, 1960, 1964, and 1976 and controlled Congress for most of this time. But the presidential wins were typically narrow, while control of Congress was often a mere technicality.

By 1952, commentators realized what has today been lost amid the zeal to find 32-year cycles in American politics: there was a new coalition of voters that included Republicans, Southerners, key white ethnic groups, farmers, and "above all...the great new middle class, from city white-collar workers to prosperous suburbanites."[3] Today we call this the "Reagan coalition," but in truth, this coalition began to take form in the late 1930s. In 1952, Dwight Eisenhower was positioned to take the rump Republican Party and finally marry three new components to that base. This coalition might not have outlasted Eisenhower, but the lengthy existential threat posed by the Soviet Union, the Democratic

Party's leftward shift, and the radical social changes of the 1960s held this unlikely bunch together. But like all coalitions, it was not immortal. As the Soviet threat disappeared and the conservative, Southern wing of the party achieved prominence, the "coalition of everybody" could no longer survive.

Because the South played such a large role in the demise of the New Deal coalition, and because it receives so much attention from scholars and pundits, much of it misinformed, we'll begin our analysis there and spend the bulk of our time on it.

SOMETHING OLD: THE SOUTH EXITS THE DEMOCRATIC PARTY

The typical narrative of Southern realignment begins around 1964, when LBJ signs the Civil Rights Act. In the words of *Salon*'s Steve Kornacki, this begins a realignment toward the GOP that "had everything to do with race."[4] Even modern realignment scholars sometimes push this narrative. Tom Schaller's *Whistling Past Dixie*, for example, begins its story of Southern realignment in 1964, when Barry Goldwater supposedly becomes the first GOP candidate to use a Southern strategy.[5] Richard Nixon then notes the potential coalition that Goldwater "made viable by carrying the five Deep South states in 1960 [*sic*]"[6] and begins a "blacklash" campaign that reaches pitch-perfect precision with Reagan's 1980 campaign against Carter.

These narratives are badly flawed. To be sure, the signing of the Civil Rights Act of 1964 and the Goldwater candidacy were important milestones in the making of the modern GOP and in the political identity of the South. But the Southern GOP did not suddenly spring to life in the 1960s. Republicans began conspiring to win Southern votes almost as soon as Abraham Lincoln passed from the scene, and these strategies are what ultimately began the shift.

For example, Rutherford B. Hayes, a former Whig, believed that by supporting the old Whig program of internal improvements and government aid to business, he could reinvigorate the old Whig coalition and win "North Carolina, with a fair chance in Maryland, Virginia, Tennessee and Arkansas."[7] But former Southern Whigs were not interested in the GOP, especially after the Civil War. Hayes's successors, James Garfield and Chester Alan Arthur, encouraged GOP fusion with the radical, agrarian third parties that popped up in the South in the 1870s and 1880s and actually had some success winning state and local elections by "fusing" with groups like the Greenbackers, Populists, and Readjusters.[8]

Democrats responded by enacting poll taxes, literacy tests, and other means of disenfranchising the blacks and poor whites who formed the backbones of these alliances, ensuring that the Democratic party would remain largely dominant in the South, and that it would, in turn, be dominated by its conservative wing.[9] The laws were brutally effective: In the mid-1890s, there were 130,000 registered African American voters in Louisiana. In 1904, there were 1,342.[10]

The Republicans under Benjamin Harrison responded by pushing for a Federal Elections Bill that was a precursor to the Voting Rights Act of 1965. Had Republicans passed the bill and successfully re-enfranchised African Americans at a time when African Americans were the majority in some Southern states, the South would have leaned Republican, and the future of electoral politics would have changed in ways we can't even begin to imagine. But a coalition of Southern Democrats and Western Republican senators killed the bill, in exchange for the passage of a pair of financial bills the West favored.[11] Four years later, Democratic president Grover Cleveland signed the repeal of the Federal Election Act of 1871, removing even the most basic federal protections for African American voting rights. Like the narrow vote of the Virginia legislature to maintain the legality of slavery in the early 1800s, the aftershocks of the Republican decision not to push through the so-called Force Act reverberate today.

Republicans then quietly abandoned African Americans and focused their attention on Southern whites. Theodore Roosevelt, like many Progressives, believed strongly that African Americans were racially inferior to whites and quietly favored restricting their voting rights to "occasionally good, well-educated, intelligent and honest colored men."[12] He sought common ground with white Southerners, announcing at a Southern gathering his belief that "race purity must be maintained."[13] Other Republicans followed this approach. William Howard Taft, for example, promised the North Carolina Society of New York that Republicans "would not interfere with Negro disfranchisement."[14] As described in the preceding chapter, this "TR strategy" eventually cost Republicans the votes of African Americans while gaining them little in return: in 1924, South Carolina senator Coleman L. Blease commented on the 1,123 votes Coolidge received in his state: "I do not know where he got them. I was astonished to know that they were cast and shocked to know that they were counted."[15]

In truth, the GOP relied on all these strategies at various times in the twentieth century to break the Democratic Party's stranglehold on the region. The movement of the South toward the Republicans proceeded in three steps, which are only just now being completed. The year 1964 is an important date, but it is at best a midpoint, not a start date. The years 1936, 1952, and 1956 are equally important, if not more so. Remember, while it is certainly important to examine the years when the GOP went from 40 percent to 50 percent in the South, it is equally important to know why the GOP could go from 20 percent support to 30 percent support. *That* happened during Franklin Roosevelt's term, as illustrated in Figures 2.1 and 2.2.

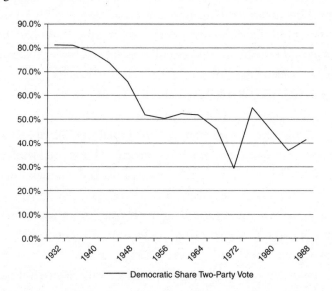

Figure 2.1   Dem. Share of Two-Party Presidential Vote in South, 1932–1988

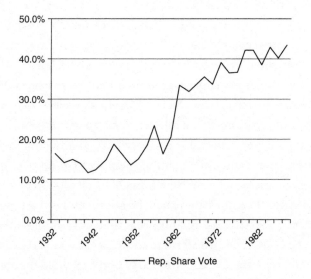

Figure 2.2   Rep. Share of Congressional Vote In South, 1932–1988

The Republican Party made gradual progress in both the presidential and congressional vote from 1932 through 1988. The first part of this—Part One of the realignment—occurs roughly from 1932 through 1960, years when the Republicans increased their share of the Southern vote in almost every presidential election. At this point, race played only an indirect role, as the GOP was still *a* party of civil rights, even if it was increasingly not *the* party of civil rights. The TR Strategy had been temporarily shelved in 1940 with the nomination of Wendell Wilkie, while Tom Dewey, the Republican nominee in 1944 and 1948, had signed the nation's first employment discrimination law. Yet the South still drifted steadily toward the Party of Lincoln. There were two factors at work at this time: the leftward movement of the Democrats and the increased wealth and size of Southern cities.

For FDR and many Progressives, pushing conservative Southerners out of the party was a feature of the New Deal, not a bug. FDR had ruminated about leaving conservative Democrats behind for a unified Progressive party as early as 1919 and famously commented to his advisor Rexford Tugwell shortly after his election: "We'll have eight years in Washington. By that time there may not be a Democratic Party, but there will be a progressive one."[16] Others were having similar thoughts; Paul Douglas, a senator from Illinois in the 1950s and 1960s, envisioned a realignment of Southern and Northern conservatives pitted against Northern liberals and Southern populists as early as 1931.[17] As FDR proved in 1932 and (especially) 1936 that the party could win without Southern votes, his resolve to bring about such a change only intensified.

The first two years of the New Deal did little to shake the South's allegiances. True, Senator Carter Glass of Virginia called the early New Deal "an utterly dangerous effort of the federal government to transplant Hitlerism to every corner of the nation,"[18] and a handful of Democratic congressmen regularly opposed the administration's first round of proposals. But for the most part, these first proposals were compatible with traditional Southern interests: shoring up agriculture, reining in the power of East Coast money, and breaking the back of Northern "economic imperialism."[19] FDR played the South like a fiddle; he later bragged that "[o]ne of the things that I am proud of is that I made men like Joe Robinson [of Arkansas] and Pat Harrison [of Mississippi] swallow me hook, line, and sinker."[20] But these men would become increasingly suspicious of FDR after the so-called Second New Deal, begun after the 1934 midterm elections, shifted its focus to social insurance programs, strengthening labor unions, and more bluntly redistributing wealth. By the 1936 elections, the average Democratic opposition in Congress to the New Deal programs had tripled, from 7 percent to 20 percent.[21] Some administration initiatives even had difficulty passing or were mangled by the conservative House, and in the 1936 elections, FDR's share of the Southern vote actually declined from its 1932 peak.

FDR's 1936 landslide win marked a turning point. Having shown that a liberal coalition could win elections, he embarked upon his "Third New Deal"—a Supreme Court–packing plan, an executive reorganization bill, the minimum wage, seven regional TVAs, and a housing bill. He bypassed Senate majority leader Joe Robinson of Arkansas, to whom he had promised the first open Supreme Court seat, and instead appointed Hugo Black, the most liberal Southern Democratic senator. He intervened on behalf of pro–New Deal senator Alben Barkley of Kentucky in the race to replace Robinson after his death; Barkley beat Pat Harrison, the heir apparent, by one vote. It proved too much for the South to swallow. Aides warned FDR of the possibility of overreach, but Roosevelt's famous ego clouded his judgment: he assured his aides, "All we have to do is to let the flood of mail settle on Congress. You just see. All I have to do is devise a better speech, and the opposition will be beating a path to the White House door."[22]

The letters never came, and his speeches fell on deaf ears. For things had changed, and Southern conservatives now knew that they were no longer in control of the Democratic Party. For one hundred years, the rule that the Democratic nominee had to receive the approval of two-thirds of the delegates to the Democratic convention had given the South an effective veto over the nomination. That rule was sacrosanct: FDR's campaign manager had nearly botched the 1932 nomination by trying to remove the "two-thirds rule." But it was removed successfully in 1936, and now FDR was trying to weaken the few remaining institutions that stood in his way: the Supreme Court, and the seniority system that effectively guaranteed that Southerners would hold the positions of power in the legislative branch. A coalition of conservative Democrats, largely Southern, and Republicans killed or emasculated the Third New Deal and even held up Black's Supreme Court nomination.[23] In historian Susan Dunn's words, "Just nine months after Roosevelt's landslide election, opposition in his own party had grown assertive, militant, and confident—and the New Deal had come to a standstill."[24]

Roosevelt decided the time was ripe to rid himself of conservative Southerners. He had actually been doing this all along by using the New Deal to strengthen the populist factions in the South. Roosevelt believed that as the New Deal sent electricity to houses and made institutions like sharecropping less advantageous, the South would become more modernized, become more progressive, and elect representatives more like the North.[25] If Roosevelt could get more Hugo Blacks and Theodore Bilbos into the party, then the New Deal could move forward. In 1938, he decided it was time to take the next step and overtly campaign against conservative Southerners. He should have known better; Wilson had done the same in 1918, with disastrous results.[26] Nevertheless, berating Democrats who, "if they lived in the North, would not be Democrats anyway," Roosevelt set forth to do battle with his own party.[27] Believing he had an incipient progressive majority in the South, he even abandoned some of his more moderate rhetoric, going so far as to compare the South directly to a fascist state while campaigning in Georgia.[28]

It was a terrible miscalculation. Almost all of Roosevelt's intended victims won easily. Having survived a direct onslaught from Roosevelt, Southern conservatives no longer feared him and were emboldened to oppose him in even greater numbers. Figure 2.3 illustrates this by showing the shift in the ideological orientation of the Southern House delegation over time.

As the 1930s wore on, there was a clear drift of Southern Democrats in Congress toward the conservative side of the House—and remember, this filters out issues having to do directly with race.[29] By 1942, the *average* Southern Democrat was positioned somewhere roughly in between the parties on

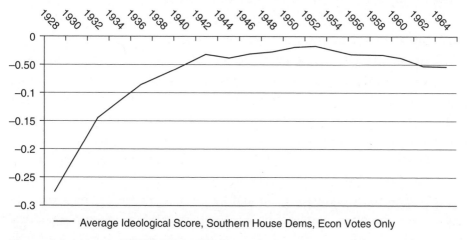

— Average Ideological Score, Southern House Dems, Econ Votes Only

Figure 2.3 Average DW-NOMINATE Score, S. House Dems, Economic Issues Only

economic issues, with many effectively voting like Republicans. As Dunn summarized, "many southerners remained *in* but not really *of* the Democratic Party."[30] With the *average* Southern Democrat voting almost like a Republican on purely economic issues, the end of the Solid South was inevitable. But it would take time. The Republican brand was still unwelcome in the South—the oldest Democrats like Carter Glass could still remember the Civil War and Reconstruction—and Southern control of local Democratic parties meant that they could still send conservative "Democrats in Name Only" to Congress. But the South had no such leverage at the presidential level, and the Southern presidential vote increasingly went to the Republicans.

At the same time, the South was growing, making the old "Hayes strategy" a viable one. Textile plants, paper mills, and even Kraft foods were moving southward, and once-sleepy towns like Richmond, Charlotte, and Atlanta became bustling cities.[31] These cities also began to provide support for Republicans; when Hoover nearly carried the South in 1928, these areas played a critical role in his success. In 1929, a prominent contemporary observer noted that "Republican rolls, once dedicated to n*gg*rs, hillbillies and other such pariahs, begins to smack of the Social Register."[32] In their award-winning book *The End of Southern Exceptionalism*, political scientists Byron Shafer and Richard Johnston carefully document the correlation between the rise of a wealthy, urban class in the South and the rise of Southern Republicanism. Shafer and Johnston thoroughly examined election data from 1952 through 2000 and found that, especially at the presidential level, the earliest steps of the Southern realignment were an outgrowth of economic development.[33]

This continued during the Great Depression. Samuel Lubell found that, in 1936, the poorest denizens of Houston gave Roosevelt 91 percent of the vote, while the richest gave Roosevelt 57 percent of the vote. In 1944, the poorest residents still gave Roosevelt 87 percent of their vote, while the wealthiest gave Roosevelt a mere 18 percent of the vote. From 1936 to 1968, the largest Republican gains in every Southern state except for Florida came in metropolitan areas.[34] As FDR's modernization campaign succeeded in changing the South, those newly wealthy voters pulled the lever not for progressive Democrats, as Roosevelt had hoped, but for conservative Republicans.[35]

The growth of Southern cities and industry also brought about the first great wave of Southern immigration. Examining the 1952 vote returns, political scientist Donald Strong is said to have exclaimed, "They're acting like Yankees!"

This was because many of them *were* Yankees.[36] Retirees from the Midwest and Northeast had begun to settle in Florida before the Depression, and the rise of Southern industry in the postwar South brought in Northern managers.[37] They brought their Republican voting habits with them. It is no accident that Roger Milliken, I. Lee Potter, and Thomas Brigham, the early Republican leaders in South Carolina, Virginia, and Alabama, respectively, hailed from New York, Pennsylvania, and Vermont.[38]

We can see how Part One of the "Southern switch" evolved plainly in Figure 2.4. Using the 1952 presidential election returns and a simple regression analysis, we can estimate how the GOP fared in succeeding elections in areas that voted for Eisenhower and Stevenson in 1952.[39] This chart basically answers the question: "In a county filled 100 percent with people who voted for Eisenhower in 1952, how would we expect that county to vote in 1956, or to have voted in 1940 (etc.)?" Because of the gradual addition of African American voters in the wake of the Voting Rights Act of 1965, we control for race in the post-1964 elections.

The two key takeaways from this chart are, first, that the areas Stevenson won in 1952 were areas where Democrats had *always* done well; and, second, even in 1944, the GOP was winning about 60 percent of the areas that would eventually pull the lever for Eisenhower. By 1960, the GOP hadn't added much of the "Stevenson" areas to its coalition.

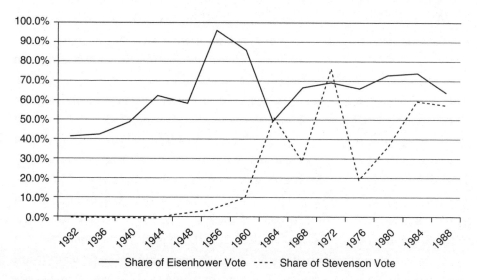

Figure 2.4 Estimated GOP Share of Eisenhower and Stevenson '52 Vote in South

In 1952, Eisenhower campaigned vigorously in the South, carried Virginia, Tennessee, Texas, and Florida, and came close in four other states. He came up only five thousand votes short in South Carolina, a state that had given Willkie 4.3 percent of the vote in 1940. Eisenhower added Louisiana, a Deep South state, to his Southern total in 1956 and came a few thousand votes from capturing a majority of all Southern voters. The party's presidential performance was buttressed by continued improvement in congressional races. Republicans won an isolated special election in west Texas in 1950, three congressional seats in Virginia and one in North Carolina in 1952 and an additional seat in Texas and Florida in 1954. Contemporary political science began taking the idea of realignment very seriously, and a number of books and journal articles began cropping up about the subject.[40] The days of the Solid South were over; its lifespan "fell just short of the Biblical three score and ten—a period of sixty-eight years from 1880 to 1948."[41]

In 1960, Richard Nixon performed almost as well as Eisenhower in the South, even though the election was much closer nationally. Virginia, Tennessee, and Florida fell into the Republican column for the third election in a row, and Nixon once again kept it close in Arkansas, North Carolina, South Carolina, and Texas. Unlike 1928, this probably was not due to anti-Catholic sentiment. Nixon's vote share closely tracked Eisenhower's, suggesting that no new factors were playing a role in 1960; the biggest shifts came *toward* Kennedy in heavily Catholic south Louisiana.[42] That Nixon could do so well in the South while part of an administration that had finished desegregating Washington, argued that segregation was unconstitutional before the Supreme Court, appointed the chief justice who wrote the *Brown v. Board* decision, implemented that decision with a show of force in Little Rock, and pushed through the Civil Rights Acts of 1957 and 1960 seems astonishing, until you realize that economics, rather than race, was primarily driving the development of Southern politics at the time.[43]

This remained the basis of the Republican coalition for years to come. Looking at the counties that Eisenhower won twice and that Nixon won in 1960, Republicans carried 36 percent of them in all seven elections from 1964 through 1988, carried 64 percent in all but one of those elections, and carried 95 percent in a majority of those later elections.[44] The Eisenhower/Nixon areas of the South became the Nixon/Ford/Reagan/Bush areas of the South.

Part One of the breakup of the Solid South was complete, and it was a result mostly of the "Hayes strategy" of allying indigenous Mountain Republicans with pro-business, Whiggish Southerners in the cities. In Part Two, the

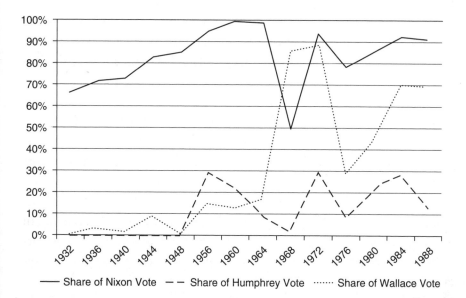

Figure 2.5 Estimated Republican Share of White Nixon/Wallace/Humphrey Vote, 1932–1988

Republicans used the Garfield and TR strategies to split the "Stevenson" areas into "Wallace" and "Humphrey" areas. To give us a better understanding of what was going on, Figure 2.5 reprises the regression analysis from above and estimates how the GOP performed in various elections in areas that supported each of the three candidates who ran in 1968.

The GOP broke through in the Wallace areas around 1964. There were three reasons for this. First, Republicans finally organized the rural South. The fact that the Republicans failed even to field candidates in almost any state or local elections from the late 1800s to the 1960s hamstrung the GOP by preventing it from building a "farm team" that could graduate to governorships or House and Senate seats.[45] It also scared off party switchers. Senator Harry Byrd of Virginia frequently contemplated switching parties, but he knew that his fearsome machine would not join him.[46] Instead, he would join a Virginia Republican party that did not have an executive secretary until 1955.[47]

Eisenhower's RNC opened a Southern division in 1957 under the leadership of I. Lee Potter, who launched an attempt to build a party infrastructure in the South called "Operation Dixie."[48] It bore fruit almost immediately. By 1961, Republican John Tower captured LBJ's Senate seat in Texas. A year later, a Republican Senate candidate came two points away from defeating longtime senator Lister Hill of Alabama, prompting Walter Dean Burnham to declare the arrival of two-party competition to that state.[49] Another Republican made a surprisingly strong showing against Olin Johnston in South Carolina, hinting at the incipient two-party competition there.[50] Jack Cox won 46 percent of the vote in the 1962 Texas gubernatorial race, while a Republican received a hitherto unheard-of 39 percent of the vote in Mississippi.[51]

Republican congressional candidates in 1962 received almost three times the number of votes in the south they had received in 1958.[52] And the Republican share of state legislative seats contested and won skyrocketed.[53] As the GOP developed a slate of experienced legislators downticket, it prepared to win races upticket, even in the Deep South.

Second, generational changes mattered. For older Democrats the Democratic Party was *their party*, and the New Dealers were the interlopers.[54] But as time progressed, it became clear that the New Dealers were not going to leave, and Southern Democrats who held onto the dream of re-creating the conservative Southern Democracy began to dwindle. Those who remembered the Civil War or Reconstruction were largely gone by the 1940s, their children not long after, and even those who remembered Hoover were becoming a minority in the 1970s. By the 1980s, many Southern voters did not remember segregated lunch counters. In 1988, Southerners aged 65 years or older (those who began voting before 1944) were split evenly between Republican and Democratic allegiance. Among those under 30 (born after 1958), Republicans had a 28-point edge.[55]

Finally, the resuscitation of the TR Strategy obviously played a major role in this phase of realignment. The outright anti–civil rights position taken by Goldwater in 1964 did not pay the dividends that he had hoped. He did well in areas that ended up voting for Wallace four years later, but he hemorrhaged support in the Nixon areas. He carried South Carolina, but Eisenhower and Nixon had both come close to doing so. His only real breakthroughs were in Georgia, Alabama, and Mississippi; he lost many of the Southern states that Eisenhower and Nixon had succeeded in placing in the GOP column. In the congressional races, the GOP fared overall a bit worse than it had in 1962, a year in which it had seen a massive jump in its Southern vote share.

In 1968, Nixon hit the sweet spot for the GOP. Like everything having to do with Nixon, his relationship with race issues is complicated. He came out against busing, requested a "slowdown" in the implementation of *Brown v. Board*, and nominated conservative Southerners to the Supreme Court.[56] But he also implemented affirmative action programs (if mainly to divide Labor), signed and expanded the Voting Rights Act of 1965, and never made a move on the Civil Rights Acts. He became the first GOP'er to carry a majority of the South in 1972, winning both the Eisenhower Southerners whom Goldwater had alienated and the Wallace voters.

It is important to remember, however, that the George McGovern Democrats were not to the left of the South only on racial issues, but also on a whole host of social, foreign policy, and economic issues. Southern Democrats had been fairly closely aligned with the GOP on such issues for quite some time, but in 1972 the gap between Southern Democrats and their national party became a chasm. After 40 years of hostility from the national Democratic Party on a range of issues—a hostility reciprocated by the South—a final divorce could not be avoided.

Nevertheless, if LBJ really did claim to have signed the South over to the GOP after signing the Civil Rights Act of 1964, he was wrong. Republican advances in the South did not accelerate after that legislation but rather progressed at their previous glacial pace, signaling that economic development, organization, and attrition still played critical roles. Between 1962 and 1988, the Republican share of the congressional vote in the South never fell below 31.5 percent (1964), but it also never topped 43.2 percent (1988). Republican Party identification likewise improved only slowly in the South, adding about 1 percent every year, in a fairly smooth line. It was not until 1988 that a majority of Southerners would consider themselves Republicans.[57] Throughout all this, the Republicans would find it frustratingly difficult to break through in the white Humphrey areas of Greater Appalachia, where racial issues were less salient and economic development was slower to arrive.

SOMETHING NEW: THE SUBURBS

The second major component of the Eisenhower coalition was suburban America, which sprang up across the country in the 1940s, 1950s, and 1960s. Although trolley lines began connecting American cities to "bedroom communities" in the late nineteenth century, Americans were still a city-dwelling people during the New Deal days. That changed in the years following World War II. In mid-1947, William Levitt and his sons began building a small planned community of bungalows in the potato fields of Nassau County.[58] Levittown was a hit; by 1951, it had built its initial plan of two thousand units eight times over. Across the country, young families of war veterans moved out of the cities to enjoy newfound prosperity. In 1940, 9 percent of the population lived in these bedroom communities. That number tripled to 28 percent by 1955.[59]

In 1948, a group of political scientists began conducting the National Election Study (NES). This study is conducted during every presidential and congressional election and seeks to track changes in political attitudes. Unfortunately, it has a relatively small sample size of about 1,500 respondents, making it difficult to engage in fine-grained analysis regarding the attitudes of different occupations or ethnic groups. This changed with the advent of exit polls, which have massive samples (usually in excess of fifteen thousand) and allow for more thorough analysis for the few questions they ask. But in the 1950s and 1960s, the NES contains the best data available. Figure 2.6 shows the percentage of the electorate the NES identified as living in suburban areas.

Republicans dominated in this growing segment of the electorate. Political scientists and sociologists have long debated the reason for this. Some hypothesize that many white ethnics and their descendants were exposed to Republicanism in the suburbs, some for the first time in their lives, and decided to conform to the extant majority.[60] Moving out of ethnic ghettoes in the city to ethnically homogenized areas could also induce white ethnics to leave their old voting habits behind, along with other aspects of ethnic identity.[61] Others argue that the new suburbanites were self-selecting—that more ambitious and upwardly mobile voters, who would be the most likely to lean Republican, moved to the suburbs.[62]

Regardless of the reason, suburbanites leaned significantly Republican from 1952 to 1988. Figure 2.7 shows the suburban vote in the United States during

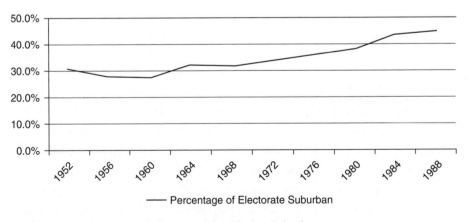

Figure 2.6   Percentage of Electorate Identified as Suburban

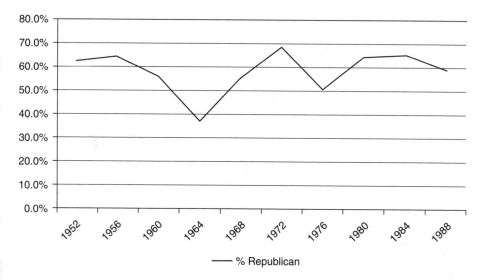

Figure 2.7 % Suburban Vote (Two Party) for Republicans

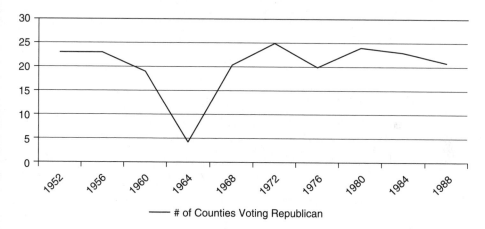

Figure 2.8 # of Counties Voting Republican Out of 25 Key Suburban Counties

this time, according to the NES. Republicans won, on average, 58.3 percent of the vote in the suburbs. During this time they leaned Democrat (that is, had a Democratic PVI) only in 1964, by one point.

The term "suburb" is vague and can include a heavily blue-collar, inner suburb like Parma, Ohio, as well as tony outer suburbs like McHenry County, Illinois. To help control for this, we also look at the vote in 25 key suburban counties and the number of times the Republican candidate carried these key counties.[63] As shown in Figure 2.8, from 1952 to 1988, Republicans carried 20 or more of these counties on all but two occasions: in 1960, the Catholic vote helped JFK carry 6 of them, while the Goldwater backlash helped LBJ carry 21 of them.

The suburbs played a critical role in the new Republican coalition. In 1920, the Philly suburbs provided about one in eight Republican voters for the state. By 1952, they provided 52 percent.[64] In New York, the New York City suburbs provided 8 percent of the 1920 Republican vote; in 1952 they provided 44 percent. When combined with the newfound votes in the South, the overall strength of the postwar Republican coalition became formidable. But there was one other crucial piece of the Eisenhower coalition.

SOMETHING BORROWED: THE WHITE WORKING CLASS

Unlike the South and the suburbs, the white working class was a transient member of the Republican coalition. Whether you define this group by geographic unit, by Catholicism, by ethnicity, or by union membership, these voters largely retained a loyalty to the Democratic Party that was hatched in their youth. Nevertheless, the Reagan Democrats who achieved prominence in the 1980s were not newcomers to occasional Republican voting. While FDR was more solicitous of white ethnics than he was of Southerners—unlike the South, they were a bedrock portion of his dreamed-of progressive coalition—many ethnic whites began shifting toward the Republicans in the late 1930s and 1940s.[65]

The renewed recession of 1938 proved devastating to the white working class and greatly weakened their belief in New Deal measures. The Democratic vote share in industrial immigrant districts fell from 57 percent in 1936 to 49 percent in 1938.[66] At the same time, Roosevelt directed his 1938 purge at a prominent conservative Irish politician, Rules Committee chairman John J. O'Connor. Indeed, defeating O'Connor was Roosevelt's one success, as James H. Fay, a World War I veteran who had lost a leg in combat, defeated O'Connor.[67] O'Connor was also running on the Republican ticket in 1938 and lost the general election in the overwhelmingly Irish district in 1938 by about 2,500 votes. In 1940, a Republican won the district.[68] Before the White House purge of O'Connor, it had never given a Republican more than a third of the vote.

As talk of war with Germany again began to stir in the mid-1930s, isolationist sentiment once again arose among immigrants. In 1936, William

Lemke did surprisingly well with his isolationist third-party bid among certain immigrants; he did well in his native North Dakota among Germans but also received 8 percent of the vote in Irish Boston.[69] Roosevelt also exhibited some tone deafness as he moved the nation to wartime footing. In 1940, after Italy declared war on France, he said in a speech that "[t]he hand that held the dagger has struck it into the back of its neighbor." Journalist Charles Peters recalls his father thinking the comment could hurt Roosevelt with Italians.[70] He was correct.

In the 1940 elections, as in the 1920 elections, voters of German, Italian, and Irish stock (the latter did not favor Roosevelt's Anglophile foreign policy) began to turn from the party that seemed to most heavily favor war against their home countries. In Minnesota, Wisconsin, and Iowa, the heaviest swings toward the GOP came in heavily German counties—about 30 points on average. Roosevelt narrowly lost Italian-Irish Staten Island and Queens after winning them by 33 points and 32 points, respectively, four years earlier. But those voters who hailed from countries that had been attacked by Hitler swung toward Roosevelt. In Minnesota, Wisconsin, and Iowa, the Scandinavian and Anglo-Saxon counties tended to swing toward Roosevelt,[71] while Polish wards in Buffalo went Democratic by nine-to-one margins.[72]

The bond between white ethnics and the Democrats was further weakened with the introduction of anticommunism as a national issue in the 1940s and 1950s. Catholics tended to be virulently anticommunist, and the Irish in particular embraced Wisconsin senator Joe McCarthy. Massachusetts governor Paul Dever once called McCarthy "the only man I know who could beat Archbishop Cushing in a two-man race in South Boston."[73] America's soon-to-be first Catholic family, the Kennedys, maintained a warm relationship with McCarthy: McCarthy dated JFK's sisters, was godfather to Kathleen Kennedy Townsend, and employed a young Bobby on his staff as assistant counsel.[74] Bobby wept upon the news of McCarthy's death and even accompanied the casket to the private gravesite where the senator was laid to rest.[75] Irish anticommunism went so deep that Joe Kennedy had endorsed Richard Nixon in his infamous 1950 campaign against Helen Gahagan Douglas (JFK delivered the news, a check, and well-wishes), and JFK later called the press treatment of Nixon in that race "disgusting."[76]

Eisenhower was keenly aware of this sentiment. As Democrats increasingly attacked the Wisconsin senator, Ike remained mute, even though he quietly loathed McCarthy.[77] It paid off, as Ike's biggest gains in Massachusetts came in Catholic strongholds like Suffolk and Bristol Counties. In heavily Catholic wards across the nation, Stevenson received a lower vote share than Truman had; in Pawtucket, Rhode Island, the Democratic vote fell 16 points; in Chicago's 32nd ward (Polish), the vote fell 8 percent; in Chicago's 18th ward (Irish), the vote fell 6 points. In 1952, the Republican carried Buffalo.[78] By 1956, a half-dozen middle-class Catholic assembly districts in New York were casting more votes for Republicans than were the upper-class silk-stocking districts of the Upper East Side.[79]

Absent JFK's nomination, Nixon probably would have taken the Catholic vote and the election—even Kennedy privately claimed that he would vote for Nixon over the other Democratic contenders.[80] In 1964, the stridently anticommunist Goldwater ran surprisingly well in Catholic enclaves; Kevin Phillips estimates that he won 44 percent of the white vote in the city.[81] Although both Goldwater and Alf Landon received about 38 percent of the vote nationwide, Goldwater ran far behind Landon in the traditionally WASP-y counties of New England. He made up for these losses not only in the South and West but also in heavily working-class counties like Camden and Hudson County, New Jersey, in Brooklyn and Staten Island, and in Brown County (Green Bay), Wisconsin. Figure 2.9 shows the volatile Catholic vote from 1952 to 1988, which swung from a high of 61 percent for Republicans in 1972 to a low of 17 percent in 1960.

Catholics always leaned Democratic compared to the general population: by 1 point in 1980 and 1972; by 7 points in 1952, 1976, and 1988; by 17 points in 1964; and by 33 points in 1960. But note that Nixon and Reagan performed

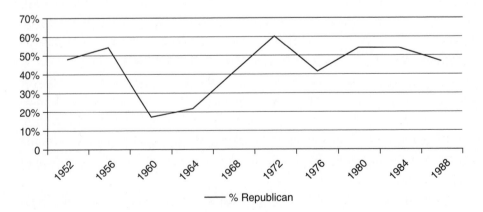

Figure 2.9   Republican Two-Party Share of Catholic Vote

little better among Catholics than Eisenhower did. This is also true if we try to isolate the "white working class" in different ways. Among members of labor unions, for example, Ronald Reagan's numbers in 1980 and 1984 (45 percent and 43 percent), George H. W. Bush's in 1988 (41 percent), and Nixon's in 1968 (44 percent) are reminiscent of Eisenhower's 1952 and 1956 showings (44 percent and 48 percent).

The Eisenhower coalition of traditional Republicans, upscale Southerners, suburbanites, and white ethnics dominated Republican strategy for the next three decades. Around 1,700 counties leaned Republican in the 1952 election. Of those counties, roughly 70 percent leaned Republican in every election from 1952 to 1988. Eighty percent leaned Republican in 1956, 1960, 1968, 1980, and 1984. To be sure, there were variants on the Eisenhower coalition in all these elections, but the basic coalition was the same.

SOMETHING BLUE: THE DEMOCRATS' COALITION, 1952–1988

Of course, the Democrats were not shut out of electoral politics during this time period. They averaged about 45.5 percent of the popular vote during these years—not a strong showing, but not on par with the 1920–1928 years, either. While the Mountain West Progressive became an endangered species as isolationism became discredited and cities and suburbs transformed former mining and ranching enclaves into the most urbanized states in the country, the white Southern Democrat had not yet become extinct, and the white working class was still sympathetic toward the Democrats on economic issues. We can see where the Democrats maintained their strength by looking at two maps. Figure 2.10 shows the counties that voted for the Democratic candidate in every election from 1952 to 1964 and again in 1976. In other words, these were the counties that pulled the lever for (1) Adlai Stevenson amid two landslide losses; (2) Catholic JFK; (3) pro–civil rights, liberal LBJ; and (4) a Deep Southerner like Jimmy Carter.

There are interesting stories behind almost all these counties (the lone Democratic county in Wyoming maintained Democratic voting habits dating back to the building of the Union Pacific railroad), but we will focus on two clusters. First, many of the major Northern cities are hidden on the map: Detroit, San Francisco, Seattle, St. Louis, Boston, and New York City all consistently

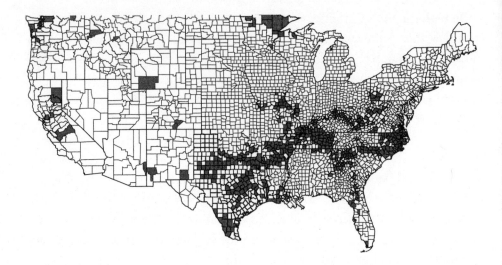

Figure 2.10   Counties Never Voting Republican, 1952, 1956, 1960, 1964, 1976

voted for Democrats. This is reflective of the Democrats' continued strength among liberals and minorities. These groups increasingly dominated the cities as white ethnics fled to the suburbs and as the Second Great Migration of African Americans from Southern farms to Northern cities continued in the postwar years.

The African American vote continued to swing against the GOP, especially in the post-Goldwater era. Even Eisenhower struggled to get above 30 percent of the African American vote, but in 1964, African American precincts where Alf Landon had received one-third of the vote in 1936 went 50-to-1 for Johnson.[82] It would be a lasting split. Even liberal Republicans like Jacob Javits and Nelson Rockefeller struggled to receive one-third of the vote in African American districts, post-Goldwater.[83]

At the same time, the African American vote in the North grew. From 1940 to 1960, the black population in St. Louis grew from 13 percent to 29 percent, in Detroit from 9 to 29 percent, in Chicago from 8 to 23 percent, and in Cleveland from 10 to 29 percent.[84] This further broke down the relationship between white ethnics and the Democratic Party, as these newcomers competed not only for jobs but for influence in the Democratic Party, and for the spoils of patronage. Northern machines, already creaky, collapsed. At the same time, the urban liberal vote was finally coalescing in the Democratic Party. The

1958 election was a watershed event for Northern liberals, as Democrats began to win districts in Massachusetts outside Boston and "Southie," won their first Senate seat in Maine since direct elections of senators began, and elected their first-ever congressman from Vermont.

But the most reliably Democratic areas were clustered in the Jacksonian Uplands. During this time, these voters proved that they were still willing to vote for just about any variant of Democrat against almost any variant of Republican. The counties were small, but together they added millions of votes to the Democratic column and reliably sent Democrats to Washington. To be sure, when the national anti-Democratic deluge was strong enough, these counties voted narrowly for the Republican. But even then, a disproportionate number of the McGovern and Mondale counties were located in Greater Appalachia.

A map of how counties *leaned* from 1952 to 1988, relative to the rest of the country, puts this in stark relief. Figure 2.11 shows a mass of Democratic-leaning counties in the heart of these upland areas.

This base was strong enough that Democrats could still win presidential elections but only under propitious circumstances. For example, in 1960 they

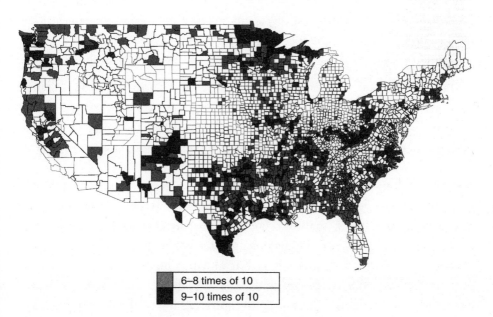

| | 6–8 times of 10 |
| | 9–10 times of 10 |

Figure 2.11   # Times County Leaned Toward Democrats, 1952–1988

nominated the one candidate who could win over the Catholic vote, who in turn selected the one running mate who could keep them from losing the South—barely. That JFK and LBJ were exceptions, rather than the rule, demonstrates that it was the Eisenhower coalition, not the New Deal coalition, that was dominant. Even then, Kennedy probably should be credited with losing the popular vote, as votes for "unpledged Democratic electors" in certain Southern states were almost certainly cast against him.[85] Similarly, Carter was able to reverse GOP advances among Wallace voters enough to eke out a narrow win, although the strength of the Eisenhower coalition was such that, even following a terrible recession and a presidential resignation, the Republicans came very close to winning the 1976 election.

The one landslide Democratic win came in 1964. But LBJ did not win with the New Deal coalition. Although Roosevelt and LBJ both won roughly the same share of the popular vote, over half the states in the country saw a net shift in the Democrats' share of the vote in excess of 20 points. Unlike FDR, LBJ ran well behind his national averages in the South, in the Mountain West, and in the Great Plains. Maine and Vermont, which had resisted FDR's entreaties four times, gave LBJ 38- and 33-point wins, respectively. Overall, only 13 states in 1964 had the same partisan lean they had in 1936. To put that in perspective, 15 states maintained the same partisan lean they had in 1964 in *every* election from 1968 through 2008. LBJ's win didn't so much represent the last gasp of the New Deal coalition as it did a precursor of what the future held for the Democrats. The only real constant came in the Jacksonian areas of the nation: Kentucky, southern Illinois, Indiana, Ohio, and Missouri all turned in similar percentages for LBJ as they had for FDR in 1936.

THE IDEOLOGY OF THE EISENHOWER MAJORITY

The suggestion that the breakdown of the New Deal coalition began in the late 1930s and early 1940s, rather than 1968 or 1980, is a novel one today. Yet in the 1950s and 1960s, analysts were keenly aware that FDR's coalition was coming unglued. Truman's 1948 campaign strategy memo, the famous "Rowe Memo," described the Democrats as "an unhappy alliance of Southern conservatives, Western progressives and Big City labor"[86] and spent the better part of 31 single-spaced pages trying to figure out how to hold them together. Samuel Lubell, writing in the mid-1950s, noted that "[i]n the winter of 1951, it seemed clear that the victorious coalition which Franklin Roosevelt brought together had disintegrated" and concluded that "[w]e are in a period of party realignment."[87] In the 1970s, Richard Scammon and Ben Wattenberg likewise suggested that the period of Democratic dominance of American politics had come to an end in 1948.[88]

While the Eisenhower coalition came together in 1952, the ideology that drove it appeared much earlier. What was this ideology? It was the simple "three-legged stool" that Republican candidates still talk about today: acceptance of the basic outlines of the New Deal but resistance toward its further expansion, a staunchly anticommunist foreign policy, and a "go slow" approach to social change.[89] The recession of 1937–1938 played a large role in changing Americans' perceptions of government action. Fifty-eight percent connected the decline with Roosevelt's policies, according to Gallup. In May 1939, 69 percent of Americans believed that Roosevelt's attitude toward businesses was delaying recovery. Fifty-five percent of respondents believed that, in order to create jobs and reduce unemployment, it would be better to follow the ideas of big businessmen, versus 45 percent who favored the Roosevelt administration. When asked in December 1937 whether government should begin spending money again in an attempt to end the slump, 62 percent of Americans answered in the negative.

Polling in the late 1930s shows consistent majorities against *expanding* the New Deal further and attitudes turning against welfare measures. Fifty-eight percent opposed Roosevelt's court-packing plan. Fifty-three percent favored relief reductions, while 79 percent opposed direct payments to relief recipients. During the General Motors sit-down strikes of 1937, 56 percent expressed greater sympathy for GM than the workers. When Congress defeated Roosevelt's $3 billion pump-priming bill in 1939, 68 percent approved.[90] To be sure, there was support for the basic idea of the New Deal; regulation of the stock market, the Social Security Act, and the Fair Labor Standards Act remained popular. But people were ready for a very, very lengthy breather from further innovation. When asked whether they supported the Roosevelt administration continuing with its agenda, improving existing laws without trying anything new, or "letting conservative elements in the party try to undo the damage already done," only 19 percent opted for expansion, 40 percent supported tinkering with existing programs, while 27 percent wanted to let "conservative elements" loose.[91]

As a result of this, New Deal candidates had increasing difficulty winning elections. The United States entered a period of "open field politics," a term that Michael Barone later used to describe post-2006 America.[92] Republicans came close to winning the popular vote for Congress in 1938, won the popular vote but not Congress in 1942, and won huge majorities in 1946. In between, Democrats won presidential elections and a congressional landslide in 1948. From 1938 through 1958, the Democrats averaged 51 percent of the vote for Congress—and this included a large number of votes for Southern Democrats who intended to vote with Republicans most of the time.

The New Deal ideology was also unable to win the White House post-1938. Absent the onset of war in Europe, it is unlikely that Roosevelt would have won a third term. In May 1939, only 33 percent of Americans favored such a third Roosevelt term. Shortly after that poll was taken, Hitler claimed Czechoslovakia. By August, support for an additional Roosevelt term was up to 40 percent. After Hitler's invasion of Poland in September, 43 percent supported a third term. During the "phony war" period, support for a third term stayed more or less stable, drifting upward a few points by April. On April 9, the Nazis invaded Denmark and Norway. On May 10, Hitler invaded France. The next Gallup poll showed support for a Roosevelt third term shooting up ten points from its prior measurement, to 57 percent; this is also when Roosevelt likely decided to try for that term, rather than take a $75,000 contract to write for *Collier's*.[93] Nevertheless, when Gallup asked, after the 1940 election, for whom respondents would have voted absent the war, 53 percent answered that they would have voted for Republican nominee Wendell Willkie—an industrialist with no experience in elective office—while only 47 percent said Roosevelt.[94] When *Forbes* asked who would do a better job on solving unemployment, Willkie led 50.4 percent to 37.6 percent. Asked who would do a better job on government spending, 56 percent favored Willkie to Roosevelt's 35.9 percent. But on foreign policy, only 42 percent favored Willkie.[95] The New Deal coalition did not propel Roosevelt into a third term; World War II did.

Roosevelt won another foreign policy election in 1944, but it was a modest, single-digit win. Truman won a stunning victory in 1948 amid an economic downturn, which was as much the result of Dewey's blundering as the public's love of Truman. Dewey, believing he had an insurmountable lead, ran a rose-garden strategy. The California campaign office was closed down in mid-October; he lost the state by four-tenths of a point.[96] At the same time, the Republican-controlled Congress stumbled through the end of its session. One contemporary observed that but for Congress, "Dewey might have made some of the very inroads that 'Ike' accomplished."[97] As for the continued vitality of the New Deal coalition, George Gallup correctly noted that Truman's win resembled Wilson's 1916 coalition more than Roosevelt's, suggesting a potential coalition for the Democrats that never came to pass.[98] Dewey surged in the cities but lost badly in the farm counties, where a farm recession was in swing and where isolationism among ethnic Germans was in retreat; Truman's argument that Dewey would put a "pitchfork in the farmer's back" may have saved him.[99] In counties where more than fifty thousand ballots were cast (accounting for about half the total ballots cast in 1948), Dewey ran four points ahead of his 1944 vote total. Similar gains in the smaller counties would have given Dewey the win, but instead he ran five points behind his 1944 totals there.

The "three-legged stool" that the GOP discovered in the 1940s remained the basic approach taken by the GOP throughout this time. Except for Goldwater, all the GOP nominees were in the Willkie/Dewey/Eisenhower line of the party, accepting the basic New Deal contours but pushing back against expansion into new areas. The only possible exception besides Goldwater was Ronald Reagan. But the distinctions between Reagan and Eisenhower are largely overblown, resting more on Reagan's rhetoric than his actions. Obviously, both were committed anticommunists. Eisenhower loathed the New Deal personally but believed that it was impossible to undo.[100] Regardless of his rhetoric, Reagan was similar. He made little effort to undo the New Deal programs that still survived in the 1980s. He abandoned his Goldwaterite opposition to the minimum wage and Social Security and even worked to shore up the latter program.[101] Contemporary conservatives were furious with much of Reagan's presidency and were apoplectic when he agreed to meet with Soviet premier Mikhail Gorbachev.

What made Reagan different from earlier Republicans was that the 1960s and 1970s had created a host of new issues for the country. While new issues frequently work to split a governing coalition, in this instance, they pushed the Eisenhower coalition together. The Democrats had overreached with the Great Society, pushing the New Deal envelope at a time when many Americans were content with the status quo. The redistributive programs of the Great Society—expanded AFDC, the Office of Economic Opportunity, embryonic affirmative action—offered perfect targets for Reagan and his budget-cutters. But Great Society programs that were outgrowths of the New

Deal social insurance programs, such as Medicare and Medicaid, were largely untouched.

The inflation of the 1960s and 1970s also brought the issue of taxes to the forefront to a degree unimaginable in the 1950s. As inflation pushed voters into higher and higher tax brackets, they saw their income tax bills shoot up while their wages were stagnant in real terms.[102] Taxes were always unpopular, even in Eisenhower's day.[103] But by 1978, 80 percent of Americans thought that their taxes were "unreasonable."[104] And of course, the surge in crime in the 1960s, the rise of the counterculture, and a series of Supreme Court decisions seeming to enshrine counterculture values gave salience to a whole host of issues that simply hadn't been on the country's radar screen in 1952. In other words, Reagan's presidency was largely consistent with Eisenhower's, with some new issues thrown into the mix. Perhaps Reagan would have governed further to the right with a Republican House, but that is unknowable.

THE EISENHOWER COALITION IN THE HOUSE

It is true that the Democrats rarely lost the House from 1932 to 1988. But this continued majority comes with a massive asterisk. As we've noted, the Southern realignment in Congress lagged behind the realignment at the presidential level largely because Southerners could still elect conservative Democrats to Congress. These congressmen were frequently more ideologically sympathetic to Republicans on a wide range of issues, and so they frequently formed coalitions with Republicans to block the national Democratic agenda. Figure 2.12 illustrates the impact of conservative Southerners on the congressional coalitions by showing the ideology of the median representative from 1932 to 1988.

After 1938, the median legislator in Congress is pretty close to the middle in terms of ideology. In fact, in the five years that Congress was controlled by Democrats—1942, 1944, 1950, 1954, and 1956—the median legislator fell on the conservative end of the spectrum; in those years, the Democrats had to appeal to legislators who were more ideologically sympathetic to Republicans than Democrats, even on nonracial issues, in order to pass legislation. From 1938 through 1974, the median legislator was just a shade to the left of center, except for the Democratic blowout years of 1958 and 1964. After 1974, reforms in the House and the expansion of the Southern electorate after the Voting

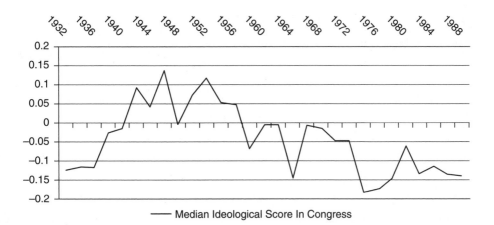

Figure 2.12   Median Ideological Score in Congress: 1932–1988

Rights Act made it more difficult to be a conservative Democrat. As we'll see in chapter 3, while this finally gave the Democratic congressional coalition a sustained leftward tilt, it also paved the way for the destruction of that coalition.

Congress essentially had a three-party system for most of this time.[105] Michael Barone has calculated that by 1944, the New Dealers in Congress made up less than a quarter of its membership. Around 45 percent of the House was typically Republican. The remainder was made up of conservative Democrats of various stripes, who frequently voted with Republicans. Because of this, neither Roosevelt nor Truman was able to significantly advance the New Deal agenda after 1937. The Works Progress Administration (WPA) and Civilian Conservation Corps (CCC) were killed in 1942, while the National Youth Administration (NYA) received the budgetary axe in 1943. The Smith-Connally Act, passed over Roosevelt's veto, began a pushback against organized labor, which was followed by an override of Truman's veto of the Taft-Hartley Act a few years later.[106] In 1944, Roosevelt asked for $12 billion in higher income taxes. Instead, he received a bill for $2 billion. It was vetoed, and the veto was overridden—the only time that has happened on a tax bill.[107]

Truman requested price controls, a full-employment bill, a higher minimum wage, national health insurance, federal aid to education, rural electrification, Alasksan and Hawaiian statehood, and a tax credit to all taxpayers.[108] He received the higher minimum wage, while Republicans and Democrats gutted the Office of Price Administration.[109] He asked for minimal tax cuts, yet

Congress enacted $5 billion more than he had requested.[110] There were a few other successes, but they came in the form of building on existing New Deal programs rather than enacting new ones: a higher minimum wage, expanded antitrust laws, an increase in Social Security.[111] America had decided that it liked the basic New Deal social insurance system but was skeptical about expanding it to other areas. Only during a brief flurry of activity from 1964 to 1966 were substantial expansions approved, and this led to a swift turnaround in American politics.

■   ■   ■

Once again, the shift in American politics was driven largely by contingencies. Had Roosevelt maintained the cautious approach that characterized the first New Deal, the politics of the late 1900s would have been very different. Had Roosevelt not succeeded in scrapping the "two-thirds rule" at the 1936 Democratic National Convention or had World War II not erupted, the South might have been able to reassert primacy in 1940, and Democrats might not have been a center-left party going into the 1940s. Even so, by 1944, the New Deal coalition was so weakened that Roosevelt had to abandon his liberal vice president and accept a fairly conservative successor in exchange for a fourth nomination. Choices by Willkie, Dewey, and Eisenhower made the creation of a new majority possible, while some fairly reckless choices by Roosevelt played a contributing role.

This coalition was given an extended lifespan by forces that would have been nearly impossible for a political observer sitting in the 1930s or 1940s to predict. The rise of the suburbs, the rise of the counterculture, the implementation of the Great Society, the continuation of the Cold War, and the leftward shift of the Democrats all were contingencies that played to Republican strengths, ensured their dominance at the presidential level, and kept the Conservative Coalition in charge in Congress. But this run of good luck was about to come to an end, and Republicans were about to learn that abandoning the positions that made the Eisenhower coalition viable would have serious consequences.

CHAPTER 3

THE RISE OF THE CLINTON COALITION

1992–2006

George McGovern stands today for the rejuvenation of the Democratic Party. He is the leader of a coalition of citizen participation, a coalition for change, as broad as FDR's in 1932....He has read more accurately than anyone else the disquietudes of the nation.

Arthur M. Schlesinger, Jr., July 30, 1972[1]

THE POLARIZATION OF THE PARTIES: 1964–1988

By 1988, a cottage industry had sprung up among political scientists attempting to explain why the Republicans could never win control of Congress yet had a seeming "lock" on the Electoral College.[2] The consensus view was something like this: The Democratic brand had a diversity that allowed Democrats to simultaneously send to Congress staunch segregationists like William Tuck and African American ministers like Adam Clayton Powell, Jr. This made it difficult for the Republicans to take more than nominal control of Congress. At the same time, this diversity precluded Democrats from unifying around a presidential candidate in most years and forced prospective Democratic nominees to attempt to make appeals to a variety of interest groups, rather than formulating a single message with appeal to a broad swath of the electorate. The result was that in the 1968, 1972, 1980, 1984, and 1988 elections, there were

38 states worth 410 electoral votes where the Democrats never once carried a majority of the votes.

Moreover, even as the country yearned for stability in the wake of the Great Society and the 1960s, the Democrats imposed structural changes that pushed the party leftward. The Voting Rights Act enfranchised tens of thousands of blacks and poor whites, who flocked into the Democratic electorates in the South. In 1966, Virginia senator A. Willis Robertson and Rules Committee chairman Howard W. Smith both lost their primaries to liberal challengers as a result of these engorged electorates.[3] House District of Columbia Committee chairman John McMillan of South Carolina almost lost his primary to an African American doctor in 1970 and lost to a relatively liberal Democrat two years later.[4] In 1974, John Rarick—whose overall voting record made him the nineteenth most conservative member of Congress from either party—lost a Democratic primary in Louisiana to Jeff LaCaze, a broadcaster who ran with the support of African Americans and labor unions.[5] In the wake of the 1968 convention, Democrats decided to base their presidential nomination process more fully on primary results, further empowering the grassroots left.

Perhaps most important, liberals were organizing the House and making life miserable for conservative Democrats. In 1959, liberals founded the Democratic Study Group, which set about trying to figure out how to break the conservatives' hold on the House agenda.[6] The problem they identified was that Southerners rarely lost their seats once elected. This allowed them to climb the seniority ladder, take over key committees, and bottle up legislation. The frustrations grew throughout the 1960s, as the Great Society Congress gave liberals a taste of success. In 1971 and 1973, the DSG pushed through a series of changes to the party's rules. They subjected committee chairmen to automatic up-or-down votes by secret ballot at the beginning of each Congress, ended the process of chairmen appointing subcommittee chairs, and limited Democrats to one subcommittee chairmanship. This forced more chairmanships down the seniority ladder and toward liberal members.[7] Other reforms enhanced the Speaker's power to force legislation to move through committee, breaking through Southern bottlenecks.[8] When the 1974 midterms added 75 new, mostly liberal members to the Democratic caucus, liberals finally had their chance to purge conservative Southern Democrats. Agriculture chairman W. R. Poage of Texas, Armed Services chairman F. Edward Hebert of Louisiana, and Banking and Currency chairman Wright Patman all were denied their chairmanships.[9]

Southern Democrats received the message. In the early 1970s, a majority of Southern Democrats voted against their party more often than not on key votes; only 14 percent voted with the party on 70 percent or more of these votes. This immediately reversed after the 1975 purge. By the end of the 1980s, only 5 percent of Southerners were in the "opposition" camp, while almost 70 percent could be considered party loyalists.[10] Perhaps the most striking turnaround came on civil rights issues, with overwhelming majorities of Southern Democrats voting to kill Republican amendments to weaken the Voting Rights Act extensions of 1981. Every Southern Democratic senator voted to override President Bush's veto of the Civil Rights Act of 1990.[11] Of course, these were still fairly conservative members who would buck the party leadership, especially on social issues like guns and abortion. But Southern Democrats were worlds apart from where they had been only a few decades before.

At the same time, the Republican Party was shifting rightward. The Supreme Court's school prayer and abortion decisions brought a new sense of urgency to religious conservatives, who organized groups like the Christian Coalition and began supporting Republican candidates in droves. Social conservatism became less associated with traditionalism and more linked with evangelicism. Unlike other countries, the religious right in America brought with it an antistatist message on economic issues, further enhancing the power of Goldwater-ites in the party.[12] Republican liberals saw their ranks depleted by primary challenges, as venerable senators like Clifford Case and Jacob Javits both lost renomination fights.

Reagan engaged in what one observer called an "awkward dance" with the Christian Right, offering enough symbolic gestures to placate them while trying not to alienate his party's moderates.[13] But this became harder as the right grew in strength. In 1988, evangelist Pat Robertson came in second place in the Iowa caucuses, ahead of George H. W. Bush, and Robertson delegates began swarming to Republican state conventions nationwide. Bush delegates split evenly between moderates and conservatives, while the Robertson delegates were almost uniformly conservative.[14] These delegates tended to be new to the political process, relatively well educated, and, most important, much younger than Bush supporters.[15] This was the future of the Republican Party, and it would make sustaining the Eisenhower coalition very difficult. In 1989, a fiery backbench congressman from Georgia named Newt Gingrich won a hard-fought race to replace Dick Cheney as minority whip. He set about trying to fulfill the promise of the Reagan Revolution and pushed the party to fight against the increasingly liberal Democratic Congress, rather than compromise with it.

At the same time, these changed parties were interacting with a changed world. In 1989, communist regimes across Eastern Europe collapsed, and in 1991, the Soviet Union itself disbanded. The Cold War was over. Crime peaked in 1991 and began to fall. Inflation began to fall in mid-1980 and was brought under control by 1982. "Bracket creep" was eliminated by the 1981 tax reforms, and the tax burden began to fall. At the same time, Americans were becoming increasingly at ease with many of the social changes of the 1960s, and the more radical elements of the counterculture tended to find themselves both subsumed and diluted in mainstream American culture. In other words, the very issues holding the Eisenhower coalition together were receding into the background.

This began to show up in the 1988 presidential election returns. George H. W. Bush experienced a solid win over Michael Dukakis, but he had to make up a massive deficit in the polls. Even then, his win represented the second-smallest victory margin for a Republican presidential candidate since 1900. Bush ran about five points behind Regan's 1984 showing. The decline was apparent in almost every demographic group outside of the South but was especially pronounced among young and first-time voters. The Eisenhower coalition was in trouble. All that held it together was the positioning of the Democrats on the left side of the football field.

THE RISE OF THE NEW DEMOCRATS

Behind the scenes, Democrats were preparing for this new world. In the wake of the 1980 elections, a group of Southern Democrats formed the Conservative Democratic Forum (CDF), an attempt to push back on the liberal drift of the party.[16] CDF founder Charles Stenholm of Texas declared: "We need to change the direction of our party, or we will soon be a minority in the House."[17] While conservative Southern Democrats held the balance of power for a brief moment during the Reagan presidency, after the 1982 midterms that was no longer the case. The CDF lost its leverage and disbanded. But other groups with similar ideas were springing up. The House Democratic Caucus Committee on

Party Effectiveness, under caucus chairman Gillis Long of Louisiana, sought not to empower conservatives so much as to bring the center of the party back toward the middle—in other words, to bring the groups together, rather than strengthen countervailing factions. In a publication titled *Rebuilding the Road to Opportunity*, two young congressmen, Tim Wirth and Richard Gephardt, spelled out an economic future for the Democrats that shifted away from economic redistribution and toward using government to empower economic growth.[18] It was politely applauded, then ignored.

In the wake of Gillis Long's death in 1985 and the appointment of Paul Kirk of Massachusetts as national party chair, these moderates opted to work outside the confines of Congress. Al From, a Long aide and executive director of the House caucus, joined with Will Marshall to found the Democratic Leadership Council (DLC).[19] From succinctly summarized the DLC views of the party's problem: "We had lost touch with middle-class voters. We were a party that in the 1980 platform spent three times as much space talking about police brutality as public safety."[20]

In 1989, the DLC set up a think tank, the Progressive Policy Institute (PPI), to act as its policy-creation arm. Through the PPI, intellectuals like Bill Galston and Elaine Kamarck argued that "liberal fundamentalism" had rendered the Democrats ineffective, unable to win elections, and out of touch with working-class concerns.[21] They declared that the white working class was becoming increasingly isolated from the upscale, liberal wing of the party and its preoccupation with issues like environmentalism and its aversion even to questioning affirmative action, crime, and antipoverty programs.[22] They concluded:

> The next Democratic nominee must convey a clear understanding of, and identification with, the social values and moral sentiments of average Americans. The firm embrace of programs, such as national service, that link rights to responsibilities and effort to reward would be a good start. The consistent use of middle-class values—individual responsibility, hard work, equal opportunity—rather than the language of compensation would also help. And finally, the American people overwhelmingly believe that the central purpose of criminal punishment is to punish—to express our moral outrage against acts that injure our community. The next Democratic nominee cannot appear indifferent to the victims of violent crime.[23]

The division between the New Democrats and Old Democrats is best illustrated by the issue of child care. Old Democrats favored the "ABC Bill," which would have set up a series of federally funded, state-supervised day-care centers with national licensing and standards. This was caricatured by fiscal conservatives as another federal big spending plan—"government baby-sitting" was the phrase—while social conservatives believed that the government should not be subsidizing working mothers at all. The DLC solution was in the middle—a tax credit to poor people in need of day care to be spent at private child-care centers of the mother's choice.[24] This eventually morphed into the child tax credit, which addressed the concerns of social conservatives by subsidizing stay-at-home mothers as well. Other New Democrat apostasies included shifting emphasis from increasing the minimum wage to expansions of the Earned Income Tax Credit.[25]

By changing their approach on fiscal matters, social change, and foreign policy, the New Democrats were able to compete for pieces of the Eisenhower coalition. They were doing so at a particularly propitious moment—when the issue was no longer how to win the Cold War but what to do with the peace, and at a time when Republican competence on economic and social issues was being challenged by a recession and a glacial recovery from it. It was a time similar to the early 1930s and late 1940s, when increasingly dissatisfied portions of one party's coalition were taking a look at the other party.

DLC CENTRISM AND THE 1992 ELECTIONS

Over the years, the most successful presidential candidates have been those with a broad range of experiences that teach them how to relate to different portions of the country. FDR was a patrician New Yorker who came to understand the South during his period of convalescence there. Kennedy was an Irish Catholic whose Harvard experience gave him credibility with the Northeastern liberal establishment. Reagan was a Goldwater-ite whose beginnings as a New Dealer taught him how to relate to disaffected Democrats.

So it was with William Jefferson Clinton, the senior governor in the country in 1992. His life experiences created what John Judis and Ruy Teixeira have described as the three faces of Bill Clinton.[26] Clinton's humble beginnings in Hope, Arkansas, in the heart of Greater Appalachia, taught him to relate to average Americans and instilled an understanding of Jacksonian economic, social, and foreign policy populism—Clinton the Southern Populist. His time at Georgetown, Oxford, and Yale Law School exposed him to the counterculture and New Left of the 1960s—Clinton the Liberal. And his time as governor of a small, conservative state during a time when the Democratic Party was shifting leftward and at a time when economic development was changing the landscape of his state taught him the utility of melding the two strains—Clinton the New Democrat. Clinton had been developing a "New Democrat" philosophy since the early 1980s: in preparation for a documentary on Clinton, Ben Wattenberg found speeches from 1981 and 1984 exploring many of the very themes that Clinton would push in his 1992 campaign.[27]

And so Clinton was better positioned to synthesize the New Democrat message than anyone else.[28] During his entire 1992 campaign, he focused on winning over the white working-class voters who had abandoned the party of FDR and the suburbanites who were alienated by the increasingly religious tone of the GOP's base. His announcement speech made ten references to the middle class in seven pages.[29] His early campaign document, the "Plan for America's Future," centered on a middle-class tax cut, a child tax credit, affordable home loans, and infrastructure development to help Americans meet the demands of the twenty-first century.[30]

At the same time, he took positions that, in DLC parlance, "inoculated" him from Republican attacks. Unlike many Democrats, he did not reflexively shy away from military action. He embraced the death penalty, hiring 100,000 new police officers, and—in a bid for the suburbs—implementing gun-control measures to combat crime. When he talked about issues from which he could not completely deviate from Democratic orthodoxy without losing his base—things like abortion and affirmative action—the rhetoric was measured: he was for mending, not ending affirmative action, and wanted abortion to be "safe, legal, and rare." And most important, he took on perhaps the greatest source of attacks against the Democratic Party, calling for *ending*, not mending, welfare as we knew it, and transitioning to a system whereby welfare was a temporary assistance program rather than a way of life.[31]

After winning the nomination, Clinton sought to reinforce his New Democrat credentials by selecting centrist senator Al Gore as his running mate (that Gore was also a Southern Democrat from the Jacksonian uplands who might help put the border states back in play was an added bonus). The pro-middle-class bent of his campaign was emphasized in the Democratic platform: "We seek a New Covenant to repair the damaged bond between the American people and their government, that will expand opportunity, insist upon greater individual responsibility in return, restore community, and ensure national security in a profoundly new era."[32] Opportunity, responsibility, and national security were not themes that the country was used to hearing from a Democrat.

At the convention, Clinton claimed the nomination, "in the name of the hard-working Americans who make up our forgotten middle class."[33] Clinton also used the postprimary time to add a new theme borrowed from H. Ross Perot's campaign—deficit reduction. Perot's campaign had moved the deficit to the forefront of the public consciousness, especially among those working-class and suburban voters whom Clinton was courting. Clinton pledged to cut the deficit in half by the end of his first term.[34] A Clinton-Gore campaign commercial summarized the themes of the campaign best: "They are a new generation of Democrats, Bill Clinton and Al Gore. And they don't think the way the old Democratic Party did. They've called for an end to welfare as we know it, so welfare can be a second chance, not a way of life. They've sent a strong signal to criminals by supporting the death penalty. And they've rejected the old tax-and-spend politics."[35] And Clinton's campaign went to great lengths to portray the Arkansas governor as a regular "bubba," constantly playing up his trips to McDonald's and regularly displaying his ability to relate to average Americans.

It paid dividends. Even though the economy was improving and political science models almost unanimously predicted Bush as the winner, Clinton won by five points. In doing so, he split the Eisenhower coalition like a melon. Setting aside Johnson's landslide win, it was the largest Democratic popular and electoral vote margin since 1944. Clinton and Gore won four Southern states, largely by performing well in the Humphrey areas, while holding their own in Wallace areas. They carried all the states in Greater Appalachia, except for Oklahoma and Texas. Clinton carried the Catholic vote handily—by nine points—and became only the second postwar Democrat to carry the suburbs.

There was an intriguing set of states where Democrats had almost been given up for dead that Clinton came three points or less from carrying—Arizona (which had not voted Democratic since 1948), North Carolina, and Florida. The last two states demonstrated an inconvenient truth about the South for the GOP: since the Southern GOP was founded largely on suburban growth, a swing against the GOP in the suburbs could be a death warrant, especially if the Democrats could find a way to appeal to rural Democratic voters as well. Bush had narrowly carried Broward County in Florida in 1988 and had won Palm Beach County by 11 points. Clinton carried them both.

Parts of the Democratic Party were euphoric. After a 12-year hiatus, they had full control of the government, with large majorities in the House and Senate. They had not only avoided the worst during the Reagan years, they had emerged stronger and ready to advance their agenda. Other Democrats were less certain that the win carried such broad meaning. They knew the sluggish economy had played a critical role in Clinton's election, that things could turn around quickly, and that their majority was heavily contingent on events. Clinton strategist James Carville famously quipped, "We didn't break the GOP electoral lock on the White House—we just picked it."[36]

THE 1994 MIDTERMS: SHADES OF THE FUTURE

Republicans viewed the election as a fluke. They fervently believed that had Ross Perot not run an independent candidacy based on fiscal conservatism and social moderation, the "Reagan Democrats" would not have split off. Looking at presidential results from 1968 to 1988, Democrats had received 43 percent, 38 percent, 50 percent, 41 percent, 41 percent, and 46 percent of the popular vote. Bill Clinton's 43 percent was consistent with those results; Bush's 37 percent was *not* consistent with what any Republican not named Barry Goldwater had received since the Great Depression. At the state level, Clinton's vote share was within five points of Dukakis's in 31 states; he ran more than five points ahead of Dukakis in only two: Arkansas and Tennessee. By contrast, Bush ran more than five points off his 1992 total in every state. He ended up finishing 16 points behind his 1988 election total—almost exactly Perot's share of the vote. Put differently, Clinton received only three million votes more than Dukakis received in 1988 and ran another three million votes behind Bush's 1988 vote total. Bush, by contrast, ran almost ten million votes behind his 1988 showing.

This was wishful thinking. Exit polling showed that, had Perot not run, these voters would have split their vote roughly evenly between Bush and Clinton, with a large portion simply choosing not to vote at all. But the GOP became even more convinced of the fluke-ish nature of Clinton's win when the Democrats drew 46 percent of the popular vote again—this time in the House of Representatives.[37] Bill Clinton had not been governing much like a New Democrat; the first half of his first term certainly wasn't in line with the Eisenhower coalition's view of the world. Judis and Teixeira summarized: "Clinton, alas, didn't grasp how tenuous his victory was. Convinced that he was the second coming of Franklin Roosevelt, and that his first year should be comparable to Roosevelt's 'First Hundred Days,' he proposed a comprehensive national health-insurance plan."[38] The new president immediately found himself embroiled in a debate over gays in the military, renewing questions about whether he was antimilitary. The middle-class tax cut turned into a tax increase that fell *mostly* on the rich. When announcing the tax hike, he used harsh language that brought to mind the rhetoric of previous antibusiness Democrats.[39] After the 1993 budget passed, only 40 percent of Americans told Gallup that they favored moving on to the health-care bill, while 38 percent favored Al Gore's "efficient government" bills, 16 percent favored welfare reform, and 2 percent favored trade.[40] Clinton chose the issue in which he was positioned furthest to the left and moved to health care. In the meantime, Congress—dragged to the left by the reforms of the 1970s—insisted on saddling his crime bill with what was viewed as pork spending, while the gun-control measures it passed proved toxic to the remaining Southern Democrats. Afterward, Clinton would say, "I became so liberal I didn't even recognize myself."[41]

Republicans, of course, gained control of the House for the first time in 40 years and won in some of the key areas that had been problems for them in previous elections. Eight of their wins came in Greater Appalachia, while 19 seats were taken from the Northern suburbs. Another 13 came from Northern rural areas. Republicans saw their share among Southern whites improve from 52 percent to 65 percent of the vote in two years, as they picked up nine Deep South districts; the national Democrats' steady nudging of Southern Democrats leftward had finally caught up with them. Republicans enjoyed a brief honeymoon during the passage of the "Contract with America"—a campaign document that few had even heard of yet was credited with bringing about Republicans' victory.[42] Five Southern Democrats switched to the Republican Party shortly after the election, and in late 1995 Republicans won a special election for a vacant House seat in Silicon Valley.

THE 1996 ELECTIONS: THE CLINTON COALITION

It was largely downhill for the Republicans from there. While previous Republicans had shied away from attacking those portions of the Great Society that were extensions of New Deal insurance programs, the Gingrich Republicans set their sights squarely on Medicare and Medicaid spending. Clinton revived his presidency by vetoing Republican spending bills due to their cuts in, in his famous words, "Medicare, Medicaid, Education, and the Environment." The federal government shut down, twice, and the public seemed to side with Clinton. He used the budget debate to pivot back to the center, embracing some Republican cuts, yet pushing back on the unpopular ones. He once again positioned himself as the champion of the middle class; his "M^2E^2" strategy formed the backbone of his 1996 campaign. Exit polls that year suggested that 27 percent of voters named Medicare and education as their top issues—combining for more than the economy and jobs—and around 70 percent of these voters pulled the lever for Clinton.[43] On the road to his successful reelection against Bob Dole, Clinton signed welfare reform, banned federal recognition of same-sex marriage in the federal government by signing the Defense of Marriage Act, and successfully pressured the Republican Congress into raising the minimum wage. The push for comprehensive health-care reform was abandoned in favor of incremental moves toward expanded coverage; in August 1996, Clinton signed the Kennedy-Kassebaum health-care bill, which enhanced health insurance portability and provided for testing the main conservative proposal for health-care reform: health savings accounts.

Bob Dole was essentially left without a platform, as the traditional Republican issues were either fading into the background or coopted by Clinton.[44] Welfare reform, gay marriage, and health care were off the table. Crime rates were falling, the deficit was disappearing, and U.S. foreign policy remained stable. By now, Clinton was similar in tone and style to that of a moderate Republican in Eisenhower's day.[45] His liberal face was hidden, and even the populist face emerged only rarely. The pragmatic, New Democrat face led the way. As a result, in 1996, the Clinton coalition came into full bloom. Clinton won by a nine-point margin, an even larger victory than Roosevelt's 1944 win. His 1996 win started with the traditional Democratic base. Of the counties that had leaned Democrat in every election from 1952 through 1988, 91 percent leaned Democrat again in 1996, and Clinton won 99 percent of them outright. Among counties that leaned Democrat in a *majority* of those years, 74 percent leaned Democrat in 1996, and Clinton carried 81 percent of these counties. In the South, he won over almost all the Humphrey areas and held most of the Wallace areas, even when controlling for the changes in the racial composition of the electorate since 1968.

But Clinton made further inroads into the Eisenhower coalition. He carried almost a third of the counties that had leaned Republican in a majority of presidential elections from 1952 through 1988 and even 12 percent of those that had never leaned Democratic in any of those years. The counties he won tended to be critical ones: suburban counties in Northern or Peripheral Southern states. He won Suffolk County, New York, Palm Beach County, Florida, and Staten Island by the largest margins of any Democrat since Roosevelt. The Palm Beach County win was especially sweet, as it was the key to his victory in the state that had narrowly eluded him in 1992. Nassau County on Long Island went Democrat by 20 points. Bergen County, New Jersey—the lynchpin of the New Jersey Republican Party—voted for Clinton by 14 points. Two key Philadelphia suburban counties, Delaware and Montgomery, voted for Clinton by ten and eight points, respectively. Table 3.1 shows the Clinton-Gore margin here, juxtaposed against the average Democratic margin in each county from 1952 through 1988.

Even allowing for the fact that Clinton outperformed the Democratic average nationally from 1952 to 1988 by about 14 points, these are impressive numbers. Every one of these counties swung toward the Democrats by more than 14 points, with several massive swings in excess of 30 points. More important, without these counties in their column, Republicans had almost no chance of

Table 3.1 Counties Carried By Clinton That Leaned Republican From 1952–1988, Population >100,000

County	Avg. Dem. Margin, 1952–1988	Clinton 1996 Margin	Clinton Improvement
Bucks, PA	−13%	4%	17%
Bernalillo, NM	−14%	5%	19%
Will, IL	−15%	5%	20%
Franklin, OH	−19%	4%	23%
Delaware, PA	−15%	10%	25%
Lake, IL	−25%	0%	25%
Fairfield, CT	−18%	8%	26%
Montgomery, PA	−20%	8%	28%
Monmouth, NJ	−20%	8%	28%
Rockingham, NH	−24%	7%	31%
Pinellas, FL	−23%	9%	31%
Orange, NY	−26%	8%	33%
Richmond, NY	−25%	10%	34%
Ocean, NJ	−29%	6%	34%
Bergen, NJ	−21%	14%	35%
Nassau, NY	−17%	20%	36%

overcoming the staunchly Democratic inner cities in these states. States like New York, New Jersey, and Connecticut were effectively off the table for Republicans so long as the Democratic victories in the suburbs continued.

All three of the marriages that Eisenhower had blessed were on the rocks. Clinton carried the suburbs nationwide by five points over Dole, the largest Democratic margin since LBJ. Of the 25 key suburban counties identified in chapter 2, Clinton carried 18—three times as many as Kennedy in 1960, almost four times as many as Carter in 1976, and better than any postwar Democrat save for LBJ. The key difference between 1996 and 1964, of course, is that Clinton carried these counties while winning by only 9 points, rather than 20. Clinton also carried Catholics by 16 points.[46] Although Republicans maintained some of their gains in the South, the region as a whole went for Clinton by a narrow tenth-of-a-point margin, only the second time since 1964 that the Democrats had outperformed the Republicans there.

Bill Clinton, in effect, took the weakest portions of the Eisenhower coalition and welded them to the Democratic base. It was a solid approach, but it came with some serious downsides. In particular, the suburbs did not move toward the Democrats so much as the Democrats moved toward them. But not *all* Democrats approved of the move. Throughout Clinton's presidency, he was constantly looking over his left shoulder, afraid that a liberal challenger would do to his presidency what Ted Kennedy had done to Carter's in 1980. Oddly enough, the left was kept in line throughout Clinton's presidency, mostly out of fear that the Republicans might be right about 1992 being a fluke, and that they could lose their last check on Newt Gingrich's Republican caucus. Senator Charles Schumer of New York later confirmed that "[w]hat kept us close to the President was the Republicans.... Their extreme nastiness pushed Democrats into Bill Clinton's arms, even those who didn't like him very much."[47] Indeed, as Bill Clinton was followed by a pair of Democratic nominees who lacked his political skills, the leftward pull of the party would help the Republicans reassemble a sort of rump Eisenhower presidential coalition. It was in *Congress* and the states that the Clinton coalition would have its greatest impact.

THE CLINTON COALITION IN THE STATES, 1996–2006

The congressional elections that fell between the "wave" elections of 1994 and 2006 are considered very quiet elections. The Republican majority moved in a

Table 3.2   Democratic and Republican Pickups, by Type

	Core Lib.	Rural South	Rural North	Greater Appalachia	Blue Collar	Mtn. West	S. Suburb	N. Suburb
Dem.	1	8	3	4	5	2	2	28
Rep.	0	9	1	9	5	2	5	11

very small range, from a high of 232 in 2004 to a low of 221 in 2000. But looking beneath the surface of these elections reveals a very noisy congressional landscape. Eighty-seven seats—one-fifth of the total body—changed hands at least once during this time.* Democrats actually captured 53 seats from the Republicans, enough to completely reverse the Republicans' gains from the 1994 midterm elections. The problem for the Democrats was that Republicans picked up 42 seats held by Democrats. Combined with a strong showing in newly created seats in the decennial redistricting, Republicans were able more or less to hold their own in the face of these Democratic gains.

As Table 3.2 demonstrates, the Democratic wins were largely due to their newfound competitiveness in the suburbs. Some of these Northern suburban districts had gone Democratic during the 1992 elections and flipped back to Republicans in 1994, but others, such as Illinois's Eighth District and Kansas's Third District, had not elected Democrats in decades. Republicans made gains in the South and in districts in Greater Appalachia, although the latter gains occurred mostly during the 2000s, after Clinton had left the scene. The rest of the country was something of a wash. These newly elected Democrats strongly identified with the New Democrats. After the 1998 midterm elections, when Clinton's Democrats became the first party to pick up seats in midterm elections since FDR's in 1934, 15 of the 20 Democratic freshmen joined the New Democrat caucus.[48] Nearly one-third of the House Democratic caucus were members of the "New Dogs" after the 2000 elections.

---

* This excludes newly created seats and seats eliminated due to redistricting in 2002. Also excluded are the Republican special election victory in NM-03, which was a result of a fluke local split between Democrats and the Green Party and which swiftly reverted to Democratic hands in the general election. The technical "pickup" that occurred in CA-31, where Matthew Martinez had switched parties only after losing the Democratic primary, is also excluded.

Table 3.3 Democratic Pickups, by Type, 2006

	Core Lib.	Rural South	Rural North	Greater Appalachia	Blue Collar	Mtn. West	S. Suburb	N. Suburb
Dem.	—	—	8	4	4	—	4	10

In 2006, the Clinton coalition broke through in Congress. Democrats picked up 30 seats from Republicans. A reasonable number of these wins were the result of scandals or flukes—it is unlikely that Democrat Chris Carney would have won in heavily Republican northeast Pennsylvania if his opponent had not been accused of choking his mistress—but the overall distribution of the pickups has an undeniable slant to it.

The Northern and Southern suburbs—and one can debate whether the Palm Beach district picked up by Ron Klein really should count as a *Southern* suburb—were where the majority was won. Democrats fared well in Appalachia, too, although many of these seats were won in part due to scandal. Even here, Democrats would not have been competitive had they not kept "farm teams" and organizations in place in these districts. Appalachia in particular played a key role in the Democrats' gains in the Senate: Claire McCaskill of Missouri and Jim Webb of Virginia both won by holding down their opponents' margins in the areas of their states settled by Jacksonians. In New Hampshire, the lone Republican redoubt in the Northeast, Democrats gained control of both houses of the legislature and held the governorship for the first time since the late 1800s.

Governors in particular were adept at using the New Democrat approach to win elections. In 1989, Democrats had emerged victorious in gubernatorial races in Virginia and New Jersey by offering up innovative variants on old Democratic ideology. Jim Florio won the New Jersey governorship big on the back of solid margins in suburban Bergen and Middlesex counties but quickly floundered by reverting to Old Democrat ideology and becoming associated with a tax hike.[49] In North Carolina, Florida, and Georgia, Governors Jim Hunt, Zell Miller, and Lawton Chiles fought off tough challenges in 1994 and 1996 with their "third way" approach to politics. In 1999 and 2001, Democrats replaced Republican incumbents in major urban areas across the country. A Democrat won the county executive race in Nassau County in New York, giving Democrats control of the county legislature and governorship for the first time since 1917.[50]

Finally, in 2001, a telecommunications executive named Mark Warner won the Virginia governorship through a coalition of rural Virginians, urban liberals and minorities, and suburbanites. His win caught the attention of two scholars who decided to investigate the phenomenon further. Their book would have a massive impact on Democratic thinking in the 1990s, just as the majority coalition that they were describing was beginning to fall apart.

PART II

WHERE WE ARE

CHAPTER 4

THE LEFT STRIKES BACK!

DEMOCRATIC PRESIDENTIAL POLITICS IN THE 2000s

It should be completely borne in mind that a coalition is just that—it is not a consensus. Both the opportunities of Johnson and Nixon—after massive victories—were lost when the responsible people came to believe that they could achieve consensus and basically ignore politics.

Pat Caddell, 1976[1]

THE EMERGING DEMOCRATIC MAJORITY

In 2002, John Judis and Ruy Teixeira published a short book with a big thesis, called *The Emerging Democratic Majority*. Playing off the title of Kevin Phillips's *Emerging Republican Majority* of the late 1960s, Judis and Teixeira amassed an impressive amount of data and argued that "the Republican era Phillips presciently perceived in 1969 is now over."[2] The theoretical basis for Judis and Teixeira's claim can be traced back to the 1950s and 1960s, to the development of realignment theory in political science literature. The term "realignment" had been used by politicians and political scientists for decades; Samuel Lubell had famously commented that one party was always the dominant "sun" to the other party's "moon."[3] But the theory really got its start in 1955, when one of the more famous political scientists, V. O. Key, Jr., published an article called "A Theory of Critical Elections." Key claimed that certain elections "reveal a sharp alteration of the pre-existing cleavage within the electorate, that tends to persist over subsequent elections."[4] Key focused on two elections and only on the North in both: the 1896 presidential election between William McKinley and William Jennings Bryan, when white ethnics moved toward the Republicans, and the 1928 presidential election, when these voters moved back to the Democrats.

Key's claim was a modest one. He even seemed to move away from the theory of critical elections in an article four years later that emphasized the gradual shifts in voting habits in New England and introduced the concept of slow-moving, "secular" realignments.[5] But other political scientists built on Key's idea, and it became a well-accepted concept in their discipline. By the 1970s, political scientists had erected complex classification systems for American presidential elections, explored the turnout surges that supposedly gave rise to them, concluded that third-party presidential runs tended to precede them, and explored the interaction between presidential realignments and congressional output. It was a case of "Key sneezing and political science catching a cold."[6]

The most important innovation for the purposes of this book was probably originated by Walter Dean Burnham. It was he who formalized the notion of critical elections occurring every 32 to 36 years. By now, some of the many problems with the theory should be readily apparent. It was, however, the starting point for *Emerging Democratic Majority*, which expressly relies on Burnham's theories of political cycles.[7]

The theory of periodic cycles in politics suggests that a realignment should have occurred around 1968. That, along with an impressive host of electoral data, is what caused Kevin Phillips to predict, prior to the 1968 election, an incipient era of Republican dominance in his now-famous (but then widely ridiculed) *Emerging Republican Majority*. The 32/36-year cycle was due to turn over that year, and indeed the 1968 election fit—or at least could be made to fit—the "critical election" mold. True, it did not bring about an immediate shift in the identity of the dominant political party, and Nixon governed as something of a liberal Republican. Judis and Teixeira ascribed this delay to Watergate and Keynesian fiscal policy's smoothing of the business cycle. They hypothesized that in the future, changes in partisan majorities would occur with "transition periods," rather than being jarred into existence by calamitous recessions (as was the case with 1896 and 1932).[8] Thus, 1968 was merely the beginning of a transition period between New Deal liberalism's collapse in 1968 and the final ascendancy of conservative, Reaganite Republicanism in 1980. In that year, "the

Republican majority finally came to pass," as Republicans won the Senate, and the Democrats retained only a narrow majority in the House.

The Republican majority that emerged in 1968 began to disintegrate in 1992, according to Judis and Teixeira, and a new Democratic majority was set to begin in 2004, on a perfect 36-year cycle. They noted the Clintonian breakthrough in suburbs dominated by professionals—or as they somewhat more broadly defined them, ideopolises.[9] They observed how Clinton had brought the white working class back into the Democratic fold and how he had overperformed among women, especially those who were college educated and single. And they saw the swing of Asian Americans toward the Democrats and the rise of the Latino vote as particularly critical. All this was leading to a situation in which Democrats would dominate Republicans and would break off portions of the Mountain West (especially New Mexico, Colorado, and Nevada), the Northeast (such as New Hampshire), and the Peripheral South (Virginia, North Carolina) from the Republican coalition.

The book was certainly inauspiciously timed, as Republicans gained seats in the 2002 midterm and George Bush carried several states in 2004 that Judis and Teixeira had identified as "Leaning Democrat" or "Solid Democrat," although the authors made several prescient predictions that were debatable at best as of 2002. But the book was absolutely correct in one critical way: it identified the *ideology* on which the emerging Democratic majority was based. Judis and Teixeira described the voters brought into the Democratic fold through Clinton's shift as "centrists," who "worry about budget deficits and are wary of large tax cuts. They want incremental, careful reforms that will substantially increase health-care coverage and perhaps eventually universalize it, but not a large new bureaucracy that will replace the entire private health-care market."[10] As Clinton moved toward the end of his first term and through his second term, he declared that "the era of big government is over," and he pursued a balanced budget, school uniforms, V-chips in televisions to block content that parents might find objectionable, expanded computers in classrooms, and ideas like a Medicare buy-in for younger retirees and the S-CHIP program to help the young obtain health insurance.[11]

Clinton *had* done something unique. By balancing the budget, cutting spending, and enacting only modest tax increases—indeed, cutting some taxes in his second term—he had rebranded the Democratic Party as the party of fiscal responsibility. They were no longer the party of radical counterculture and antiwar protests; Clinton's social moderation and intervention in Haiti and the Balkans had successfully shifted the public's perception of the party. Democrats had come to "own," or at least own a share of, traditionally Republican issues. Polling data found that the Republican edge as the party of "prosperity" that had opened up in the 1980s was gone. Democrats maintained their traditional edges as the party best able to handle health care, social security, and education while moving toward parity with Republicans on taxes and gaining an edge on the deficit.[12] As Judis and Teixeira noted, a broad coalition could be built around this ideology. But while the link between this particular ideology and the party's national majority was a strong one, the party's overall commitment to that ideology was weak.

A WOBBLY DEMOCRATIC MAJORITY: 2000 AND 2004

Clinton's unique persona had played a larger role in developing this New Democratic majority than many had credited. His "three faces" appealed to broad swaths of the country. Individual congressional candidates did not need to be adept at showing all three faces; they just needed a national party leader to whom the voters in their districts could relate, whether it was in the outer suburbs, in Appalachia, or in Harlem. At the presidential level, though, the New Democrat hold on the country remained tenuous. Less talented politicians would have a more difficult time appealing to Clinton's coalition of liberals, suburbanites, working-class voters, Jacksonian Democrats, and minorities. These interests almost immediately bumped up against each other with the candidacy of Clinton's vice president, Al Gore. Gore lacked Clinton's three-faced persona. Although nominally from Tennessee, he had spent most of his life in Washington, DC, and had never perfected Clinton's "down-home" appeal. If Clinton oozed empathy, Gore seemed to suck it out of the room. As pollster Ken Warren put it, "Gore came across as a snob and a Northeast, Washington bureaucrat. Clinton never came across that way. And [opponent George W.] Bush came across as folksy. You have no idea how rural people hate that Northeast, Washington image."[13] And while Clinton had always managed to keep a serious challenge from brewing on the left, Gore found himself challenged by Green Party candidate Ralph Nader, who took 3 percent of the vote nationwide and played a critical role in costing Gore the election.[14] Gore found himself pushed leftward, both in an effort to head off the Nader candidacy and to distance himself from the scandals that surrounded Bill Clinton in his second term. Rather than running on the Clinton legacy of balanced budgets, welfare reform, and crime reduction, he ran a "people versus the powerful" campaign against big polluters, HMOs, tobacco companies, and the like. Michael Kinsley famously summarized Gore's dissonant campaign theme as "You've never had it so good, and I'm mad as hell about it."[15] *Slate*'s Jacob Weisberg observed that "middle-class Americans actually own big chunks of the oil, insurance, and pharmaceutical companies that Gore was vilifying. Instead of running the first campaign of the new economy, he ran the last campaign of the New Deal."[16]

At the same time, Republicans were taking a page from the Clinton triangulation playbook. The challenge facing Texas governor George W. Bush was straightforward: how to run a campaign when most of the old Republican issues had been taken off the table. Instead, he embarked upon a triangulation campaign of his own, seeking to inoculate himself from Democratic charges of heartlessness. "Compassionate conservatism" was his watchword, and he used it to appeal to various factions of the old Eisenhower coalition that Democrats were now competing for. To appeal to suburbanites, Bush made clear that, unlike Newt Gingrich and the congressional Republicans, he would not work to disband the Department of Education. Instead, he would expand it. For the white working class, he would favor a mild expansion of Medicare and a Patient's Bill of Rights. He even tried to compete among minority groups, using the 2000 convention to showcase prominent African Americans and flirting with comprehensive immigration reform. In a year when the economy was growing smartly and most political scientists were predicting a large Gore win, the incumbent vice president barely won the popular vote, and he lost the Electoral College after a drawn-out dispute over the proper procedure for counting ballots in Florida.

Some Democrats argue that Gore lost because of his perceived abandonment of Democratic advocacy for small government. Others argue that he lost because of his appeal to the suburbs and his advocacy of gun control, abortion rights, and the scandals surrounding the Clinton administration.[17] There is some truth to both of these claims, however this only illustrates the inherent difficulty in maintaining a coalition as broad as Clinton's. Professional whites and the white working class may have interests that are aligned on some issues, but they are inevitably at loggerheads on others. As Gore moved to placate Nader voters on the left, he took positions that made it difficult to maintain the center. When he appealed to moderate professionals, his positions looked elitist to the white working class and Jacksonians; when he tried the populist route to bring the white working class on board, he lost suburbanites. Bill Clinton could pull it off because he was a remarkably adept politician. Al Gore was not. He lost ground among the white working class: in Missouri, Clinton had won whites without college degrees by 3 points; Gore lost them by 28 points.[18] At the same time, Bush swung suburban voters in his direction, who made up a much larger share of the electorate than working-class whites.[19]

Four years later, Democrats would nominate a candidate who was further to the left than Gore. John Kerry was not even a New Democrat. Kerry was a decorated Vietnam veteran who had come home to Massachusetts and embarked upon a career in politics. In 1972, he was the only Democrat to lose a contest for an open seat that George McGovern carried. Ten years later, he was elected lieutenant governor of Massachusetts on a ticket with Michael Dukakis. In 1984, he won an open Senate seat and spent most of his career as the junior senator from Massachusetts developing a voting record that was among the most liberal in the upper chamber. His patrician demeanor and wealthy wife—the widow of liberal Republican John Heinz—made it difficult for him to claim even an arguable tie to the party's populist tradition. Kerry saw his margins drop even further off Gore's. In 2004, Bush won over suburban voters 52 percent to 47 percent and even held Kerry's margins in the big cities to 20 points (Gore had won by 45 points).[20] Bush lost Latinos by only 9 points, improving by 8 points over his 2000 showing and by 22 points over Dole's in 1996.[21] Among voters without high school educations, Bush fared better than any Republican since Reagan in 1984 and did so without carrying the country in a landslide. Against Roman Catholic John Kerry, senator from Massachusetts, Bush carried the white Catholic vote. This is something that no prognosticator in 1960 would have thought possible, especially without a Republican winning in a landslide.

Perhaps most important, the Democrats finally began to lose their grips on Jacksonian America. Part Three of the South's shift to the Republicans was beginning. Republicans had never won more than 30 percent of the white vote in the Humphrey areas largely because of Greater Appalachia's continued allegiance to the Party of Jackson. That changed in 2000, when Bush won

42 percent of that vote. Four years later, he won 51 percent. Whereas Clinton had carried Kentucky, Tennessee, West Virginia, Arkansas, and Louisiana, and had kept Texas close in both of his runs, Gore and Kerry lost all these states. Kerry fared so poorly here that he lost all these states save for Missouri by double digits.

This weakness in the old heartland of the Democratic Party was responsible for a poor showing by both Gore and Kerry in the counties that had leaned Democrat in presidential elections from 1952 through 1988. Gore carried only 61 percent of these counties, while Kerry edged Bush in only 56 percent of them. While many of these counties were small, they totaled almost two million votes. There was a related Kerry/Gore weakness in those counties that had leaned Democrat eight or nine times from 1952 to 1988 that subtracted many more votes from the Democratic column. Put simply: If either Kerry or Gore had been able to maintain Clinton's strength in Greater Appalachia, they would have won the presidency. Unlike Clinton, neither Gore nor Kerry took much from the traditional Republican coalition. Kerry won less than 3 percent of the counties that had leaned Republican in every election from 1952 to 1988. Among the broader group of counties that had leaned Republican in simply a majority of elections from 1952 to 1988, Kerry emerged victorious in just 9 percent of them (Clinton had won almost one-third of these counties).

We can summarize all of these trends by revisiting some charts that were introduced in chapter 2.[22] Figure 4.1 shows the continued trend in the suburban

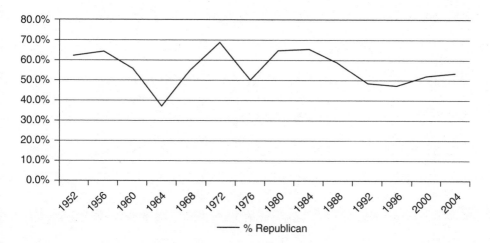

Figure 4.1 % Suburban Vote for Republican

vote for Republicans from 1952 through 2004. After sagging in the aftermath of Ronald Reagan's presidency, the Republican performance in the suburbs gradually ticks upward during the Bush years.

We see similar, although less pronounced, trends among Catholic voters in Figure 4.2.

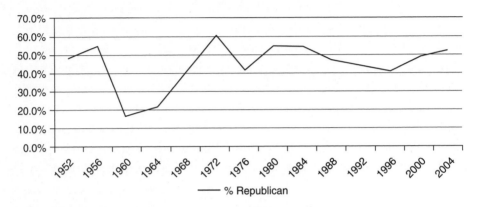

Figure 4.2 Republican Two-Party Share of Catholic Vote

Finally, we can see, in Figure 4.3, how the GOP progressed in the South after Reagan's presidency—both the Clinton advances in the Wallace, Humphrey, and Nixon areas, and George W. Bush's success in stalling and even reversing some of these trends.

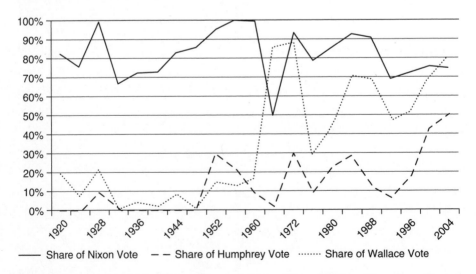

Figure 4.3 Estimated Republican Share of White Nixon/Wallace/Humphrey Vote, in South, 1920–2004

The Democratic Party was moving steadily away from Clintonism at the presidential level, and it was paying the price.

BARACK OBAMA AND THE CHALLENGE TO CLINTONISM

Although Gore and Kerry had drifted leftward from Bill Clinton's approach, they had never abandoned Clintonism entirely. Neither called for general tax increases. Neither adopted the stance of a foreign policy dove—Al Gore had called for a larger defense budget than Bush in 2000. Kerry emphasized his military training and refused to disavow his vote for the Iraq War.[23] On health care, both favored incremental steps toward universal coverage, but neither announced a plan for comprehensive reform. Both largely avoided social issues, especially Kerry, who preferred to focus on the war effort. This worked both ways; even though both candidates were progressively further to the left than Clinton had been, the general rebranding of the Democratic Party that Clinton had accomplished helped inoculate subsequent nominees who didn't stray too far from the Clinton label. Of course, these Democrats also got a hefty assist from George W. Bush.

George W. Bush's presidency—especially his second term—was an upper-middle-class suburbanite swing voter's nightmare. On social issues, Bush was perceived as uncompromisingly conservative. This was not entirely fair: his position on stem cell research was a compromise on a polarized issue, and the law to intervene in the Terri Schiavo affair passed on a bipartisan vote in the House and by voice vote in the Senate. But white professionals saw a Republican party that was no longer content with giving the religious right symbolic victories. It was now giving them substantive victories as well, a perception that was likely reinforced by Bush's Southern twang and evangelical religiosity. The uncompromising social conservative label stuck. On fiscal issues, while Bush's expansion of federal education funding and tax cuts might have appealed to suburbanites at first blush, the massive deficits that arose from the spending, tax cuts, wars, and recessions stood in stark contrast to the surpluses of the later Clinton years. During Bush's two terms in office, the national debt had increased from $5.73 trillion to $10.63 trillion.[24] The American people already associated the Democratic Party with deficit reduction, and now the Republican Party was on a fast track to becoming the "spending party." At the beginning of

Bush's presidency, the Democrats had a slight edge over Republicans as to who voters perceived as the "party of prosperity." By 2007, before the onset of the "Great Recession," that had exploded into a 20-point Democratic advantage.[25]

Finally, the wars in Iraq and Afghanistan eroded the Republican advantage on national security. At the end of the first President Bush's term, Republicans maintained roughly a 40-point edge over Democrats as the party best able to handle national security issues. This gap narrowed during Clinton's presidency, but Republicans maintained a 30-point edge. During the Bush years, the gap closed sharply, particularly after the Iraq War began. By 2007, the two parties were in near equipoise when adults were asked who was better able to handle national security issues.[26] Republican actions on fiscal, social, and foreign policy were weakening the party.

This presented Democrats with a unique opportunity. The right Democratic candidate probably could have put together a massive 2008 presidential majority, combining minorities, liberals, Jacksonians, Catholics, and suburbanites. The mood of the country was certainly similar to the mood in 1920/1932/1952/1980. The Clinton coalition could have become dominant; the Democrats even had a Clinton running to claim the mantle. In the days of smoke-filled rooms choosing candidates, party bosses would choose a candidate capable of appealing to wide swaths of the electorate, and there would be no pressure to run leftward in the primary. Those days, of course, were gone, and the Democratic candidates found themselves competing for the votes of a Democratic electorate that was feeling its oats after the wins of 2006.

Three top-tier challengers arose to compete for the nomination. Former first lady Hillary Rodham Clinton, now a senator from New York, started out as the unquestioned front-runner. She was the logical heir to the mantle of Clintonism. This, however, actually caused her trouble. Despite her husband's political success, there was a general perception of the Clintons as unprincipled scoundrels willing to do anything and say anything in order to win an election. In particular, bad feelings toward her husband among the left-leaning portions of the Democratic Party cost her dearly. For example, media mogul David Geffen, a major player in Democratic politics in Hollywood, had abandoned the Clintons when Bill Clinton pardoned Marc Rich on his last day in office but did not pardon Leonard Peltier.[27] Clinton had problems of her own making, to be sure, including her struggles to explain her vote for the Iraq War, which many viewed as "weaseling."[28] Throughout the campaign, she struggled to appeal to the newly energized Democratic base, to improve the perception of her among Independents, and to become seen as her own candidate without disowning her husband's positions. But at the end of the day, liberal Democrats were most concerned that she would not go far enough for them—odd, given that she was a fundamentally more liberal person than her husband[29]—while conservative Democrats fretted that she might be electoral poison up and down the ticket.[30]

Concern about the Clintons at a very fundamental level abetted the rise of a second contender for the nomination.[31] Barack Obama, a charismatic, African American senator with barely two years in office under his belt, had burst onto the national scene in 2004 with his famous address to the Democratic Convention. If Bill Clinton had three faces that empowered him in the general election, Obama had three faces that made him potentially formidable in a Democratic primary. The first was his African American heritage. In the South, African Americans made up majorities of the vote in many Southern primaries, a potentially decisive advantage if Obama could convince these voters that he was a real threat to win the nomination. Second, his background as a civil rights attorney and community activist carried great weight with liberal activists. Finally, his position as a law school professor and his eloquent, scholarly manner appealed to upper class professionals, who saw him as "one of them." But there was one critical issue where he was clearly defined, and it set him apart from Clinton and the other major challenger. Obama had opposed the war in Iraq from the start. Although he later made statements that sounded like a hedge, he had never really abandoned that opposition. That would prove critical among the 2008 Democratic electorate.

John Edwards, a former senator who had run as Kerry's vice presidential candidate in 2004, was running a populist campaign in 2008. Edwards's positioning in the campaign was odd. He was a former New Democrat who was running to Clinton's left, yet who drew votes from her among more conservative Democratic voters. His appeal to downscale white voters, who did not warm to Obama's message or aloof persona, threatened to squeeze Clinton if he were to catch fire.[32]

For all these stylistic differences, there was little difference between the three Democratic candidates' platforms. All of them positioned themselves substantially leftward from 2000 or 2004. While none endorsed single-payer, they were all endorsing near-universal health-care bills, which was a big step away from what the country had been hearing from Democrats since 1994. On this issue, at least, gradualism was out the door. All favored significant revisions to the Defense of Marriage Act (DOMA). All favored pulling out of Iraq, and all favored repealing the Bush tax cuts on high earners. Even Clinton sounded skeptical notes on her husband's signature free-trade agreement, claiming that "NAFTA was a mistake to the extent that it did not deliver on what we had hoped it would."[33]

There were differences, but they were subtle. Obama favored repealing DOMA in its entirety, while Clinton wanted only to reverse the federal ban on recognition of state same-sex marriages. Obama had a 100 percent rating from the League of Conservation Voters, while Clinton scored only a 71.[34] It was truly a minor distinction between different flavors of liberalism.

The Democratic electorate was not only shifting leftward, it was increasingly against further compromises with the right. There was a portion of the Democratic electorate, especially upscale white liberals, that had always loathed the very idea of Clintonian triangulation, viewing it as a giant sellout to corporate interests.[35] They were a familiar face in Democratic primaries. In 2000, Bill Bradley had criticized Gore as being too timid, while Howard Dean—who had actually governed Vermont as something of a centrist—had castigated the Clinton presidency as unsound at the same time Kerry was surrounding himself with DLC leaders.[36] Dean's critique argued that Clinton shifted so far to the right that he validated the right-wing narrative about government incompetence and enabled the Bush presidency. Robert Borosage, codirector of the Campaign for America's Future, claimed that "[Clinton's] budget policies were pretty much an extension of Bush I, and his economic policies were largely an extension of Wall Street. . . . Clinton's presidency fit snugly into the era of Reagan and Bush."[37]

The anti-triangulation chorus grew louder and louder throughout Bush's presidency. Rather than leading to the hoped-for progressive resurgence, it had delivered only a steadily more conservative government. The vote for the Iraq War, and the direction that the Iraq War took, was the final straw for many Democrats. The left wondered, "What if the path to victory lay not in compromising with Republicans but in having the fortitude to fight ruthlessly and to defend your own convictions, no matter how unpopular they might be?"[38] This line of argument resonated especially among younger activists, many of whom had not yet achieved political consciousness when the DLC had engaged in the very same debate with the New Left during the 1980s. The level of vitriol against the DLC was particularly high among the so-called Democratic netroots, which had grown largely out of the Dean insurgency. Markos Moulitsas, founder of the influential blog Daily Kos, fought a lengthy war to make the DLC "radioactive."[39]

Hillary Clinton, of course, could not run against Clintonism wholesale. Her opponents could. One opponent in particular seemed the perfect foil for the "Big Dog," and he seemed to relish the task. Barack Obama's famous motto, "Hope and Change," was not only directed at Bush and the Republicans. It symbolized his desire not only to put an end to the Reagan coalition's dominance at the national level but also to Clintonism's dominance of the Democratic Party. Obama readily decried what he called "triangulation and poll-driven politics," arguing that while Clintonian incrementalism may have captured the heart and mind of the country in the 1990s, by the late 2000s, the country was ready for bold and decisive movements.[40] In his November 11, 2007, address at the Iowa Jefferson-Jackson Day dinner, he enthralled the audience by promising a new transformational agenda that, implicitly, would bring about a majority beyond anything the Clintons had dreamed of:

> We have a chance to bring the country together in a new majority.... That's why not answering questions because we are afraid our answers won't be popular just won't do. That's why telling the American people what we think they want to hear instead of telling the American people what they need to hear just won't do. Triangulating and poll-driven positions because we're worried about what Mitt or Rudy might say about us just won't do.[41]

Obama continued this line of argument throughout the campaign. He famously identified Reagan as someone who had changed the course of the country, while calling out Bill Clinton as a president who had not.[42] Rather than offering something to each of the various blocs in the country—trademark Clintonian coalition building—Obama promised to use his powers of persuasion to convince a broad swath of people of the rightness of his cause. He aimed to put an end to the supposed Reagan Era and open the door to a new, progressive shift in politics. In particular, he emphasized the generational shift that he represented as a 45-year-old, offering a chance to move past what he termed the "psychodrama of the Baby Boom generation" that had played out during the

Clinton/Gingrich years.[43] For Democrats who were sick of the Clintons, it was a powerful message. For the general electorate, it was more problematic.

THE DEMOCRATIC PRIMARY SEASON

During the early stages of the Democratic race, the Democratic coalition split into two camps. In September 2007, Clinton held a 59 percent to 20 percent lead over Obama among Democrats making less than $30,000 a year. But among those making more than $75,000 a year, the lead was a much narrower 37 percent to 30 percent. She also had a smaller lead among 18- to 49-year-olds than among those over the age of 50.[44] Clinton was winning the votes of the blue-collar workers whom Bill Clinton had helped move back into the Democratic camp, the one group to whom Obama's life experiences offered little. To them, Obama seemed too slick, too liberal, too effete, too urban—and for some, too black. Yet even when his candidacy was not being taken seriously by many pundits, Obama was performing better among more upscale voters. Perhaps most ominously for Clinton, she led 53 to 38 percent among African Americans[45]—ominous because it suggested the existence of a large, untapped source of votes for Obama if he could only catch fire somewhere and demonstrate that he was a credible threat to claim the nomination.

Even so, for much of the early primary season, it looked as though Clinton was going to walk away with the nomination. By September and October, pundits were declaring her nomination "inevitable."[46] In early October, Gallup declared that "Democrats have rarely had a front-runner as dominant as Clinton."[47] All that changed in late October, when Clinton found herself unable to give a straightforward answer to a question regarding giving driver's licenses to illegal immigrants. To many, her indecisive response seemed like a sign of classic Clintonian dissembling. Her opponents pounced, and the press finally found an interesting storyline in what had been a boring Democratic primary. Almost immediately, her standing in the polls began to plummet. The beneficiary was Barack Obama.[48] While the Clinton campaign stumbled and fought among themselves over how to respond to Obama's surge, Obama passed her in the polls.

On January 2, 2008, Obama shocked the world by defeating Clinton in the Iowa caucuses. It wasn't even close. Clinton received 29 percent of the caucus vote, former senator John Edwards took another 30 percent, while Obama received 38 percent of the vote. More important, though, was the intraparty breakdown. Entrance polls showed that Obama defeated Clinton by over 20 points among those making over $100,000 per year. Clinton, by contrast, tied Obama among those making between $15,000 and $30,000 per year. Among very liberal Democrats, Obama won by 16 points; John Edwards won conservative Democrats, but Clinton tied Obama in this demographic. Probably the biggest split played out among age groups. Obama won by 44 points among those aged 17 to 29, while Clinton carried voters 65 years or older by a strong 27 points.[49]

As the Democratic primaries turned into a lengthy slog between Clinton and Obama, African American voters lined up behind Obama, while Latinos backed Clinton. But the age and class differential persisted. Clinton won New Hampshire, even though Obama carried 18- to 24-year-olds by 38 points. Clinton countered by walloping Obama by 36 points among Democrats and independents with only a high school degree and by 21 points among those making $15,000 to $30,000 per year. By the time Super Tuesday had passed and a few other early primaries were completed, Jay Cost of *RealClearPolitics* calculated that Clinton had carried Northern voters with annual incomes of less than $50,000 by 15 points, while Obama had carried those making more than $50,000 per year by 1 point.[50] Clinton carried union workers by 14 points and nonunion workers by only 4 points. This caused John Judis great concern; he observed that "if Obama doesn't find a way now to speak to these voters, he is going to have trouble winning that large swath of states from Pennsylvania through Missouri in which a Democrat must do well to gain the presidency."[51]

A war had erupted in the Democratic Party, splitting the party neatly in two. The day-to-day back-and-forth was fascinating, but a full exploration of that is beyond the scope of this book. In the end, Obama claimed the requisite number of delegates, but it was not because he became the consensus pick of the Democratic Party. Analysts would ultimately dispute who won the popular vote; it depended on how you counted the caucus votes and whether you counted the unsanctioned primaries in Florida and Michigan, two states that had favored Clinton demographically. Regardless, it was a virtually even divide. Obama won, but he had not captured the hearts and minds of all the component groups of the Democratic Party.

Perhaps the most interesting thing about the split in the Democratic Party was how lasting it was. It was obvious on May 6 that Obama had clinched the nomination, after he held Clinton to a modest two-point win in the Indiana primaries. Yet one week later, West Virginia Democrats showed up in droves to reject the Democratic nominee. Clinton won a resounding 67 to 26 victory in the Mountaineer state. Every county went against Obama, typically by massive margins. A week later, Kentucky echoed its neighbor, giving Clinton a 40-point win. On the very last day of the primary season, 55 percent of South Dakota Democrats cast their ballots for Clinton's lost cause. Once again, Clinton won by 32 points among Democrats over 60, while Obama won by 34 points among those aged 18–29. The electorate in that state was still divided along educational and class lines, even with the nomination settled.

All this added up to a stunning portrait of the Democratic primary vote by region. Figure 4.4 shows the Democratic vote in primaries nationwide. States that held caucuses are not shown, nor are the results of Michigan's and Florida's unsanctioned Democratic primaries. The dynamics of those races were simply too dissimilar to those of primaries to perform an apples-to-apples comparison with sanctioned primary races.

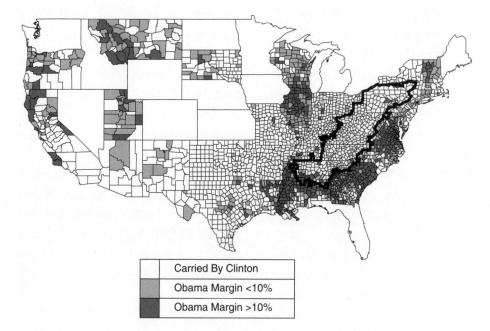

| | Carried By Clinton |
| Obama Margin <10% |
| Obama Margin >10% |

Figure 4.4 Vote for Obama and Clinton in 2008 Democratic Primaries

The counties included in the federal government's definition of Appalachia are outlined by the bold line. It shows Obama's key weakness in the primaries. Obama performed poorly in Jacksonian America and in Greater Appalachia in general. He and Clinton had splintered the Democratic Party in a critically dangerous way. He was holding on to liberals, minorities, and upscale suburban voters. She was winning over blue-collar workers and rural Appalachian whites. In other words, Clinton's coalition was strongest among the voters who had some of the weakest relationships with the Democrats. And, it bears repeating, Obama wasn't just "sort of" weak among these groups. In Floyd County, Kentucky, a Democratic bastion at the national level, Obama received 5 percent of the vote on primary day. These voters weren't just skeptical of him. They were rejecting him outright.

The danger to the Democrats, of course, was never really that Obama would lose *Democrats* in these regions. After all, both candidates' supporters told exit pollsters that they would support the opposing candidate in the general election. The danger lay among Independents who shared a similar demographic profile with these voters but lacked the party loyalty. These were voters who had been brought into the Democratic coalition through Bill Clinton's extraordinary political talent. As the Democratic nominees became progressively more urban, more Northern, and more liberal during the 2000s, the Democrats' grip on them weakened. Democrats now had a nominee who was urban, liberal, of an odd ethnic background, had a strange name, and was African American. While his background and soaring rhetoric of transformation and hope gave upper- and upper-middle-class whites goosebumps, for many Americans the reaction was more akin to chills. The Democrats would soon find out just how important rural and blue-collar voters were to their coalition.

CHAPTER 5

MR. JACKSON VOTES FOR MR. CLAY

THE ELECTION OF 2008

The Republican party cannot find, outside of the performance of its presidential nominee, a single encouraging indicator of a general sort from its 1976 electoral performance.... We have criticized the common tendency of political commentators to overreact to the last election, but what we see manifested here is a secular deterioration of the GOP position. The Democrats have emerged almost everywhere outside the presidential arena as the "everyone party."

Everett Carll Ladd, Jr., 1976[1]

THE CONVENTION SEASON

Few pundits remember this today, but for a time in the summer of 2008, there were real doubts about whether Barack Obama could win the election. From the breaking of the Jeremiah Wright scandal in mid-March through the beginning of the Democratic National Convention in August, Obama's average lead in the *RealClearPolitics* average of polls (RCP Average) was a little bit less than three points. Even if we start our measurement from the beginning of June, when Obama clinched the nomination, his lead averaged a modest four points. And for most of the campaign, Obama found himself unable to top 50 percent in the polls. Indeed, it was not until October 7, in the midst of the financial collapse, that he first hit that mark in the RCP Average. Figure 5.1 shows the trend in the

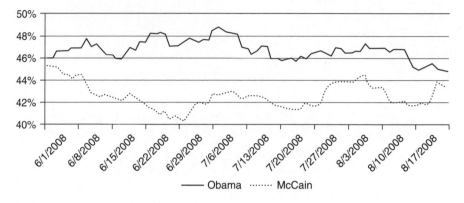

Figure 5.1   Obama and McCain in RCP Averages, Pre-Convention

RealClearPolitics averages for Obama and his opponent, Arizona senator John McCain, as the candidates moved from the primary season to the convention season.

By the end of June, Obama had opened up a large lead over John McCain—in fact, on June 24, shortly before his "unity rally" with Hillary Clinton, his average margin in the polls was higher than his actual margin of victory in November. But over the course of the summer, McCain steadily whittled away at Obama's margin. McCain began ridiculing Obama around that time with a series of commercials comparing Obama to Britney Spears and Paris Hilton. It was a brilliant act of political jujitsu by the McCain campaign, turning Obama's greatest strength into a glaring liability. At the same time, gas prices soared. McCain battered Obama with ads contrasting his support for drilling to Obama's opposition; ads came with the tagline "Don't hope for more energy, vote for it."[2] As energy rose in importance in the public's mind, McCain cut down Obama's advantage on that issue from 17 points to zero. Even David Axelrod, Obama's chief strategist, admitted that they fumbled the issue; Obama's opposition to drilling was much less popular than McCain's support for it.[3]

By the time the Democratic convention opened on August 25, Obama's lead was down to two points in the RCP Average. In Gallup's tracking poll of registered voters, McCain had pulled even with Obama by mid-August, and on August 25, the first day of the Democratic convention, McCain actually led, 46 percent to 44 percent.[4] Many had suspected that Latinos might be the real problem for Obama. These voters had given Bush 44 percent of the vote in 2004, John McCain was a prominent advocate for immigration reform, and the relationship between African Americans and Latinos is complex, to say the least. They had supported Clinton heavily during the primaries, but Obama actually brought them on board fairly quickly—he led by 40 points by June.[5]

The real problem for Obama came from the same white working-class voters who had bedeviled him in the primary season. By now, the Obama staff was referring to this group as the "bitter people," a reference to Obama's controversial statement before the Pennsylvania primaries that, due to economic frustration, people "get bitter, they cling to guns or religion or antipathy to people who aren't like them or anti-immigrant sentiment or anti-trade sentiment as a way to explain their frustrations."[6] It was an update of sentiments expressed by Franklin Roosevelt about the South in the 1930s, and it proved equally as explosive. At the beginning of August, Obama trailed McCain among whites with high school diplomas by 13 points, among those with some college by 14 points, and among white college graduates by 11 points. Only among those with postgraduate degrees did he lead, by 11 points. By the opening day of the Democratic convention, McCain's lead among high school-educated whites had ballooned to 23 points. Among whites with some college, he led by 21 points. The voters whom Eisenhower had borrowed from the New Deal coalition, and whom Clinton had snatched back, now threatened to defect again.[7]

Of course, elections are not won in the popular vote but rather in the Electoral College. But even at the state level, Obama's weakness with whites, especially those without college educations, was threatening to upend a candidacy in a year that seemed like a "gimme" for Democrats. On the opening day of the Democratic convention, McCain was competitive in more than enough states to win the Electoral College—the map was looking a lot like the Bush/Kerry map of 2004. In the RCP Averages, McCain led by half a point in Colorado, four points in Florida, four points in Indiana, seven in Missouri, three in Nevada, four in North Carolina, and a point in Ohio, and they were tied in Virginia. He trailed by only four in Michigan, five in Pennsylvania, three in Minnesota, one in New Mexico, and by three-tenths of a point in New Hampshire. In other words, the traditional "purple" states that many Americans remembered from the Bush/Gore days were almost all close.

Both Obama and McCain had successful conventions, but the net result favored McCain; he wiped out Obama's convention bounce and then some.

His selection of Sarah Palin as his running mate may have undercut his message of Barack Obama as the inexperienced, "Britney Spears" candidate, but it energized his base. More important, Palin was perhaps the only candidate on either ticket who shared a strong cultural tie with the blue-collar voters who were most skeptical of Obama. Her speech to the Republican convention was almost universally well received and watched by almost as many Americans as Obama's. The shine would come off the Palin selection fairly quickly, but in the short term, it looked like a master stroke by the McCain campaign.

As the Republican National Convention drew to a close on September 4, the freshly minted McCain-Palin ticket had whittled Obama-Biden's six-point postconvention lead down to four points (figure 5.2). Three days later, McCain and Palin led. In Gallup's postconvention polling, Republicans led by four points—50 percent to 46 percent among registered voters. Among likely voters, the Republican lead stretched to ten points, 54 percent to 44 percent.[8] McCain had nearly tied Obama on who was better suited to handle several key issues, including taxes, energy, and, most important, the economy.[9] Perhaps most surprisingly, Republicans led by five points in the generic congressional ballot.[10]

In the states, McCain was in solid shape. As of September 14, almost two weeks after the Republican convention concluded, the RCP Averages showed him leading by five points in Florida, five points in Indiana, seven points in Missouri, a point in Nevada, two points in Ohio, and three in Virginia. Obama led by a point in Colorado, two points in Michigan, five points in Minnesota, three in New Hampshire, and two in Pennsylvania. North Carolina, which looked at one point like it might be competitive, showed an 11-point McCain

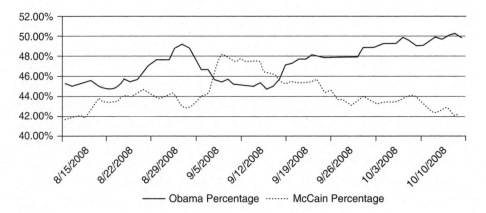

Figure 5.2 Obama and McCain in RCP Averages, Convention Period Onward

lead. Obama had a lead in the Electoral College based upon these poll averages, but it was a narrow one.

There were two things that were critical to this convention turnabout. First, McCain continued to grow his support among whites, particularly working-class whites. In Gallup's polling from September 8–14, McCain maintained a 22-point lead over Obama among white voters with high school educations and grew his lead seven points among those with "some college," to 28 points.[11] Second, for the first time, Republicans closed the "enthusiasm gap" with Democrats. For much of the year, more Democrats had claimed that they were enthusiastic about voting than did Republicans. This reached a peak during the Democratic primary season, when 79 percent of Democrats said that they were more enthusiastic than normal to vote, while only 44 percent of Republicans made the same claim. On the eve of the Democratic convention (August 21–23), that gap had shrunk, but Democrats still had a 57 percent to 39 percent enthusiasm edge over Republicans.[12] But in the wake of the convention, that gap had closed; 67 percent of Democrats were more enthusiastic than usual about voting, while 60 percent of Republicans were more enthusiastic than usual about voting.[13]

McCain's postconvention bounce seemed to have lasting legs, and Democratic leaders started to worry about the election outcome, particularly with Sarah Palin's appeal to blue-collar workers. David Bonior expressed "real concern" and observed: "We can't lose white women and expect to do well in this race." Another Democratic strategist described a campaign that had been "knocked off stride."[14] Matt Stoller of OpenLeft began to wash his hands of the Obama campaign,[15] while blogger Chris Bowers began to worry that the Democrats had underestimated McCain,[16] and that Obama's campaign was disastrous.[17] A few days later Jerome Armstrong, in many ways the founder of the Democratic netroots, posted a video of Obama/Dukakis comparisons.[18] While Democrats were not in a state of panic, they were taking the McCain bounce very seriously. In a year when they should have been winning by double digits, they were behind. It would ultimately take a catastrophic event to help heal the rift between Obama and the Democrats' estranged blue-collar base.

THE GENERAL ELECTION

On September 15, Lehman Brothers, the fourth-largest investment bank in the United States, filed for bankruptcy protection. The Dow Jones Industrial

Average fell over 4 percent, its worst day of trading since the September 11 attacks. This set off a chain reaction of events that kept the U.S. financial system on the brink of collapse throughout the rest of the election season and into the early days of Barack Obama's presidency. On September 16, the Federal Reserve agreed to bail out the American International Group (AIG) insurance conglomerate. Four days later, the Bush administration proposed a $700 billion bailout of American financial institutions. On October 9, the Dow fell below 9,000 for the first time in five years, just as Obama passed the 50 percent threshold in the RCP Average for the first time.

The financial collapse and bank bailout did for Obama what almost two years of campaigning could not do: it swung white voters into his column in sufficient numbers to enable him to win the presidency. In Gallup's early October tracking, McCain's lead among whites with no college experience had shrunk from 22 points in September to 6 points. Among those who reported having "some college," his lead contracted from 28 points to 11 points. Whites with college degrees were now reporting a mere three-point lead for McCain. Combined with Obama's stable, sizable advantage among African Americans, Latinos, and whites with postgraduate degrees, it was enough to ensure that John McCain could not touch him. At the same time, with the passage of the bank bailout bill, Republican enthusiasm collapsed. Democrats regained a 20-point edge in enthusiasm that ensured a significant turnout advantage.[19]

The economic collapse helped Obama in other ways. It threw the McCain campaign completely off balance. McCain had planned to run a campaign based on gas prices and taking on party insiders and had picked Palin precisely because of her record on those issues. But the slowing economy drove down gas prices; by mid-October the price of a barrel of crude oil was down 50 percent from its earlier highs.[20] Worse, it shifted the debate to the economy, an issue in which McCain had little interest or knowledge. When Fed chairman Ben Bernanke tried to explain the collapse to McCain, McCain tried to analogize it to management problems at Home Depot, much to Bernanke's horror.[21] While the McCain campaign had intended on using September 15 to begin its assault on Obama's record,[22] the candidate had to speak about the Lehman Brothers collapse, uttering the fateful words in a garbled response: "[f]undamentals of our economy are strong." The full statement reveals that, in context, McCain was acknowledging the hardship around the country, but news outlets and the

Obama campaign ran with the snippet.[23] It took its toll and reinforced the image of McCain, like Bush, as being disastrously out of touch on the economy.

By Election Day, the economy was in absolute freefall, feeding a narrative in which, according to McCain's pollster, "everything's broken."[24] In the fourth quarter of 2008, homebuilding was down 23.6 percent. Gross domestic product (GDP) was shrinking by 6 percent. McCain pollster Bill McInturff observed that the Michigan consumer sentiment had been in the 70s on Election Day three times, when Jimmy Carter, Gerry Ford, and George H. W. Bush lost. In October 2008, it was at 58.[25] It surprised few when Obama won the election.

Republicans like to fantasize that, absent the financial collapse that began September 15, John McCain would have won the election. Democrats retort that this argument is absurd, that Obama's final poll numbers merely ended up close to where they had been over the summer, and that Lehman Brothers' collapse simply happened to coincide with the normal erosion of the postconvention bounce. In truth, both of these arguments have some merit. With President Bush maintaining a sub–30 percent approval rating in Gallup's polling for most of the postconvention period and with an economy in a deep recession, it is virtually unimaginable that a member of his own party could be elected to succeed him.[26] McCain's support was likely soft, and many of those supporters would have deserted him at the slightest inevitable gaffe.

At the same time, it strains credulity to suggest, as have many pundits and academics, that the financial collapse merely brought about the inevitable. To argue that the evaporation of trillions of dollars of stock market wealth in the weeks before the election did not have a substantial effect on the outcome is simply not credible. Moreover, it is inconsistent with the data. McCain and Palin were maintaining their postconvention bounce. As of September 14—more than a week after the conclusion of the Republican convention—McCain's lead in the RCP Average was 2.1 points, demonstrating only a slight drop-off from its 2.9 percent peak of September 8. More important, the poll averages demonstrate a sharp, immediate reaction to the events of the financial collapse. During the postconvention period, there were seven days when the RCP average showed over a one-point net shift toward Obama. Those were: September 17 and 18, September 24, October 10 and 11, October 14, and October 21. These dates all coincide with major events in the unraveling of the financial markets:[27] the unraveling of Lehman Brothers and the bailout of AIG from September 14–16 and the Dow Jones collapse of October 9. The Colin Powell endorsement of October 18 seems to be the only noneconomic event that had a significant impact on the size of Obama's lead.

Absent the financial collapse, the only major events between September and November were the debates. While it is difficult to resolve a purely counterfactual chain of events, it is noteworthy that, at least in terms of the polls, the debates were largely washes. After the three presidential and the one vice presidential debate, Obama's margin rose .4 points, shrunk .2 points, rose 1.1 points—this debate coinciding with the October 9 collapse of the Dow—and shrunk 1.7 points. And had McCain been able to run the campaign that he had planned to run, rather than rethinking his strategy on the fly, he probably would have done better.

The financial market collapse and $700 billion bailout of Wall Street fired the populist engine among whites without postgraduate educations in a way that Barack Obama could not. Perhaps most important, it played directly to Barack Obama's strengths. He looked calm, cool, and collected, while John McCain behaved erratically, suspending his campaign to sit in negotiations in an area where he had little expertise; the image of McCain sitting at the end of the bargaining table with little to say is one of the most enduring images of the campaign. After a decade of Republican profligacy, the base saw John McCain, whose only real tie to the Republican base was his strong anti-spending stance, attempting to take the lead on what was viewed as yet another massive spending spree by the Bush administration. Without this, McCain probably still would have lost, but it would have been a much closer affair than the fundamentals of the campaign would have suggested was even possible. Republican senators in close races like Norm Coleman, Gordon Smith, and Ted Stevens probably would have won. Senator Elizabeth Dole, who represented North Carolina, a state where a Republican needs strong support from the white working class to win, might have even pulled out the win, as she was up eight points in nonpartisan polling before the Lehman Brothers collapse.[28] Republicans probably would have held their ground in Congress.

THE REALIGNMENT THAT WASN'T

The Clinton coalition was predicated upon Democrats nominating talented politicians who could appeal to the "progressive center," while holding together minorities, professionals in the upper-middle-class suburbs, and enough of the white working class to win. In 2008, Democrats did not do that. They nominated a candidate who was culturally and stylistically distant from the white working class. To the extent that his policy specifics attempted to be cautious and centrist, Obama undermined this with his soaring rhetoric of hope, change, and transformation of American politics. They certainly didn't sound like the words of someone who sought Clintonian gradualism. In a year when the economy was collapsing, wars were going poorly, and the Republicans were being badly outspent—a year when all the intangibles suggested Democrats should "max out" on their potential electorate—Obama won by seven points. In the midst of probably the most favorable election year environment for a party since 1952—if not 1932—he achieved a smaller victory margin than George H. W. Bush had received in 1988 or Bill Clinton had received in 1996. That should have been a warning sign for Democrats. If the Clinton coalition was tenuous, the Obama coalition was downright fragile.

Instead, Democrats were ecstatic. Many commentators seemed to accept the Obama campaign's argument that it had remade the political map.[29] The term "broad coalition" appeared repeatedly when people described Obama's win.[30] They spoke of a "permanent progressive majority" and argued that the conservative movement and the Gingrich revolution had been "crushed." They urged "a dramatic change agenda" to solidify the win.[31] Books predicting the death of the Republican Party, if not conservatism writ large, began filling the shelves. Sam Tanenhaus declared that it was impossible for movement conservatives to make their case in the wake of the Bush years and dismissed the post-Bush conservatives as noisemakers.[32] Dylan Loewe proclaimed that Democrats were poised to control Congress and the White House for "three consecutive two-term presidencies and twelve congressional elections" and would use their control of state governments in the 2010 redistricting to pick up over a dozen seats from redistricting alone.[33]

These predictions were based on a faulty understanding of both past and present. Neither FDR nor Reagan had actually produced the type of majority that many were projecting for Obama; Eisenhower came close, but his coalition's successes were due to a unique set of circumstances that was unlikely to repeat itself. If neither FDR nor Reagan had actually brought about a radical, long-lasting realignment, it seems unlikely that Barack Obama would be able to either. Had pundits been possessed of a fuller understanding of the limits of the coalitions assembled by Obama's predecessors, perhaps they would have been more cautious discussing the prospects for Obama's own coalition.

These incautious analyses were also wrong in a more limited sense. Obama had not, in fact, remade the map. His coalition was narrow but deep. And it was most certainly not new. Between 2004 and 2008, only three states saw their partisan lean, or PVI, switch. Colorado had leaned one point toward the Republicans in 2004; it leaned one-quarter of one point toward the Democrats in 2008. Nevada had leaned six-hundredths of a point toward Republicans in 2004; it leaned two points toward the Democrats in 2008. And Ohio had leaned two-tenths of a point toward the Democrats in 2004; it leaned two points toward the Republicans in 2008. Only seven states saw their PVI shift more than five points in either direction: Hawaii moved 13 points toward Obama, while Arkansas, Louisiana, Oklahoma, Tennessee, Alaska, and West Virginia all moved toward the Republicans. If realignments *do* exist, this was not it. It did not resemble 1932, when Roosevelt completely remade the political map and 16 states leaned in a different direction than they had in 1928. Nor was it like 1952, when 13 states changed their partisan orientation. To put it differently, the average change in PVI from 1928 to 1932 was eight points, and from 1948 to 1952 it was six points. From 2004 to 2008 it was three.

Geographically speaking, much of that movement was away from the Democrats—a fact that is of minor importance in presidential races but of much importance in Senate and House races. Figure 5.3 shows the swing in PVI from 2004 to 2008 at the county level.

There were a few areas where the state's PVI shifted heavily toward Obama: the Rio Grande Valley, where Bush had made some serious inroads among Latino voters, Montana, especially in the traditionally Democratic western regions; North Dakota, particularly in the Fargo area, where Obama had made a campaign stop and run unanswered television advertisements; and in Indiana. But the Jacksonian/Appalachian/Humphrey areas refused to join the national shift toward the Democrats. To the extent there was any radical redefinition of the country's basic political alignment, it occurred here. These counties collectively cast several million votes. They likely made the difference between a seven-point Obama win and a double-digit Obama win.

A close examination of the returns further reveals that Obama's coalition was merely a truncated version of the Clinton coalition. The average state shift in PVI from 1996 was only four points, with eight of the largest nine shifts coming

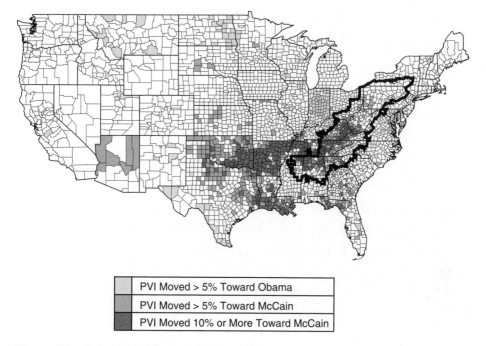

Figure 5.3 Swing From Kerry to Obama, PVI

in states that moved toward the Republicans. Clinton had built his coalition by appealing to the traditional Democratic base of minorities and liberals and adding upper-middle-class suburbanites and blue-collar workers, buttressed by sufficient traditional support among rural Southern whites of Appalachian descent to remain competitive in the border states. Obama collapsed among the last group and brought the second-to-last group into his coalition only at the last minute. The reason he received roughly the same portion of the popular vote as Bill Clinton overall is because he ran up huge majorities in the first three categories and engendered a massive turnout among the first group. Indeed, somewhat amazingly, Obama improved his showing among whites only a net of two points over John Kerry. Had African American voters and Latinos turned out at their 2004 levels, and had these two groups swung toward Obama only as much as had whites (i.e., by two points), Obama would have barely won the election.

We can understand this better by examining the 2008 election at the regional level. We won't pay too much attention to the Northeast—that area simply remained heavily Democratic. The big changes occurred in the South, West, and Midwest.

THE WEST SOUTH CENTRAL AND
EAST SOUTH CENTRAL

The Census Bureau defines the South Central United States as Alabama, Arkansas, Kentucky, Louisiana, Mississippi, Oklahoma, Tennessee, and Texas. By now, these states should automatically conjure up images of hawkish, individualist evangelicals of Scots-Irish descent: our Jacksonians. These were the voters who stayed loyal to Stevenson and with whom Humphrey had a solid showing. The maps in Figure 5.4 show the performance of Democratic presidential candidates in these regions in 1996, 2004, and 2008.

Clinton won almost every county that Obama won. Both performed well in the Rio Grande Valley and the black belt, and both won in scattered urban areas throughout the region. Obama ran behind Clinton overall in small cities and large cities throughout the region, but he ran well in the largest metropolitan areas. Of the 834 counties in this region, Obama carried only four counties that Clinton had not. But these counties were critically important in balancing out the areas that he lost, as three were counties that hosted big cities: Harris (Houston) and Dallas in Texas, and Jefferson (Birmingham) in Alabama. These flips were largely due to the Obama surge among African Americans, as well as his improved showing among upper-middle-class whites.[34]

In the small-town and rural areas, it was another matter. Clinton carried a good portion of the vote in the "Little Dixie" area of southeastern Oklahoma, in Arkansas, in the rural Fourth and Sixth Congressional Districts in Tennessee and the Fifth District in Alabama, and in the "Old Seventh" congressional district (dismembered in 1992) in eastern Kentucky. Obama did poorly in all of these areas. Even though Obama ran evenly with Clinton nationwide and well ahead of Kerry nationally, his Southern map looked more like Kerry's than Clinton's.[35]

Overall, Obama ran about as well as Clinton in the counties that both Clinton and Kerry had won and performed slightly better in the counties that Clinton and Kerry had both lost. But the Democratic showing in the counties that Clinton had carried but Kerry had lost plummeted, from about 55 percent of the vote in 1996 to 40 percent in 2008. These cannot be written off as small, insignificant counties either; they cast a total of almost five million votes in 2008. Obama received the worst vote total of *any* of the previous four Democratic candidates (Kerry, Gore, Clinton, or Dukakis) in the rural and

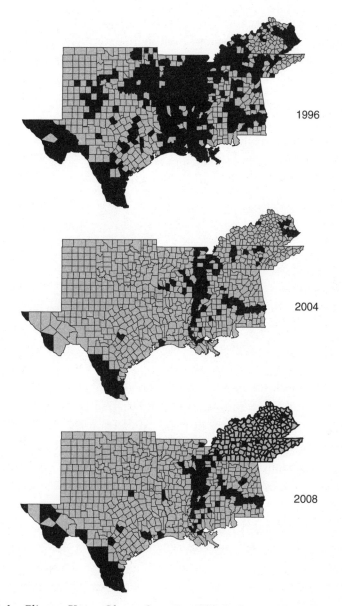

Figure 5.4   Clinton, Kerry, Obama Counties, W.S.C. Census Div.

small-town counties in this census division. Obama's gains came largely among African Americans and Latinos; Bush won 10 percent of the African American vote here in 2004. McCain won just 2 percent. Kerry won 50 percent of Texas Latinos; Obama won 63.7 percent.[36]

Obama was unable to rebuild the coalition that had enabled Democrats to remain competitive in these states, even in an extremely favorable environment for the Democrats. In this region, at least, the Democratic coalition was narrowed significantly. This was fraught with significance for the Democrats. Three Democratic senators hailed from these states. Even after excluding minority-majority districts, 15 Democratic congressmen came from these states. Democrats controlled half the governorships and 11 of the 16 state Houses. If these states began abandoning the Democrats at the state level at the same rate that they had abandoned Democrats at the national level, it would present a huge problem for the party.

THE SOUTH ATLANTIC

The South Atlantic consists of the states located south of the Mason-Dixon line and, with one exception, that touch the Atlantic Ocean: Delaware, Florida, Georgia, Maryland, North Carolina, South Carolina, Virginia, and West Virginia. Two of the three states nationwide that Bill Clinton was unable to win, but that Barack Obama put into the Democratic column, were located in this region. Overall, Obama lost only a handful of counties that had gone for both Clinton and Kerry in this region and carried 13 counties that neither Kerry nor Clinton carried. None of these latter counties was as populous as Harris County, Texas, but Wake County, North Carolina (Raleigh), and three suburban Virginia counties (Henrico, Loudoun, and Prince William) offered Obama impressive victories where both Kerry and Clinton had failed to claim a majority. But once again, Obama faltered in the counties that Clinton had carried but Kerry had not.[37] There were over 159 such counties, and Obama won only 31 of them. In so doing, he sacrificed counties that cast almost two million votes.

Maryland and Delaware remained reliably Democratic; little changed there. In West Virginia, however, we see trends similar to what we saw in the South Central regions (figure 5.5).

The weakness that dogged Obama in the primary reappeared in the general election. The traditional Democratic coalition in the state collapsed. While Bill Clinton had carried most of the state, both Kerry and Obama carried only a handful of counties, the worst Democratic showings in West Virginia since

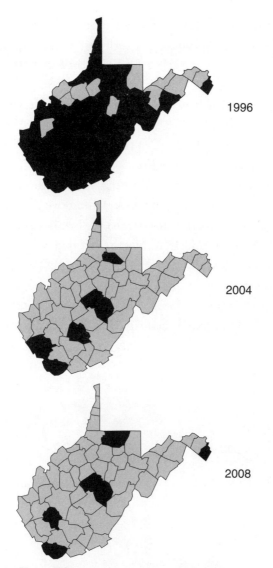

Figure 5.5   Clinton, Kerry, Obama Counties, West Virginia

McGovern ran in 1972. To make matters worse, McGovern lost a national land-slide; Kerry and Obama did not. There were *some* slight shifts toward Obama. The Eastern Panhandle, increasingly a part of the Virginia suburbs, followed the rest of the DC metropolitan area toward the Democrats. Unlike Kerry, Obama carried Monongalia County, perhaps reflecting his strength among college students at West Virginia University.

The rest of the state shifted dramatically toward the Republicans, including, shockingly, the coal-producing southwest. This region began voting Democratic when literal class warfare broke out in the 1920s—at one point, as many as fifteen thousand coal miners were engaged in trench warfare with the local constabulary in what became known as the "Battle of Blair Mountain." Obama became only the second Democrat since Woodrow Wilson ran for president to lose Logan County, the site of that uprising. Even George McGovern won here by three points; Al Smith lost.

We see the same trend even in Virginia and North Carolina (figures 5.6 and 5.7). Bill Clinton nearly won them both, falling two points short in Virginia and four points short in North Carolina. Kerry lost both states by larger margins—8 points in Virginia and 13 in North Carolina. Obama won Virginia by seven points and North Carolina by four-tenths of a point, fairly significant improvements over Clinton.

Despite outperforming Clinton and Kerry significantly in these states overall, Obama failed to expand the map. He just went deeper into areas where

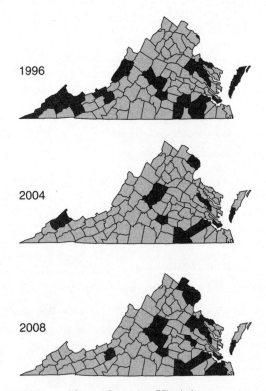

Figure 5.6   Clinton, Kerry, Obama Counties, Virginia

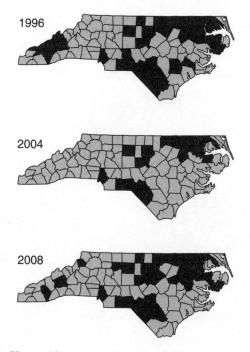

Figure 5.7 Clinton, Kerry, Obama Counties, North Carolina

Clinton and Kerry had been successful. West of the Blue Ridge, Obama carried only one county in Virginia and three in North Carolina—three of these four counties are home to major universities. But once again, there was a tradeoff. In Virginia he carried the northern Virginia suburbs to an extent that would have been unthinkable for a Democrat only a decade earlier, and he ran well in the greater Richmond, Hampton Roads, and Charlottesville areas. He carried a few heavily African American counties in the South. But he lost areas where Democrats had traditionally been competitive. In North Carolina, it was the same idea. He ran well in heavily African American areas and in urban areas, but he lost the rest of the state.

Obama won in part because he ran well ahead of Clinton and Kerry among African Americans in both states. He also outperformed Clinton and Kerry in urban and suburban areas. In Virginia, Obama won almost 60 percent of the vote in northern Virginia, compared to 50 percent and 52 percent for Clinton and Kerry, respectively. In Richmond and the Hampton Roads area, Obama won 55 percent of the vote, compared to 52 percent for Kerry and 50 percent for Clinton. In small- and large-town Virginia, he ran behind Clinton and only

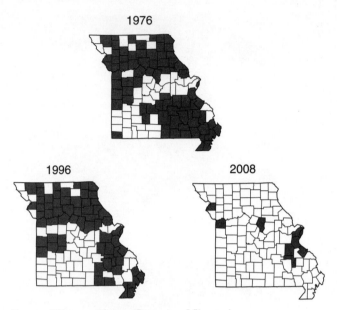

Figure 5.8 Carter, Clinton, Obama Counties, Missouri

slightly ahead of Kerry. It was much the same story in North Carolina, with Obama running seven points ahead of Clinton in the large cities, while running behind in the rural and small-town areas.[38]

The same trend applied to South Carolina, Georgia, and Florida. In Georgia, Obama ran about three points ahead of Clinton in metro Atlanta to keep the state close, but he was blown out in the rural areas, where he ran almost 20 points behind Clinton. In Florida, Obama lost several northern counties that Clinton had carried, but he outperformed Clinton in the Miami, Tampa, and Orlando areas. Clinton's coalition was narrowed as rural voters there finally fled from the Democratic Party.

THE MIDWEST, PLAINS, AND WEST

The story continues in much the same fashion across the Midwest and Great Plains states. Bill Clinton won these states overall with 51.9 percent of the vote, while Obama won 50.4 percent of the overall vote here. Once again, Obama consistently outperformed Clinton in the urban areas, while Clinton did better in rural areas, especially those along the Ohio River. Even in Indiana, Obama succeeded largely where Clinton failed, and vice versa. Obama shed voters in the southern, Jacksonian area of the state but made up for it through an impressive showing in the northwest portion of the state, which is part of greater Chicago, and in the greater Indianapolis area.

Nowhere was the danger of an Obama-type coalition more evident than in Missouri (figure 5.8). Jimmy Carter had carried the state by four points in 1976, and Clinton had won by six in 1996. Obama lost the state, and it takes only a quick glance at the maps to see why. Clinton and Carter both lost in the southwestern portion of the state. The Ozarks had been reliably Republican since the Civil War and showed no signs of flipping in either year. Similarly, both lost a band of counties across the center of the map that had been settled by German Americans rather than Jacksonians. They both ran well in the urban areas. Clinton did a bit better than Carter in the St. Louis suburbs, but both ran well in the northern and southeastern rural counties, which had largely been settled by Jacksonian Southern Democrats.

Obama ran well ahead of Clinton and Carter in the urban centers and carried a few rural counties. His overall weakness in the rural areas of this state, however, overwhelmed his surge in the urban counties, causing him to lose the state by the narrowest of margins. This pattern repeated across the Midwest and plains, with urban and suburban areas moving toward the Democrats, while rural areas turned red. In Pennsylvania, Obama became the first Democrat to win the state while losing the blue-collar southwestern quadrant, making up

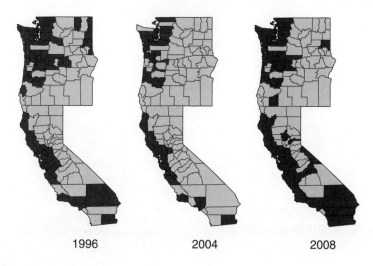

1996   2004   2008

Figure 5.9   Clinton, Kerry, Obama Counties, West Coast

the lost votes by becoming the first Democrat since LBJ to sweep the Philly suburbs. This was something new. But remember, Clinton had achieved a win of a similar magnitude in the Keystone State in 1996 by winning both sections of the state, albeit by smaller margins in the suburbs.

On the West Coast, there was little variation from Clinton's win (figure 5.9). Obama ran a touch better in the "grass belt" counties of coastal Oregon and Washington State, while running slightly behind Clinton in the interior counties. In California, Obama outperformed Clinton in the Central Valley and in the "Inland Empire" of Southern California. This is also known as "subprime central." It is unsurprising that Obama ran so strongly here.

Analysis of the Mountain West is a bit more difficult because of the sprawling urban counties and because it is such a broad, diverse region. Comparing Mormon Utah to heavily Latino New Mexico is difficult. Obama won three states here that George W. Bush had carried, and if John McCain had not been the nominee, he probably would have added Arizona to his total. But once again, he was only building off Clinton's successes in the region rather than breaking new ground. The three states that Obama took from the Republican column—Nevada, New Mexico, and Colorado—had all been carried at least once by Clinton. Although all these states have broad,

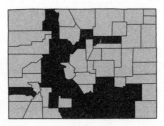

1996

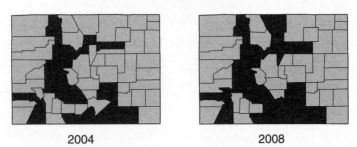

2004   2008

Figure 5.10   Clinton, Kerry, Obama Counties, Colorado

rural expanses, these rural counties are largely uninhabited. Overall, these are some of the nation's most urbanized states. In Nevada, for example, 86 percent of the state's vote is cast in Clark (Las Vegas) and Washoe (Reno) counties. These cities grew up in the 1940s and 1950s, and so even the inner cities have an almost suburban feel to them. Thus, when the suburbs swing against the GOP nationally, it hits hard in the Mountain West. A growing Latino population adds to the GOP's woes, although it is easy to overstate this problem; Latinos constitute only about 15 percent of the region's population.

Colorado demonstrates the power of the state's urban vote (see figure 5.10). Obama ran about seven points ahead of Kerry and about five points ahead of Clinton. It was not, however, due to any major change in the voting patterns of the state.

The same basic "C" is evident whether Democrats lose the state (2004), carry it narrowly (1996), or carry it handily (2008). All three Democrats ran strongly in the historically Latino counties in the South, up through the Front Range of the Rocky Mountains, and then into Denver. What changed is that Bush carried the white vote in the state by 15 points, while Obama carried it by 2 points. This swing was concentrated in metro Denver, where the Democratic share of the vote increased by almost ten points relative to 1996 and 2004. The other areas of the state were mostly unchanged. The same pattern repeated in Nevada and New Mexico.

THE OBAMA COALITION

As we've already noted, Clinton carried 99 percent of the counties that had leaned Democratic in every election from 1952 through 1988. Obama carried only 39 percent of these counties, even while winning nationally by a similar margin. Clinton won 81 percent of the counties that had leaned Democratic in a *majority* of elections from 1952 through 1988, while Obama carried just 38 percent. While this was a slightly better showing than Kerry, who had won 33 percent of these counties, Obama was running much better than Kerry nationally. Obama also shared Kerry's weakness in counties that formed the traditional Republican base. Clinton won 12 percent of those counties that had traditionally leaned Republican, while Obama won 11 percent. Overall, Obama won only 28 percent of the nation's counties, the smallest percentage of counties carried by a victorious candidate since John Quincy Adams in 1824.[39] The counties that he shed were largely concentrated in the old, Jacksonian areas of the country, which had been voting Democratic for generations. To be sure, neither Gore nor Kerry ran well in these regions. But Obama accelerated long-term trends against the Democratic Party here.

At the same time, Obama was able to run roughly even with Bill Clinton nationally because he ran extremely well among the remaining areas of the Democratic coalition. Minorities, liberals, and upscale suburbanites all rallied behind him. This is especially evident when examining the 25 "key" suburban counties identified in chapter 2 (table 5.1).

Obama outperformed Clinton by about ten points on average here. He would have performed better but for a Democratic setback in populous Nassau and Suffolk counties in New York. Had Obama performed only as well as Clinton in these 25 counties, he would have received 500,000 fewer votes and

Table 5.1   Dole Margin and McCain Margin, Key Suburban Counties

County	Dole Margin	McCain Margin	Democratic Swing, '96–'08
Orange, CA	14%	3%	11%
Riverside, CA	3%	–2%	5%
Adams, CO	–12%	–18%	6%
Jefferson, CO	6%	–9%	15%
DuPage, IL	11%	–11%	22%
Lake, IL	0%	–20%	19%
Johnson, KS	22%	9%	13%
Baltimore, MD	–7%	–15%	8%
Montgomery, MD	–24%	–45%	20%
Macomb, MI	–10%	–9%	–1%
Oakland, MI	–4%	–14%	10%
Jefferson, MO	–12%	–3%	–10%
St. Louis, MO	–6%	–20%	14%
Bergen, NJ	–14%	–9%	–4%
Morris, NJ	8%	8%	–1%
Nassau, NY	–20%	–8%	–11%
Suffolk, NY	–16%	–6%	–10%
Westchester, NY	–21%	–28%	7%
Bucks, PA	–4%	–9%	5%
Chester, PA	8%	–9%	17%
Montgomery, PA	–8%	–21%	13%
Arlington, VA	–26%	–45%	19%
Henrico, VA	13%	–12%	25%
Fairfax, VA	2%	–21%	23%
Racine, WI	21%	26%	–5%

knocked half a point off his national total. Obama's personality, style, background, and position on the issues played well in the suburbs. This is very important to acknowledge. But we also must acknowledge what we've mentioned time and again in this chapter and the preceding one: these gains came at a cost.

There is nothing inherently wrong with a narrow, deep coalition. In theory, the Obama coalition could become so heavily concentrated in a few states that it makes an electoral victory difficult—much like what happened to the Democrats in the late 1800s—but that seems unlikely. A potential threat lurks in Congress, where the geographic dispersion of congressional districts and the allocation of Senate seats requires parties to form broad coalitions. But the real threat with a narrow, deep coalition is that there is not much room for error. The party cannot afford for another portion of the coalition to become dissatisfied with the direction it is taking.

CHAPTER 6

STORM CLOUDS

VIRGINIA, NEW JERSEY, AND MASSACHUSETTS

Margaret Truman recalled that her father's happiest months in office, when all political success seemed before him, were from November 1948 until the invasion of Korea in June 1950; Democrats from Truman to Bolling looked forward to "smashing Democratic victory in the fall elections" of 1950.[1]

THE AMERICAN ATTITUDE ADJUSTMENT THAT WASN'T

Barack Obama has been accused of many things. Modesty is not one of them. During the 2008 campaign, he constantly spoke of his desire to preside over a transformative presidency, one that supplanted Reaganite conservatism with a new, progressive majority. He didn't just want to be someone who survived presidential politics. He wanted to change them.[2] In an interview with a Nevada newspaper, Obama famously commented that "I think part of what's different are the times. I do think that, for example, that 1980 was different. I think Ronald Reagan changed the trajectory of America in a way that, you know, Richard Nixon did not and in a way that Bill Clinton did not. [Reagan] put us on a fundamentally different path because the country was ready for it."[3] This started a miniature war in the Democratic primary when Obama was accused of having complimented Reagan's policies. He clearly did not, but what actually is remarkable about his comments is how they misunderstood our political history. Obama's statement implied a belief that Reagan somehow *made* his coalition and *engineered* the supposed realignment that came about in 1980. That most certainly was not the case. As this book has demonstrated, Reagan's majority looked an awful lot like Eisenhower's majority. To the extent Reagan was transformative, it was merely because the issue agenda had been changed by the dislocations of the 1960s and 1970s. Reagan was an effect much more than he was a cause.

But was the second part of Obama's statement correct? Was America in 2008 really ready to turn onto a different path? There were strong warning signs that it was not. Exit polls in 2008, as well as the Annenberg Public Policy Center's polling data, showed that the number of Americans identifying as conservative, moderate, or liberal had remained basically static for decades.[4] Survey data buttressed these exit poll results. Every few years, the Pew Research Center conducts a wide-ranging poll on political attitudes. Its early 2007 poll revealed that American attitudes had changed little on many issues since 1987, two years before George H. W. Bush handily defeated Michael Dukakis.[5] Pew updated this survey in 2009 and found similar results.[6] A summary of the key findings is presented in Table 6.1.

Table 6.1 Responses to Poll Questions Regarding American Attitudes, 1987–2009

Question	1987	2007	2009
Most elected officials care what people like me think (answering "no")	49%	61%	59%
The government is really run for the benefit of all the people (answering "yes")	57%	45%	49%
There need to be stricter laws and regulations to protect the environment	90%	83%	83%
Voting gives people like me some say about how government runs things (answering "no")	78%	71%	68%
Prayer is an important part of my daily life (change in "completely agree")	76%	78%	78%
Government should take care of those who can't take care of themselves	71%	69%	63%
Rich just get richer, poor get poorer	74%	73%	—
Business corporations make too much profit	65%	65%	62%
Government regulation of business does more harm than good	57%	57%	54%
Government should help the needy even if it means greater debt	53%	54%	48%
When something is run by the government, it is usually inefficient and wasteful	63%	62%	57%
It is best for the future of our country to be active in world affairs	87%	86%	90%
I have old-fashioned values about family and marriage	45%	41%	40%
Books that contain dangerous ideas should be banned from public school libraries	50%	46%	46%
The strength of this country today is mostly based on the success of American business	76%	72%	76%
The best way to ensure peace is through military strength	54%	49%	53%
Women should return to their traditional roles in society (agree)	30%	20%	19%
School boards should have the right to fire homosexual teachers	51%	28%	28%
I think its all right for blacks and whites to date each other	48%	83%	83%

The poll revealed attitudes that were in many ways not appreciably less "conservative" than they had been in the heyday of the Reagan administration. Americans did not appear more trustful of government's responsiveness to their needs or its ability to run things and indeed appeared to be a bit less sympathetic toward the poor. The number of people who believed government was inherently inefficient and wasteful was roughly unchanged from 1987. After a dip during the worst phases of the Iraq War, the "peace through strength" number had rebounded. The only areas in which Americans seemed appreciably more liberal were social issues: Americans were more receptive toward women in the workplace, homosexual rights, and interracial dating. To the extent that "liberalism" is narrowly construed as "tolerance," America could be considered more liberal. Beyond that, the shifts were slight.

On a host of other issues, Americans maintain a complex host of attitudes compatible with both conservatism and liberalism. Only 32 percent believed that success in life was determined by forces outside their control, down from 2007. Thirty-three percent agreed that "[t]he police should be allowed to search the houses of people who might be sympathetic to terrorists without a court order," a remarkable result given the wording of the question. Pew did show that pro-conservative views were down from 1994 and 2002—two very good Republican years—but were nevertheless still around the level that they had been during Reagan's presidency.

Nor was Pew the only pollster finding this. For 15 years, Gallup had been asking Americans whether government was "doing too many things that should be left to individuals and businesses" or whether it "should do more to solve our country's problems." The "government should do more" response had claimed a majority only twice in the poll's history: during 1993 and after 9/11. In September 2008, the "doing too many things" answer led by 12 points, a larger margin than Gallup had found in early 1993, at the beginning of the Clinton presidency.[7]

Nor did Obama's election signify a wholesale embrace of his agenda. Americans retained deep doubts about whether he had the judgment to be president and whether he was ready for the job. In 2008, the Annenberg Public Policy Center maintained a tracking poll of various questions of Americans' attitudes about the election. One question probed whether the public believed that each candidate for president and vice president was ready to be president. The final Annenberg survey showed McCain and Biden receiving strongly positive ratings, Palin receiving weak ratings, and Obama receiving tepid ratings.[8]

Moreover, while those who voted against Obama generally expected liberal governance, many of Obama's supporters were unclear exactly what type of change he would bring, supporting him simply because the status quo had become so untenable. Obama had once proudly proclaimed that he was a "blank screen on which people of vastly different stripes project their own views."[9] This became especially pronounced in the general election. During the debates, and especially during his 30-minute "closing argument" advertisement, he railed against accumulated debt and promised to cut taxes.[10] He promised a "responsible" exit from Iraq. He offered a nod to the notion that government could not fix every problem, and he pledged that his plans would result in a net spending cut.[11] These types of statements permeated the close of his campaign and were sufficiently vague that liberal listeners could find what they wanted. They also allowed a voter who wished to imagine Obama as a Clinton-style centrist to find adequate support for that proposition. This wasn't dishonesty—both parties engage in this type of rhetorical campaigning for similar reasons. But it cut against the argument that President Obama had won a mandate beyond "fix it, please." Or, at least, it should have.

Once in office, Obama's politics quickly became more defined in the minds of voters. On February 17, 2009, President Obama signed the American Recovery and Reinvestment Act of 2009, better known as the "stimulus," which provided for approximately $800 billion in spending and tax incentives. The bill was surprisingly controversial for the first major legislation put forward by an administration. The public supported it, 59 percent to 33 percent, but that support was weighted heavily Democratic. Only 28 percent of Republicans and 56 percent of Independents supported the law.[12]

Obama's approval rating slipped immediately following passage of the stimulus, from 68 percent to 63 percent, largely as the result of an 11-point drop among Republicans from 41 percent approval to 30 percent approval.[13] A few days later, it dipped below 60 percent for the first time as his support among Independents trickled downward to 54 percent.[14] His approval stabilized in the low 60s, where it remained until early June. During this time, Democrats were cheered by their ability to hold a seat in upstate New York, which had historically been Republican and had elected a Democrat only in the wake of Republican scandals in the 2006 midterms.

Beginning in early June, the president's approval ratings began a steady decline, outpaced by the increase in his disapproval ratings.[15] Clearly the economic situation was taking a toll on him; the unemployment rate had risen past 9 percent by that point and showed little sign of reversing course. But at the same time, Americans approved of Obama's job performance on the economy, 55 percent to 42 percent. Where they disapproved of him was *spending*.[16] The government's decision to loan money to General Motors and Chrysler in return for a government share in the companies proved highly unpopular. Majorities disapproved of this move in every region, including the auto-producing Midwest.[17] On controlling federal spending, 45 percent of Americans approved of the president's performance in June 2009, while 51 percent disapproved. At the time, the only other issue on which the president's approval rating was "upside down" was his handling of the federal budget deficit; 46 percent approved, while 48 percent disapproved.[18] By mid-June, the share of the country that self-described as "conservative" showed a statistically significant uptick to 40 percent, and for the first time since the 1990s, a plurality of Americans viewed the Democrats as too liberal.[19]

Bill Clinton's rebranding of the Democrats as the party of fiscal responsibility had taken a hit, as the Democrats gradually moved away from "progressive centrism" and incrementalism, toward support for a more activist government. By mid-July, the president's approval rating in the RCP Average had declined to the mid-50s. Once again, the leading issue, according to Gallup, was not the economy. Twenty-four percent of Americans claimed that they disapproved of Obama's job performance because he was "spending too much," while another 15 percent cited "leading nation toward socialism/government takeovers/bailouts."[20] The notion that the economic stimulus plan was not working came in third, at 10 percent. By mid-July, his approval rating on the deficit had slipped to 41 percent, while his approval rating on the economy slid just under the "break-even point," with 47 percent approving and 49 percent disapproving. Sixty-six percent of Independents expressed concern that the president was calling for too much spending, while 60 percent believed that he was calling for too much government expansion.[21]

By November, the Democrats were in serious trouble. The number of Americans who agreed that government was trying to do too much spiked to 57 percent, the highest number seen since the 1990s.[22] The president's approval rating in the RCP Average was consistently in the low 50s, while his disapproval was in the mid-to-low 40s. His signature legislative measure, the health-care law, was unpopular, while the number of Americans who believed that it was the government's responsibility to provide health care registered the lowest in Gallup's history.[23] Republicans had moved within two points of Democrats in the Gallup congressional ballot, majorities viewed the president as "mostly liberal," and the public was evenly divided over whether he was keeping his campaign promises.[24] Democrats were about to endure serious electoral tests in Virginia and New Jersey, two states that were at the heart of the new Democratic coalition.

VIRGINIA SLIPS

Virginia has always had special importance in America. It is, after all, the birthplace of five of our first six presidents. It was among the last of the Southern states to secede from the Union, and it led the way out of the Old Confederacy by picking up Republican voting habits earlier than any Southern state save Tennessee. It always had a strong Mountain Republican contingent in the southwestern corner of the state. The growing Virginia suburbs provided an additional base for the party: as early as the 1920s, Arlington County had supported Republican candidates for the presidency, and in the 1930s it registered relatively lukewarm support for Franklin Roosevelt. By the 1940s, Virginia Republicans were threatening Democratic congressmen outside the historic Republican base in the mountains: after being held below 60 percent in the 1944, 1946, and 1950 elections, conservative Democrat Howard Smith demanded that Fairfax and Arlington counties be removed from his district. They were removed in 1952, and the newly created district elected a Republican, as did two of the three districts west of the Blue Ridge. Republicans would have captured the Virginia governorship in 1953 but for a severe misstep by their candidate in the closing weeks of the election.[25] And when the Voting Rights Act made the Virginia Democratic Party inhospitable to conservative Democrats, many jumped ship and provided enough support to the Republicans to make them a majority party in the commonwealth.[26]

Given Virginia's primacy in Southern political trends, it is only appropriate that Judis and Teixeira began their *Emerging Democratic Majority* with a vignette from Virginia. They begin by telling the story of Mark Warner, a telecommunications executive who surprised most observers by almost defeating John

Warner in a 1996 Senate race. Some dismissed it as a case of mistaken identity, but in truth, Mark Warner ran about evenly with Bill Clinton that year. Five years later, Warner was back. He focused his campaign on winning over rural Virginians, who still make up roughly one-third of the Virginia electorate, and suburbanites, who had voted heavily for John Warner in 1996. Mark Warner promised not to raise taxes, embraced the death penalty, and emphasized his opposition to gun control. Aided by dissension in the ranks of the Virginia Republican Party and a staunchly conservative opponent, he enjoyed a solid five-point win.

Warner's coalition stretched across the Old Dominion, from the coal-producing counties in the western Appalachians, to rural southside counties that had voted for George Wallace, to Fairfax County and the northern Virginia suburbs (see figure 6.1). It was, in other words, the consummate New Democrat coalition.

But over the course of the 2000s, the Democratic nominees in Virginia became more liberal. Tim Kaine in particular did not share Warner's embrace of the death penalty, although he promised to enforce the law as governor. As mayor of Richmond, he had supported some gun-control measures, and there were claims that he had supported subsidizing Richmonders who had traveled to the pro–gun control "Million Mom March" in Washington, DC. He campaigned on increased government programs, especially a plan for universal pre-school. At the same time, though, the country was beginning to turn against the Bush administration, especially in the suburbs. With President Bush's approval rating hovering at around 40 percent, Kaine managed a six-point win. But his map was markedly different from Warner's (see figure 6.2). It represented something of a halfway point between Obama's 2008 map and Warner's 2001 map.

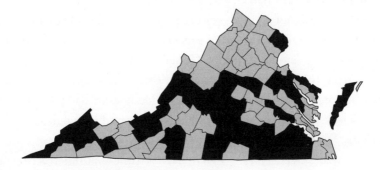

Figure 6.1   Counties Carried by Mark Warner, 2001

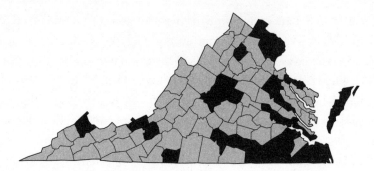

Figure 6.2   Counties Carried by Tim Kaine, 2005

Kaine retained some residual Democratic support along the West Virginia border and in southside Virginia. Overall, however, he lost a substantial amount of rural support. But he advanced deeper into the northern Virginia suburbs than had Warner. Three years later, faced with vanishing 401(k)s, diminishing home values, and general disgust with Bush's presidency, moderate suburbanites flocked to Obama. Liberals were enthused to finally have the opportunity to elect one of their own as president. And minorities turned out heavily for the opportunity to elect the first black president. But as we saw in chapter 5, Obama lost all of western Virginia, save for Montgomery County, home to Virginia Tech. Buchanan and Dickenson counties had cast their ballots for Dukakis, Mondale, and Stevenson (twice). Obama was the only Democrat other than George McGovern to fail to carry these counties since they were unionized in the early 1900s.

As the 2009 election approached, Virginia Democrats had good cause to be optimistic about the chances of their candidate, Creigh Deeds. Deeds, an affable state senator with a moderate voting record, hailed from the western portion of the state. He had defeated a pair of formidable opponents in the Democratic primary and seemed—at least on paper—capable of recreating the Mark Warner map. Democrats were especially hopeful about Deeds's chances because he had run against Attorney General Bob McDonnell, a conservative Republican from the Hampton Roads area, nearly four years earlier, and lost by only a few hundred votes. Since that election, Democrats had picked up both of Virginia's Senate seats and three of its House seats and had gained its electoral votes for only the second time since 1948.

But this year, Deeds had a much harder time finding traction against McDonnell. McDonnell slipped briefly when his master's thesis from Regent

University, a school affiliated with Pat Robertson, surfaced. It criticized gays, working mothers, and feminists, and generally portrayed McDonnell as a culture warrior in the Robertson mold.[27] Democrats sensed an opportunity to make up ground in the northern Virginia suburbs, and Deeds's poll numbers did improve. But Deeds's bounce was only temporary, and he slipped after appearing unable to offer a straightforward answer to a question on taxes.[28] McDonnell won in a landslide. He received almost 59 percent of the vote—the highest percentage (although not the highest victory margin) for *any* gubernatorial candidate since 1961. The entire Republican ticket won by similar margins, and the GOP picked up six seats in the General Assembly. It could have been even worse there—five Democrats won their Assembly races by fewer than one thousand votes.

Figure 6.3 shows how Virginia changed from Bush's 2000 election to Deeds's loss. Counties that moved significantly toward McDonnell are white, while those that moved significantly toward Deeds are black.

The gray pockets in the state represent places where there was little movement from 2000 to 2009. Roughly speaking, these are the DC suburbs in the northeast, Hampton Roads in the southeast, and Richmond and its suburbs. McDonnell essentially reversed a decade of Democratic progress in the Virginia suburbs, performing almost as well as Bush had in 2000. But the advances McDonnell made in rural Virginia made the difference between Bush's 54 percent showing in 2004 and McDonnell's 59 percent of the vote in 2009. This suggested not only that Democrats were losing ground in the suburbs, but more important that the deterioration of the Democrats' fortunes at the presidential level was filtering downticket. As I noted at the time, *"Even with Obama off the ticket, and a much less cosmopolitan figure atop the ticket, rural Virginia went solidly Republican."*[29]

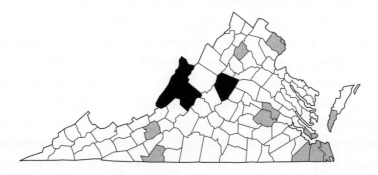

Figure 6.3   Countywide Movement, 2000–2009

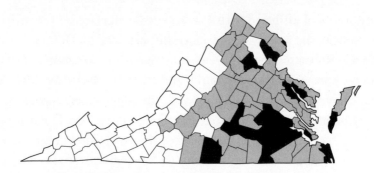

Figure 6.4   Countywide Movement, PVI, 2005–2009

Comparing the 2009 results to the results of the 2005 McDonnell-Deeds attorney general race shows similar trends. Almost every county in the state moved significantly toward McDonnell in that race, so instead of comparing absolute movement, we'll compare the shift in county PVI. A county that is white saw its PVI move toward McDonnell, while a county shaded black shifted toward Deeds (figure 6.4).

Once again, we see that rural Virginia moved heavily against the Democrats. The suburbs remained steady, while heavily African American counties in the southside swung, relatively speaking, toward Deeds.

At the same time, comparing Deeds's 2009 map to Obama's 2008 map (shown in chapter 5) shows a slightly different result. The western counties don't shift much mainly because the Republican vote in this area was largely maxed out in the 2008 elections. McDonnell made the biggest gains over Obama in the outer DC suburbs, with Loudoun and Prince William counties swinging heavily toward the Republicans. Some of this was doubtless due to the economy, but remember, it was Obama's handling of fiscal matters that drew the poorest reviews from voters at the time. As we've seen, the president was heavily upside down on his handling of government spending and the economy but roughly even on his handling of the economy. Obama may have had few choices in the policies he pursued, especially with regard to the stimulus bill and the automobile bailout, and the flailing economy may have made it nearly impossible to run deficits of under a trillion dollars, much less to balance the budget. But regardless of whether he had a choice, he was making Bush's fiscal profligacy look mild by comparison, and by now very few voters were likely putting much stock in his campaign promise to enact a net spending cut.

In other words, after the Gore/Kerry/Obama succession, the Jacksonians finally seemed to be deciding that they could no longer pull the lever for the Party of Jackson, even downticket. That alone might have been a problem for Deeds, had he been able to run as well as Obama among African Americans and in the DC suburbs. But the DC suburbs were also moving toward the Republicans. Two pieces of the basic Clinton coalition were moving away from the Democratic Party. This presents the Virginia Democrats with a sizable medium-term problem. They can endure the loss of suburbanites, and they can endure the loss of Jacksonians, but they cannot endure the loss of both in the same election if they hope to remain competitive in Virginia. If both groups head for the exits, the Democrats are left in a weaker position than they were in even with Michael Dukakis; hence McDonnell's historic win. In the longer term, this becomes less of a problem; as we will discuss in chapter 8, as the state becomes browner, it arguably becomes more winnable for Democrats. In the meantime, unless the party has a charismatic leader atop the ticket who, like Obama, can generate truly massive enthusiasm among the Democratic base, it simply cannot lose both groups simultaneously and survive.

NEW JERSEY SLIDES

Virginia's election of a Republican governor was not all that surprising—the state had a history of going against the political grain. The Republicans broke through in Virginia in the late 1960s and early 1970s, and ever since the establishment of truly competitive two-party politics in the 1970s, the state had selected a chief executive from the party that did not hold the presidency. McDonnell's massive margins were a potential cause for concern in a state that had seemed to be trending blue, but the basic result was not unexpected.

New Jersey was another matter entirely. Like Virginia, it epitomized many of the "macro-trends" observed as early as chapter 1. It was one of the few swing states in the aftermath of the Civil War. But the Panic of 1893 and the William Jennings Bryan candidacy repelled many of the conservative Democrats and white ethnics who had made the state competitive. Democrats overwhelmingly controlled both statehouses in 1892, but by 1896 Republicans held a six-to-one edge in the state Senate and a fourteen-to-one edge in the Assembly. Three decades later, Irish/Italian Hudson (Jersey City) and Essex (Newark) counties were instrumental in handing New Jersey's electoral votes to FDR. The subsequent white ethnic shift back toward the Republicans is evident here, as Roosevelt's percentage of the vote plummeted 10 points in Essex County and 12 points in Hudson County from 1936 to 1940, making the state close again.

Today, 90 percent of the New Jersey electorate lives in suburban areas of Greater New York or Philadelphia. These suburbs are also wealthy. Using just about any measure of household incomes places New Jersey among the three wealthiest states in the union. And like wealthy suburbanites across the country, they demonstrated their discomfort with the rightward drift in the state and national Republican Party in the post-Goldwater era. In 1973, conservative congressman Charles Sandman defeated moderate Republican William Cahill in the Republican gubernatorial primary, only to lose to the Democrat by over 30 points in the general election. Five years later, Clifford Case, a four-term Republican senator who typically received near-perfect scores from the liberal group Americans for Democratic Action, lost a primary to conservative activist Jeffrey Bell, who in turn lost badly to Bill Bradley.

The national Democratic ticket still had little purchase in the Garden State, as George H. W. Bush carried the state by 14 points. But Bill Clinton's message aimed at suburban moderates enabled him to carry the state by two points in 1992. Four years later, Bill Clinton's rebranding of the Democrats paid dividends as the state went Democrat by 18 points and handily elected a Democratic senator in what was expected to be a competitive race. When Democrats have overreached and Republicans have nominated a sufficiently moderate candidate, the Republicans have been able to win—Christine Todd Whitman rode a taxpayer revolt into the governor's office, for instance. Conservative Republicans, however, have found very little success statewide.

The year 2009 proved to be different. Democratic governor Jon Corzine had never been especially popular in New Jersey. He had barely defeated moderate Republican Bob Franks for a Senate seat in the generally good Democratic year of 2000 and had won the governorship against a conservative insurgent in 2005. Corzine showed the damage that perceived fiscal liberalism could do to a Democrat in a heavily suburbanized state, especially if suburbanites felt that they would be expected to pay the bill. Among other things, in January 2008, Corzine proposed a steep increase in tolls to fund construction and pay off debt. In October 2007, Corzine's approval was 46 percent and his disapproval 32 percent. By April 2008, those numbers had reversed to 34 percent approval and 52 percent disapproval.[30] His poll numbers never really recovered, and Corzine's approval rating outpaced his disapproval only once for the remainder of his term.[31] At the same time, while Barack Obama won the state handily in 2008, he did so by a narrower margin than Bill Clinton had in 1996.

It was unclear, however, that Republicans would be able to capitalize on their opportunity. They chose U.S. attorney Chris Christie as their nominee. Christie was more liberal than his primary opponent, Bogota mayor Steve Lonegan, but he was still a staunch fiscal conservative who held views on social issues that were further to the right than the state had generally been willing to accept previously. Christie was pro-life, was anti–gay marriage,[32] and supported school vouchers.[33] He also defeated Corzine in the fall. His four-point margin may seem slender at first blush, but it was the largest margin of any newly elected Republican governor since the 1960s.

As was the case in Virginia, the traditional Democratic strongholds in the state—Hudson and Essex counties—showed little movement from 2008. In the wealthier outer suburbs, however, the shift against the Democrats was severe. While McCain had barely carried Morris County, Christie won with two-thirds of the two-party vote.[34] Christie improved on McCain's showings by 15 points in Monmouth, Somerset, and Hunterdon counties, all of which are among the 50 wealthiest counties in the United States. He narrowly won Middlesex County, which had given Obama a 22-point margin and had gone for every Democratic presidential candidate since 1992 by double digits. It was the closest thing to a rout that a conservative Republican could probably achieve in the Garden State. Once again, a state that had been brought securely into the Democratic fold by Clintonism was looking shaky for a Democratic Party that was turning distinctly non-Clintonian.

MASSACHUSETTS SHAKES

Two states that were crucial to the Clinton coalition had swung heavily against the Democrats, and not uniformly either. The losses had been the most severe in rural areas, suggesting that the final remnants of Democratic strength were being cast off. At the same time, Democratic gains in the suburbs were being eroded across the country. Republican Joan Orie Melvin won a seat on the Pennsylvania Supreme Court, carrying the Philadelphia suburbs in the process. Republicans won a pair of city council seats on the outskirts of Queens, New York, and won a special election in a Westchester County Assembly district that had given Obama over 60 percent of the vote. Conservative Republicans won county executive positions in two suburban New York counties that had shifted toward the Democrats in the 1990s and 2000s. Shortly afterward, Parker Griffith, a conservative Democrat representing Alabama's Appalachian Fifth District, one that had never elected a Republican and that had histori- cally served as the base for populist Democrats in the state, announced that he was switching parties. Party-switchers have a terrible history of survival, especially if they do not allow themselves sufficient time between their switch and the party primary to endear themselves to the base of their new party.[35] But Griffith evidently saw something in his polling that made it worth the risk.

Of course, nothing prepared the political world for what happened in Massachusetts a month later. Liberal icon Ted Kennedy passed away in August 2009, and most observers believed that his successor would easily carry the state. After all, the state had last elected a Republican senator in 1972 and had become even more Democratic since then. A little-known fact about Massachusetts, however, is that the dominant political faction in the state is Independents, not Democrats. While Republicans make up a pitiful 12 percent of the state's regis- tered voters, Independents make up 51 percent.[36] Of course, these Independents tend to vote for Democrats, but Republicans had been able to control the gover- norship from 1990 through 2006 by building coalitions with these voters.

In early 2010, these Independent voters were as infuriated by the Democrats' health-care bill and the state of the economy as were Independents everywhere. Nationally, the president's approval rating had fallen below 50 percent in the Gallup poll in November and dropped below 50 percent in the RCP Average a few weeks later.[37] Republicans picked an obscure state senator named Scott Brown as their nominee, while Democrats selected the state's attorney general, Martha Coakley, as their nominee. At the end of December, Brown still did not even have a picture up on Wikipedia.

Brown turned out to be an outstanding candidate, however, far exceeding Republican expectations. His first advertisement played on the Kennedy theme, showing JFK announcing his support for tax cuts, while his second advertise- ment showed him driving his pickup truck to his home in the suburbs. He was pitching his candidacy simultaneously to suburbanites and blue-collar voters. Coakley's 30-point lead was cut to 9 points by January.[38] As Brown's perfor- mance earned rave reviews from observers, Coakley proved to be a terrible candidate. The list of her gaffes was lengthy, but the most inexplicable were insults to Red Sox fans: she called Curt Schilling "another Yankee fan" and testily suggested that she was reluctant to stand outside Fenway Park to shake hands in the cold.[39]

In the end, it wasn't even close. Brown won by five points, in a victory that showed the scars of the Obama-Clinton primary contest. Obama had lost the Massachusetts Democratic primary, despite receiving Ted Kennedy's endorsement, carrying only the Eighth District, which consists largely of downtown Boston and Cambridge and is home to most of the state's minorities. The only other district where he received more than 45 percent of the vote was the First District, the bucolic rural district in western Massachusetts that had been represented by Silvio Conte, one of the last liberal Republicans in the House, until his death in 1990. Its collection of liberal expatriates from New York and concentration of college towns had swung the First decisively toward the Democrats in the 1990s and 2000s. Coakley carried both of these districts. But the truly "liberal" vote in the state is concentrated in these two districts. The remainder are either working class or suburban. Brown carried all eight of these, running narrowly ahead of Coakley in the working-class districts and far ahead of her in the suburban districts.

By winning the state of Massachusetts, Scott Brown effectively won a district that had given President Obama 62 percent of the vote. There were literally one hundred seats held by Democrats that were more heavily Republican than Brown's. If the Democrats were truly being reduced to their liberal rump, they were in for a catastrophic November.

CHAPTER 7

HURRICANE

THE 2010 MIDTERMS

Forget it, the [Pennsylvania] suburbs are just too blue for the GOP to win.

Chuck Todd, 2009[1]

THE FRAGILE DEMOCRATIC CAUCUS

In retrospect, perhaps the most shocking thing about the 2010 midterm elections is how few people saw the Democratic collapse coming until very late in the game. Top-notch prognosticators like Stu Rothenberg were declaring in May 2009 that the idea of a GOP takeover of the House was "lunacy [that] ought to be put to rest immediately."[2] Around the same time, veteran horse-race analyst Charlie Cook wrote that "the 1934 model [in which FDR's Democrats picked up nine seats] probably represents Democrats' best-case scenario and 1982 [in which Reagan's Republicans lost 26 seats] their worst-case scenario. As of now, Obama's Democrats are heading down a track much closer to 1934's."[3] Even as late as April 2010, pundits were treating a special election in a southwestern Pennsylvania House seat that McCain had barely carried as a must-win for the GOP if it was going to even "make a reasonable case that the majority is in play this fall."[4]

This isn't to disparage these writers in any way, but it should serve as a vivid reminder of how quickly our politics can change, and how subject they are to events. Throughout most of 2009, the 2008 elections were still seen as having fundamentally changed our politics and the electoral map. Most of the "big picture" analyses of politics during this time focused on the concept of the Republican Party as a regional party confined to the South. This applied not only at the presidential level, pundits argued, but at the congressional level as well. Ronald Brownstein, one of the most respected electoral analysts in the country, wrote a lengthy cover story for *National Journal* in May 2009 titled "Southern Exposure." His thesis was simple: The Republican Party was increasingly dominated by Southerners, and this was a very bad thing. It threatened to leave the party isolated and unable to put together a winning congressional majority, just as Barack Obama's win in 2008 threatened to put the presidential Republicans out of business.[5] The Republican Party, he wrote, was being reduced to a regional rump party, unable to compete outside the South:

> [T]he regional challenges now confronting the GOP resemble those that Democrats faced in the first decades of the 20th century, when Republicans dominated Congress and the White House.... [T]he Democrats' pervasive identification with the South made it harder for them to loosen the Republicans' commanding grip on the rest of the country.[6]

But in truth, it was the Democratic caucus that was shaky. We've already seen that the 2006 congressional elections and 2008 presidential election were based on versions of the Clinton coalition, and that this coalition was unraveling in 2009.

The 2008 congressional elections had followed the same pattern (see table 7.1). Almost half the Democrats' gains in 2008 came from suburban districts, this time from the South as well as the North (aided in part by significant African American turnout).

This congressional majority was dependent upon two contingencies. First, the Appalachian voters who had stuck with the Democrats at the congressional and local levels throughout the 1990s and 2000s had to continue to stick with the party in the Obama years. But Democrats had already received a warning signal during the Virginia gubernatorial race that this might not happen.

Table 7.1 Democratic Pickups, by Type, 2008

	Core Lib.	Rural South	Rural North	Greater Appalachia	Blue Collar	Mtn. West	S. Suburb	N. Suburb
Dem.	—	2	4	—	3	5	4	8

Second, the Democrats had to maintain their "progressive centrist" stance. Judis and Teixeira were right when they described the voters who sent the new Democratic majority to Congress as people who worried about deficits, did not want tax increases, and wanted incremental improvements to the health-care system.[7] Straying too far from this agenda could be as damaging to the party's prospects in Congress as at the presidential level.

In truth, the playing field in 2010 was tilted against the Democrats from the start. The Democrats had struck deeply into GOP territory in 2006, and a number of members held seats in heavily Republican districts. In fact, 2010 saw the largest number of Democrats representing Republican districts since 1994. In that year, there were roughly 79 Democrats who represented districts that leaned toward the Republicans. Forty-six represented districts that Bush actually carried in 1992, even while he was losing nationwide.

The GOP had won many of these seats back in 1994, but after the 2006 and 2008 blowouts, the Democrats had returned to their inflated numbers. At the beginning of the 111th Congress, 68 Democrats occupied districts that leaned toward Republicans.[8] Even while John McCain was losing nationwide by eight points, 49 Democrats managed to win elections in districts he carried.[9] Needless to say, if these districts shifted at the congressional level to match their presidential voting, Democrats could find their majority in trouble. Moreover, McCain's performance was a sign that Republicans *weren't* actually confined to the South. He had carried vast swaths of the North at the district and county levels. Voters there split their tickets at the congressional level, but they could probably be persuaded by strong candidates to return to their Republican roots.

The Republicans, by contrast, had found themselves demolished in swing districts. While several dozen Republicans occupied districts that Obama had won, that would be expected after a year when he had won by a relatively large margin nationally. Only 15 Republicans, however, represented districts that Obama had won by more than his national average, and several of these were from Obama's home state of Illinois.

Perhaps more important, these Democrats turned out not to be the progressive centrists that Judis and Teixeira had envisioned as the basis for their emerging Democratic majority. Instead, they were part of the most homogenous group of Democrats in decades. When Keith Poole and Howard Rosenthal compiled the DW-NOMINATE scores for the 111th Congress, the results revealed a Democratic caucus with an average score of -.362, and with only five members voting mostly on the right side of the aisle. This was easily the most cohesive Democratic caucus since before the New Deal.

Perhaps most important, the Democratic leadership in Congress represented some of the most liberal districts in the country. This put a distinctly liberal imprint on legislation. Speaker Nancy Pelosi's district leans 35 points toward the Democrats, while the chairmen of the critical districts charged with developing domestic policy—Appropriations, Education and the Workforce, Energy and Commerce, Financial Services, Judiciary, Rules, and Ways and Means—reported back to districts that leaned on average 21 points toward the Democrats. They share an average DW-NOMINATE score of -.552, substantially to the left of even this historically liberal Democratic caucus. With these members responsible for crafting most legislation, it was highly unlikely that a centrist agenda would emerge.

Virtually every assumption regarding the nature of the Democratic Party that had given rise to the Clinton coalition was eroded in 2009 and 2010. The first major act of Congress was the stimulus, which involved almost $800 billion in deficit spending. The bill itself marked a rare instance in which a party simultaneously did too little and too much. We've already explored the effects of the "too much," which was the massive price tag.

At the same time, though, the stimulus did too little because, although the administration had been sent to Washington in large part to fix the economy, this was the last many voters would hear about economic plans until much later in the president's term. President Obama had always preferred transformative plans to incremental ones, and he had promised to pursue policies that were, for lack of a better word, audacious. But this bill had so many policies and programs crammed into it that people could not see the trees for the $787 billion forest. It was as if FDR had crammed the SEC, AAA, SEC, PWA, and NRA bills into one giant legislative measure passed at the beginning of the 73rd Congress, then turned to Jack Garner and said, "Let's go on to Social Security."

This approach allowed Republicans to take potshots at provisions they didn't like and use them as reasons for voting against the bill. Had the administration been less focused on transforming the country's politics and proving it could do big things, it might have broken the bill up into several parts. It is hard to imagine Republicans universally voting against a "pure" tax-cut bill, a bill that funneled public works to their districts, a bill that extended unemployment benefits, and so forth. Such an approach also would have kept economic efforts in the news for an extended period of time and would have been simpler for members to explain and defend. Instead, the omnibus bill provided Republicans with a gigantic target that they could unanimously oppose and use to define the administration.

After the stimulus, Democrats in vulnerable districts were forced to take a vote on a cap-and-trade bill that effectively raised the price of energy at a time when the economy was barely recovering. The administration's near-universal health-care bill did little to dispel concerns that Obama might not be a "New Democrat." It was a conservative way to achieve universal health care...but it was still a huge, complicated bill. Once again, the ambitiousness of the bill and its price tag obscured several popular provisions, and it reinforced the image of the administration as paleoliberal. And because Democrats were so extended into Republican territory, they could not pass the bill without significant support from Democrats in swing districts and senators from swing states. Even after Scott Brown claimed Ted Kennedy's Senate seat in 2010, Democratic leaders pushed the measure—which was by then deeply unpopular—through the House.

Finally, high unemployment persisted throughout the congressional term, incomes flatlined, and inflation slowly crept back into the picture. Altogether this was a triple punch to the party's New Democratic image: it became increasingly difficult to argue that balanced budgets, incrementalism, and economic competence defined the party. This was not what many had expected from Barack Obama or the Democrats. And these were still the same congressional districts that had only four years ago sent 232 Republicans to Congress.

BLOWOUT

In November 2010, the Clinton coalition came unglued. Democrats lost 66 House seats, while picking up three seats from the Republicans. It was the worst showing for any party in House elections since 1948 and the worst showing for either party in a midterm election since 1938. Other losses were more modest: Democrats lost six Senate seats, abetted by the choices of the Republican primary electorates in Colorado, Delaware, and Nevada. Republicans picked up 11 governorships from Democrats, but they once again gave up even larger gains due to primary choices, this time in Colorado and Illinois. Republicans also lost five of their own governorships to the Democrats, for a net gain of six governorships.

The national exit polls show the effect that the Democratic Party's shift away from Clintonism had on the party's coalition. The Democratic vote in the suburbs had remained relatively strong throughout the 2000s, even at the presidential level. Al Gore and John Kerry each won 47 percent of the suburban vote, while Barack Obama improved to 50 percent.[10] But the congressional Democrats in 2010 won only 43 percent of the suburban two-party vote.[11] To put this in perspective, Michael Dukakis won 42 percent there. Among white Catholic voters, the Democratic vote share dropped from 47 percent in 2008 to 39 percent in 2010, quite possibly the Democrats' worst showing among this group since the 1920s.[12] And white voters without college degrees—the final group to join up with Obama in 2008—swung from a 40 percent Obama group to a 33 percent Democratic group.[13] In short, suburbanites and white working-class voters peeled away from the Democratic coalition in 2010.

Minority turnout was down, along with turnout among other core Democratic groups, but not as much as one might suspect. Whites made up 77 percent of the electorate, African Americans 11 percent, and Latino voters 8 percent.[14] While this was down from 2008, when whites were 74 percent of the electorate, African Americans 13 percent, and Latino voters 9 percent, these numbers were also nearly identical to that of the 2004 electorate, when Democrats had fared substantially better than they had fared in 2010, especially at the presidential level.[15] The liberal share of the electorate was down only two points from 2008 levels and only one point from 2004.[16] In other words, 2010 was not simply about liberals staying home.

The 2010 elections further underscored the importance of the relatively new Republican base among white evangelical Protestants. As described in chapter 3, these voters had flocked to Republicans in the 1980s. Today, they function in the Republican Party much as minority groups function in the Democratic Party, providing a solid basis for the Republican congressional and presidential vote. In 2010, Democrats won only 19 percent of the white evangelical Protestant vote, which constituted a full quarter of the electorate.[17] Altogether, Republicans won almost four million more votes from white evangelical Protestants than Democrats won from African Americans and Latinos combined. Of course, as we've already seen, this affiliation may have made it difficult for the GOP to make even deeper inroads with suburban and moderate voters.

House majorities are not won at the national level—they are actually a result of 435 local elections. And while we've discussed elections at the demographic level, we've also focused on geographic regions. Table 7.2 continues our series of charts showing Democratic pickups or losses by "type."

The largest Democratic losses came in Greater Appalachia, where voters who had been giving up on the Democratic Party at the national level for the past decade also abandoned the party at the congressional level. Democrats also gave up huge gains in suburban districts, and half the Mountain West districts could probably be characterized as Northern suburbs as well. Democratic gains in the rural South during the late 2000s were reversed, and Republicans even made inroads into blue-collar congressional districts.

Looking at how the Democrats' total vote share varied over the course of the 2000s in both Democratic-leaning and swing districts, rather than simply seats gained and lost, tells a similar story. Table 7.3 tracks the average Democratic performance over the course of the decade in all districts that the Democrats won at least once during the 2000s.[18] These districts are broken down into various "types" that represent the core components of the Democratic coalition. The categories are somewhat different from those in the tables we have used earlier, but our focus here is on the Democratic Party as a whole, and not just the seats the Democrats have been able to pick up. Unopposed members were not included in the tallies.

Table 7.2 Democratic Losses, by Type, 2010

	Latino	Rural South	Rural North	Greater Appalachia	Blue Collar	Mtn. West	S. Suburb	N. Suburb
Dem.	2	9	11	14	8	6	4	13

Table 7.3 Democratic Performance, Sorted by Year and District Type

Type of District	2002	2004	2006	2008	2010	Change, 2008–2010
Appalachia	60.7%	59.8%	62.8%	60.0%	45.9%	−14.1%
Deep South	52.6%	49.5%	51.7%	58.1%	44.8%	−13.3%
Working Class	61.2%	63.1%	65.6%	69.5%	58.2%	−11.3%
Northern Rural	49.5%	49.6%	57.2%	58.1%	48.1%	−10.1%
Suburban	50.2%	53.7%	58.9%	62.0%	52.9%	−9.1%
Latino	70.4%	69.7%	75.7%	74.6%	66.7%	−7.9%
Core Liberal	68.8%	71.4%	72%	74.2%	67.8%	−6.4%
Black Majority	76.3%	77.7%	80.5%	82.2%	77.5%	−4.7%

As we might expect, the Democratic vote share in Appalachia was demolished in 2010. For probably the first time in the party's recent history, it fell below 50 percent in this core Democratic area. This wasn't just attributable to the bad Democratic night, as Democrats had been able to hold on here in bad Democratic years like 1994, 2002, and 2004. Indeed, this area had been largely immune to the Democrats' national difficulties. The difference here between the Democrats' performance in a good Republican year like 2002 and a great Democratic year like 2006 was negligible. Something deeper was going on. The congressional Democratic vote here had become nationalized; Jacksonian America had finally fully embraced the Party of Clay. More important, Phase Three of the Southern realignment now appears to be fully underway, as areas of the South that had remained loyal to Humphrey are swinging into the GOP column. It isn't enough to write this off to racism against Obama, either. These areas had stayed loyal to Democrats even as whites in the black belt had left the party in droves.

The Democratic losses here were among the most surprising of the night. Rick Boucher in western Virginia saw a 28-year congressional career come to an end. Democrats lost three districts in Tennessee, including the district that Davy Crockett had once represented in Congress. Lincoln Davis, a congressman from the central part of the state who had won by over 20 points in 2008, lost by an almost identical margin to an inexperienced challenger, for a stunning net change of almost 40 points. Members who had not seen a close election in years, like Ben Chandler in Kentucky, Dan Boren in Oklahoma, and Nick Rahall in West Virginia, watched their vote shares dip below 60 percent. The Democratic experience in Greater Appalachia is probably best exemplified by Rusty Farley, who spent $170 on his bid for the Oklahoma state House in McCurtain County, tucked away in the southeast corner of the state. Farley toppled a Democratic incumbent in a district where 81 percent of the voters register as Democrats. Farley commented after the race: "I'm still just kind of in a state of disbelief.... I never thought I'd live to see the day a Republican would be elected in McCurtain County."[19]

Democratic districts in the Deep South, excluding the minority-majority districts, saw similar results. The decline would have been less steep had increased African American turnout across the South not bolstered Democratic numbers in 2008, but nevertheless, this was an historic result. Are Democrats locked out here? Not at all—as we'll see in chapter 11, elections and coalitions are contingent upon the choices of the party, both in how they govern and whom they select as candidates. Republicans could absolutely blow it in Appalachia and the Deep South, and Democrats could absolutely move toward the center and regain competitiveness here. But in the short-to-medium term, the latter option seems unlikely.

Voters in Appalachia and the Deep South had been trending Republican for a while, and even Bill Clinton had really only stanched the bleeding here for Democrats. But the next two groups that showed declines in their vote shares were at the core of the Democratic revival of the 1990 and 2000s. As we've noted, suburban and working-class districts had actually produced increasingly strong showings for Democrats in the 1990s and 2000s. But in 2010, Democrats had perhaps their worst showing since the early 1900s in working-class districts. They didn't *lose* many of these districts, but the decline was nevertheless significant. Anthony Weiner of Queens/Brooklyn fell to 59 percent of the two-party vote, from 71 percent in 2004 (the last time he had major party opposition), while James Oberstar of Duluth fell to 49 percent, from 68 percent in 2008, becoming the first Democrat to lose this district since the 1940s. Dale Kildee of Flint, Michigan, fell from 72 percent of the vote in 2008 to 54 percent, and Marcy Kaptur of Toledo plummeted 15 points to 59 percent of the vote, even after her opponent was revealed to have reenacted World War II battles in a Nazi uniform. Peter Visclosky of Gary, Indiana, sank to 60 percent, while John Dingell of Dearborn, Michigan, the Dean of the House, sank to 59 percent, from 74 percent in 2008.[20] These results are all the more surprising when one considers that none of these Democrats faced experienced opponents; this was entirely the national environment at work.

Democrats in suburban districts had a poor showing as well. Pickups in these suburban districts formed the backbone of the Democrats' congressional majorities of 2006 and 2008, but in 2010 the party gave many of these districts back. Even in districts where they did not lose, the Democratic vote share declined markedly. Overall, Democrats did better here than they had done in 2002, but this was cold comfort: many of these districts had been represented by Republicans in 2002 and did not swing toward the Democrats until 2004, 2006, or 2008. Democratic gains in many Northern suburban districts were reversed, as Republicans swept the Philadelphia and Chicago suburban districts for the first time since 2002. In New York City, the 13th and 19th districts had gone Democratic in the 2006 and 2008 landslides but reverted back to Republican form.

Steve Israel, who won his Suffolk County district in 2000, defeated an underfunded opponent with only 57 percent of the vote. His companion in the New York delegation, Carolyn McCarthy, who had famously won in 1996, dropped from 64 percent of the vote to 54 percent of the vote, a perilously low margin. On the other side of the Hudson River, Rush Holt won with 54 percent of the vote in his meandering suburban New Jersey district, while on the West Coast, Adam Smith of Washington saw an 11-point drop from his 2008 showing, to 54 percent of the vote.

Democrats really held their own only in two types of districts. First, they performed well in "core liberal" areas. Places like Madison, Wisconsin, and Seattle, Washington, had no taste for Republicans, and moved little off their 2008 support for Democrats. Second, Democrats performed well in minority-majority districts. Even here, there's an asterisk, as Democrats had several surprisingly close races in Latino districts in the Southwest and even lost a district that is over 70 percent Latino in southeast Texas. Puerto Rican voters in the Northeast didn't shift their Democratic loyalties, but it seems that Mexican American voters in the Southwest may have.

The Democratic debacle was probably most pronounced in state legislative races. When examining the map in Figure 7.1, bear in mind that four states did not have any legislative races in 2010 (Louisiana, Mississippi, New Jersey, and Virginia), while another three (Kansas, New Mexico, and South Carolina) had races only in their state Houses. Nebraska, of course, has a nonpartisan, unicameral legislature.

Republicans saw limited gains in states where they had maxed out their possible share of the legislature; there simply were not many seats for them to gain in Florida, Georgia, or Idaho. Similarly, they had a lukewarm showing on the West Coast, in the Mountain West, and in much of the Northeast.[21] But in the rest of the country, they scored major successes. The final Southern Democratic bastions were either wiped out or substantially weakened. Republicans picked up 21 seats in Alabama and 27 seats in North Carolina, gaining control of the respective legislatures for the first time since the 1800s.[22] They also took 24 seats in Arkansas; they did not take control of the legislature, but they enjoyed their best showing there in decades.

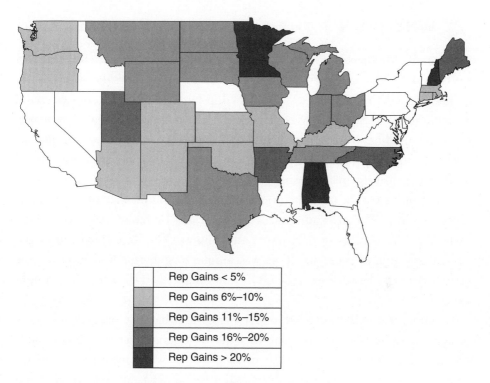

	Rep Gains < 5%
	Rep Gains 6%–10%
	Rep Gains 11%–15%
	Rep Gains 16%–20%
	Rep Gains > 20%

Figure 7.1   Republican Gains in State Legislatures, 2008–2010

Strong Republican performances in the upper Midwest flowed from Democratic weakness in suburban districts, and here, at this local level, Republicans actually scored wins in working-class districts. The biggest shocker of the night, though, came in the far Northeast. In New Hampshire, Republicans picked up a total of 123 seats, for their strongest performance in the New Hampshire legislature since the early 1900s.[23] In Maine, Republicans seized control of both houses of the legislature for the first time since 1972 and added control of the governorship to win unified control of the government—a first since the 1960s.[24]

Overall, Democrats suffered their worst electoral debacle in living memory. They had underestimated how shaky their coalition was and how contingent it was on perceptions of moderate, centrist governance. Republicans were ecstatic, and for a party that had been widely left for dead only two years earlier, there was good reason. But there were also significant warning signs, which should serve as reminders that, regardless of whether the country leans center-right or center-left, the word "center" always comes first.

WHY DIDN'T THE GOP DO EVEN BETTER?

Despite all this success, the 2010 elections had a bit of an anticlimactic feel for the GOP. After all, they had won the Virginia governorship by almost 20 points, carried the New Jersey governorship by 4 points, and even elected a Republican to the Senate in Massachusetts. Many had thought that Democratic bastions would be overrun completely, and the GOP would enjoy seat pickups not seen since the 1800s. Why did these even larger gains not materialize? There were three primary reasons.

First, at least at the gubernatorial level, Republicans just had some old-fashioned bad luck. Six governors' races were decided by fewer than two points, including critical races in Minnesota and Illinois. The Republicans managed to win only one of these six. This was unique to gubernatorial races: in the close Senate and House races, the GOP won roughly half the time, as we might expect.

Second, if pundits were late to the party in 2010, they nevertheless were in agreement by late summertime that the Democrats' majority was in serious trouble. This stood in stark contrast to 1994, when most pundits never showed up for the party; most dismissed a Republican takeover as unthinkable as late as Election Day. This gave Democrats a bit of an advantage. The tough votes stopped in March 2010; there was no equivalent to the disastrous September 1994 crime bill vote. Also, in 2010 Democratic incumbents had at least some advance notice of the impending wave, giving them an opportunity to fundraise, activate their voting base, and, most important, research their opponents.

Viewed in this light, the unevenness of the GOP victory makes perfect sense. Gubernatorial and Senate candidates are the most high-profile in the country. These statewide races gather a lot of attention, as well as money. Voters and newspapers focus on them. It was relatively easy to focus voter attention on the records of candidates like Sharron Angle and Bill Brady. At the House level, however, it is more difficult to focus voter attention on particular candidates. Accordingly, Republican gains here were bigger than they had been in the Senate and gubernatorial races. Finally, hardly anyone pays attention to state House candidates. Voters here voted purely the party line, and it resulted in massive wins, even for the most unlikely Republican candidates. Had the Republican wave developed later, or had the Democrats not had such an efficient fundraising and research effort, the House and Senate races might have looked a bit more like the state House results.

But even this doesn't explain everything. Scott Brown effectively picked up a district that had given Obama 62 percent of the vote. No other Republican could claim such a win. Scott Brown defined the upper limit of where GOP candidates could win. But it must also be remembered that Brown won an *open seat*. This is a critical distinction, as defeating an incumbent is a more difficult task than flipping an open seat. The GOP wave didn't advance very deeply into blue territory among Democratic incumbents (nor did it in 1994). However, it did go pretty deep in open seats (in fact, it went deeper than it had in 1994).

If we confine our analysis to open seats only, Brown looks like much less of an outlier. As we might expect, Republicans won every open seat in jurisdictions McCain carried except for two: Pennsylvania's 12th District and the West Virginia Senate seat. But even in districts that had leaned Democrat in 2008, Republicans performed very well, up to a point (see table 7.4).

If we focus not on win/loss results, but rather on the amount by which the candidate ran ahead of John McCain in open seats, we see that Brown's performance was much more typical of GOP gains this cycle. Of the 25 races in

Table 7.4 Republican 2010 Performance in Open Seats Where McCain Won <47% of the Vote

Race	McCain Performance	GOP 2010 Performance	Difference
CA-33	12.1%	13.8%	1.7%
MI-13	16.0%	18.9%	2.9%
AL-7	26.0%	27.5%	1.5%
RI-1	33.7%	46.8%	13.2%
CA-10	33.7%	44.8%	11.1%
FL-19	34.0%	36.2%	2.2%
MA-Sen	36.7%	52.4%	15.7%
DE-Sen	37.4%	41.4%	4.0%
DE-At Large	37.4%	41.9%	4.5%
IL-Sen	37.4%	51.0%	13.6%
CT-Sen	38.4%	44.0%	5.6%
IL-10	38.4%	51.2%	12.8%
WI-7	42.9%	53.9%	11.0%
NH-2	43.4%	50.9%	7.5%
PA-7	43.4%	55.6%	12.2%
MA-10	43.9%	47.5%	3.6%
PA-Sen	44.9%	51.0%	6.1%
NH-Sen	45.5%	62.1%	16.7%
WA-3	45.9%	53.2%	7.3%

this category, just under half the candidates (12) showed improvements within 5 points of Brown's performance. While Brown's 15.7-point improvement over McCain's showing was substantial, it wasn't the largest such improvement. That honor actually goes to Kelly Ayotte, who ran 16.7 points ahead of McCain.

In other words, Brown didn't represent a fluke so much as he represented the outer limits of what a low-double-digit improvement over McCain's showing could accomplish. Had there been more open Democratic seats among the "35–40 percent McCain" districts, Brown's win probably would have looked even less like an outlier.

But looking at these data, we see that not all GOP candidates performed as well as Brown. In fact, the distribution is somewhat "bi-modal," to use a political science term. That is, the data points aren't evenly distributed around a central point—instead there are two clusters: one in which the GOP candidate ran about 2–8 points ahead of McCain, and another cluster in which the GOP candidate ran 11–17 points ahead of McCain. The explanation for this goes a long way toward revealing Scott Brown's secret. The truth is that it isn't *Scott Brown's* secret at all. It is merely the difference among Scott Brown, Mark Kirk, Bob Dold, and Pat Meehan versus Christine O'Donnell, Charlie Bass, Jeff Perry, and Glen Urquhart.

Simply put, Republicans nominated several candidates who were too stridently conservative for their states and districts, even in 2010. It wasn't just their actual views on issues that were too conservative, although this was certainly sometimes the case. Style played an important role as well. For example, consider Kelly Ayotte. She was a pretty conservative candidate: she is pro-life, opposes gay marriage and allowing same-sex couples to adopt, opposes increasing the minimum wage, supports an Arizona-style immigration law, is a climate-change skeptic, and never met a tax cut she doesn't like. She ran in a state (New Hampshire) that was only about six points more Republican than Delaware, and yet she ran almost a full 20 points ahead of O'Donnell.

It isn't just that Ayotte figured out a few key areas to moderate herself on a few key issues, although that was certainly part of her appeal. It's that she was conservative without being in-your-face about it. To borrow an analogy from our earlier depictions of Bill Clinton, her style is multifaceted. Ayotte didn't act as though there was a conservative majority in her swing state. While she probably would have voted with Sharron Angle or Ken Buck on about 95 percent of Senate roll-call votes, unlike Angle and Buck, she didn't launch into tirades about Second Amendment remedies or compare homosexuality to alcoholism. It is the same skill set that Marco Rubio used to capture a near majority in the three-way Florida Senate race.

This isn't just true of Republican candidates in 2010 either. In 2008, only five Democratic Senate candidates ran further behind Barack Obama in their states than Al Franken; three of these were minor candidates. The difference between Franken's share of Minnesota's two-party vote and Obama's was greater than that of obscure Democratic candidates like Vivian Figueres in Alabama and Erik Fleming in Mississippi. His strident approach to politics turned off swing voters and nearly cost him an election in a state where President Obama was winning by double digits. As we've noted, even the Gipper understood this. Reagan studiously avoided making Goldwater-like comments on the campaign trail about "wanting to lob one into the men's room at the Kremlin"; it was crucial for his success.

Looking back at Table 7.4, Republicans of various stripes managed to perform about as well as Brown. Those races with Republicans who performed worse than Brown fell into two categories: ones in races in which there was no national party support, such as California's 33rd District, and ones in which the Republican candidate had some type of major image problem. Scott Brown was among the group of Republicans who outperformed Obama, despite being a rough ideological fit for his state, because he always couched his rhetoric carefully and was conscious of his image as an "everyman." Deviating from this model cost the Republicans dearly, and if they continue to do this in moderate or Democratic-leaning districts, or if the national party recasts itself as substantially outside the mainstream, they will lose their majority as quickly as they gained it.

CONCLUSION

This, then, is the real story behind how things came apart so quickly for the Democrats from 2008 to 2010. They had assembled the closest you could come in modern times to a "coalition of everyone." Yet, as has been the case with such coalitions time and again in the past, it proved unstable. The leftward pressure from the Democratic leadership made it impossible for the Democrats to hold on to more moderate voters in suburban districts and to more traditionally populist voters in blue-collar districts. Moreover, contingent events—namely, the economy—intervened to keep the Democrats from maintaining their majority. It was the exact same story we have seen play out time and again in this book since the 1920s. It happened to the Republicans in the 1920s, it happened to the Democrats in the late 1930s, and it happened to Republicans in the early 1990s. Pundits who thought this result was impossible, or even merely unlikely, in early 2009 just didn't have a long enough view of history.

But what of the future? We've made oblique references to the demographic underpinnings of the supposed emerging permanent Democratic majority, but we haven't examined these claims in any systemic fashion. Likewise, we've danced around some of the problems with realignment theory, without examining them in depth. Part III examines these issues in detail. Just as pundits should not have expected the Democrats' 2008 majority to become permanent, neither should they expect a permanent majority to emerge in the near future (for either party). The coalitions they describe are inherently unstable and *cannot* exist.

PART III

WHERE WE GO FROM HERE

CHAPTER 8

THE GOP AND THE LATINO VOTE

Unless the Republican Party is delivered from its reactionary leadership and reorganized in accordance with its one time liberal principles, it will die like the Whig party of sheer political cowardice.

William Borah,1934[1]

UNTIL NOW, THIS BOOK has largely been backward-looking. It has focused on the development of voting patterns in the United States over the past century and how these patterns affected the 2010 midterm elections. Now the focus shifts to the future. Where do the parties go from here? With the breakdown of regional parties largely accomplished and the rise of ideological parties nearly complete, what types of changes to the political system can we expect in the next two or three decades and beyond? And, although Obama's majority appears to be a lost one for now, can he reclaim it?

Despite the massive GOP gains in Congress, very few observers take seriously the idea that a permanent Republican majority is in the offing. Yet the notion of a permanent Democratic majority remains very much in vogue. Proponents of this theory suggest that Democrats will lose very few elections over the course of the next few decades, because demographic trends are so decisively in that party's favor. The 2010 midterms are dismissed as a fluke resulting from decreased Democratic participation and a poor economy.

There is no doubt that these factors were critical in the 2010 elections. But there is also no doubt that there is no permanent Democratic—or

Republican—majority anywhere on the horizon. Permanent majorities simply do not exist in American politics. Politics rarely travels in a straight line; contingent events constantly pop up that alter the country's trajectory, and different parts of coalitions bump up against each other. Just as the same factors that contributed to Obama's expansion of the Democratic appeal to minorities and suburbanites decreased the party's appeal to white working-class voters and Jacksonians, its appeal to youth and racial minorities will affect its ability to appeal to other groups in the electorate.

Probably the central feature of the emerging-Democratic-majority thesis is the argument that the growth of the minority electorate will eventually overwhelm the white vote. Judis and Teixeira mention African Americans, Asians, and Latinos, but the real analysis centers on Latinos alone. Asian Americans are not yet numerous enough to significantly affect the balance of national politics and are concentrated largely in already-blue states. While the party switch of a few African American state officials in Southern states in the wake of the 2010 elections is intriguing—if only for the tantalizing possibility that more African Americans in heavily red Southern states will join the GOP rather than toil in political irrelevance in their states—African American voters will probably remain Democrat for the foreseeable future.[2]

But the analysis regarding Latinos is far more controversial. *If* Latinos continue to immigrate to the United States at their present rates, *if* the Republican Party fails to adapt to a changed political environment, *if* Latinos continue to vote Democratic at their present rates, and *if* this expanded Latino electorate doesn't push other portions of the electorate toward the GOP, then a Democratic majority will emerge. But these are all very big "ifs." The experience of the 2000s suggests that none of these factors is a given, and some may actually be unlikely.

THE TRUE TREND LINES

The salience of the Latino vote is nothing new. It has loomed as the basis for a potential Democratic counterrevolution in the South since at least the late 1960s. In *The Emerging Republican Majority*, Phillips noted that "¡Viva Kennedy!" clubs provided a new level of political consciousness for the Mexican Americans in Texas, who flocked to the polls to support the first Roman Catholic president, much like their Northern brethren, and probably swung Texas's votes to

Humphrey.[3] From 1960 through 1972, it is estimated that Mexican Americans gave 84 percent of their vote to Democratic presidential candidates.[4]

What has changed since the 1960s is the size of the Latino population, and hence the salience of that vote. In 1980, Latinos constituted a relatively modest 6 percent of the population. By 1990, that number had increased to 9 percent.[5] Ten years later, the Latino population reached 12 percent of the American population.[6] From 2000 to 2010, Latino growth accelerated, to the point where Latinos now account for 16.3 percent of the U.S. population. Non-Hispanic whites in the United States are expected to become a minority by 2050.

It is easy to look at this trend and conclude that the Republican Party, at least as we know it, is on the road to extinction or at least permanent minority status. But what if these trends are wrong or at least substantially off? In *The Emerging Democratic Majority*, Judis and Teixeira followed the trend lines and suggested that minorities would constitute 25 percent of the electorate by 2010.[7] They further explained that, when combined with increased Democratic strength among professionals and women, the Republicans would rarely be able to win elections.

Using a similar approach, Professor Alan Abramowitz of Emory University predicted that in the 2010 elections, "no more than 76 percent of voters will be white while at least 11 percent will be African-American and at least 13 percent will be either Hispanic or members of other racial minority groups."[8] Abramowitz went a step further and predicted that because "Republican candidates would have to win almost 60 percent of the white vote in order to win 50 percent of the overall national popular vote in 2010," and because Republicans hadn't done that even in the very good Republican year of 1994 (when they received 58 percent of the white vote), it would be "extremely difficult" for Republicans to take control of the House. To underscore the difficulty facing Republicans, Abramowitz accompanied his column with a chart that suggested explosive minority population growth (see figure 8.1).

All of these projections were wrong. In 2010, minorities did not constitute 25 percent of the electorate, whites were more than 76 percent of the electorate, and Republicans won more than 60 percent of the white vote. In House races, whites constituted 77 percent of the electorate, a larger share than in the 2004 or 2008 elections, and Democrats received only 37 percent of their votes. Latinos made up 8 percent of the electorate, just as they had in 2006 and 2004. Using a

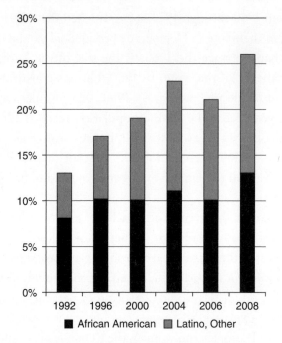

Figure 8.1 Racial Composition of U.S. Electorate, 1992–2008

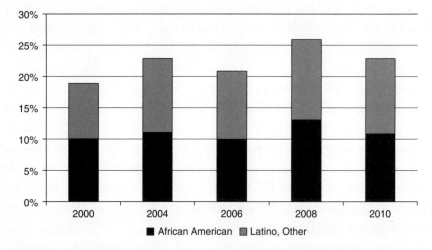

Figure 8.2 Racial Composition of U.S. Electorate, 2000–2010

more reasonable chart shape and including the 2010 data suggest a much more gradual increase in the Latino share of the electorate (see figure 8.2).

The speed with which the Latino population grows is of critical importance for any potential Democratic majority. Holding all other votes constant, the

Latino portion of the electorate in Arizona would have to more than double before Jan Brewer would have found herself in any danger of losing and would have to triple before John McCain was threatened there. In Texas, the Latino share of the electorate would have to almost triple before Rick Perry would have been threatened with a loss. This is not to dismiss the challenge that the growing Latino population presents for the GOP, but rather to put it in perspective—the critical mass necessary to create the problem is probably still some years off. And if the Latino vote falls off trend, as it did in 2010, those numbers will take longer to arrive.

The standard response of permanent-Democratic-majority advocates to this tempered view is that the Latino vote is akin to the white working-class vote of the 1920s after the surge of immigration at the turn of the century—large, but mostly dormant. It needs only to be mobilized. This is evident in the low participation rates relative to the Latino share of the population. As the latent Latino population becomes naturalized, and as their children come of age, it will overwhelm the GOP more quickly than these recent trend lines suggest.

But this analogy also illustrates the difficulty inherent in engaging in accurate straight-line projections. If one were to look at the state of the parties in the 1920s, especially in 1920, one would have to conclude immediately that the white working class represented a ticking time bomb for the *Democrats*. After all, Northern ethnic minorities voted Republican at the time, the nation was majority urban for the first time in its history, and, as a result, the Democrats' sole bastion in the South had begun bleeding population (as a result of the First Great Migration) and Electoral College votes. Of course, an utterly unforeseeable event occurred in 1928, followed by another such event in 1929, shifting the voting patterns of this group.

The shift in the voting patterns of white ethnics in the 1920s is especially relevant given one additional, little known fact about the Latino vote: Republicans are doing better among Latino voters today than they have in the past; after a steady decline in Republican fortunes from 1980 to 1996, the trend has reversed (see figure 8.3). This is true even when we examine the Latino PVI, rather than the absolute results (figure 8.4).

Not shown on this chart are earlier estimates suggesting that the Mexican American vote was as high as 84 percent for the Democrats during the 1960s. This represents a significant shift toward Republicans over the past 50 years.

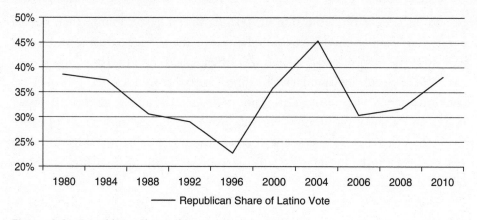

Figure 8.3 Republican Share of Latino Two-Party Vote

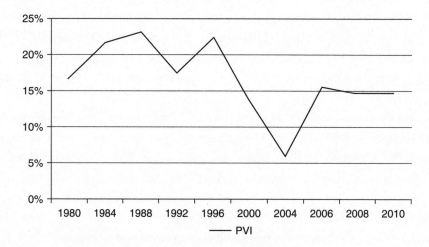

Figure 8.4 Democratic Lean of Latino Electorate, by Year

And there are critical distinctions in Latino voting patterns that suggest this trend will continue over the next few decades. Like other white ethnic groups before them, Latinos tend to vote more Republican as they climb the socioeconomic ladders of society. Consider Figures 8.5 and 8.6.

The non-Hispanic white vote in America is sorted pretty well by ideology: conservatives vote for Republicans, liberals vote for Democrats, and moderates split their vote. The African American vote, by contrast, clusters toward the Democratic Party regardless of ideology. This is a particularly disheartening sign for Republicans who would like to see the GOP expand its appeal among African American voters. But what of Latinos? If they vote like African

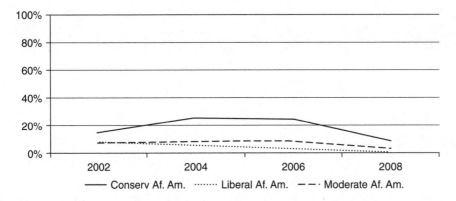

Figure 8.5   Republican Share of African American Vote, by Ideology

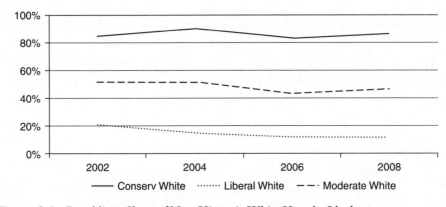

Figure 8.6   Republican Share of Non-Hispanic White Vote, by Ideology

Americans, it seems that Republicans would be in very deep demographic trouble. However, if they vote like Anglos, it suggests that as more and more Latinos become wealthier and, presumably, more conservative, they will also become more Republican (see figure 8.7).

As it turns out, the Latino vote looks a lot more like the non-Hispanic white vote than the African American vote. Latino voters in each group are roughly 10 points more Democratic than white voters, while Latino conservatives are about 50 points more Republican than conservative African Americans.[9] The critical distinction is that there are more Latino liberals than there are white liberals and fewer conservatives.[10]

There are likely a variety of factors driving the larger number of Latino liberals, including Republican positions on immigration, health care, and such. But differences in socioeconomic status are also a crucial factor.

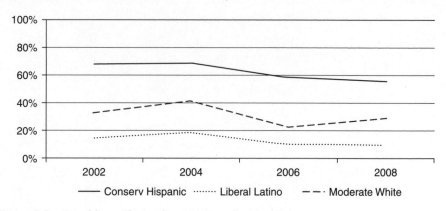

Figure 8.7   Republican Share of Latino Vote, by Ideology

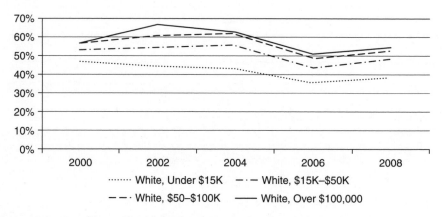

Figure 8.8   Republican Share of White Vote, by Income

Figures 8.8, 8.9, and 8.10 show the effect of different levels of income on different groups' voting patterns.

Once again, the Latino vote begins to look an awful lot like the non-Hispanic white vote. Over the past decade non-Hispanic whites who make in excess of $100,000 per year have given Republicans around 58 percent of the vote, versus 44 percent of Latinos and 19 percent of African Americans with similar incomes. Non-Hispanic whites making less than $15,000 per year have given Republicans 41 percent of the vote over the past decade, as opposed to 29 percent of Latinos and an abysmal 7 percent of African Americans. It is striking that wealthy Latinos actually vote more heavily Republican than poor non-Hispanic whites. The difference, again, is that there are simply more wealthy non-Hispanic whites. This will surely change over the next few decades, however,

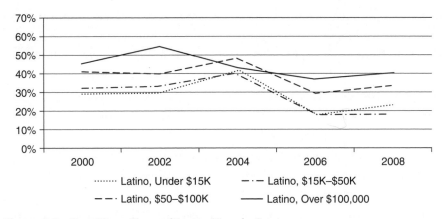

Figure 8.9   Republican Share of Latino Vote, by Income

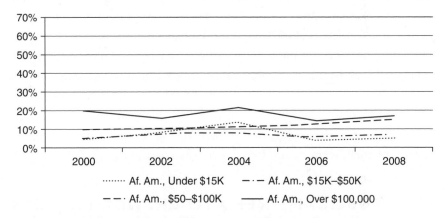

Figure 8.10   Republican Share of African American Vote, by Income

as Latinos become more established in this country, and their children join the ranks of the middle class. Again, it is difficult to extrapolate from the present, but there is at least significant evidence that as this occurs, the Republican trend among Latinos will continue.

Assimilation is an incredibly complicated, controversial topic that is well beyond the scope of this book. I certainly don't wish to argue the relative merits, drawbacks, or morality of assimilation. It is simply worth observing that there is a strain of scholarship that suggests that America never becomes majority nonwhite and at the same time became majority nonwhite long ago. At one time, according to this line of thought, the Irish were not considered white but were slowly redefined as a part of white society.[11] The great wave of immigrants from southeastern Europe was likewise only gradually accepted into American society; perceived racial distinctions retreated first, followed by ethnic distinctions. In 1922, for example, the Alabama Court of Appeals overturned a miscegenation conviction of an African American man because testimony regarding his wife's Sicilian origins "can in no sense be taken as conclusive that she was therefore a white woman."[12] Indeed, it wasn't until the 1980s that scholars began talking about the end of Italian ethnicity.[13]

According to this line of argument, Irish, Italian, and other groups once retained the dual ethnic/racial identity that to some extent characterizes the Latino community today. The racial connotation disappeared gradually, and then the ethnic connotation lost much of its meaning. The differentiation of the Latino vote by ideology and income suggests that a similar process is occurring today; as one expert on Latino voting patterns put it, "The trajectory of Latino political development, however, mirrors earlier European immigrant experiences to a much greater degree than does the black American experience."[14] Of course, Republicans could put a halt to this were they to embrace some of the more virulently anti-immigrant political positions. But even this seems unlikely; Teddy Roosevelt inveighed violently against "hyphenated-Americanism," while Harding and Coolidge shut off the immigration spigot in the 1920s. Yet it did not prevent the gradual assimilation of turn-of-the century white ethnics, nor did it prevent them from voting Republican throughout the 1920s.

DO REPUBLICANS NEED TO CHANGE POLICIES TO ATTRACT LATINO VOTERS?

Almost every discussion of the growth of the Latino population eventually comes around to the same conclusion: the GOP must swing leftward on immigration if it is to survive. This is usually declared after a discussion of the fate of the California Republican Party. It has become an article of faith among pundits that the California Republican Party was doomed by a series of racially charged initiatives in the mid-1990s.[15] In 1994, Governor Pete Wilson backed Proposition 187, which prohibited noncitizens from receiving government-funded services, including health-care services and public school enrollment. It was approved 59 percent to 41 percent, with only the San Francisco Bay area rejecting it. It was followed two years later by Proposition 209, which effectively prohibited affirmative action programs in public institutions. It passed

55 percent to 45 percent, losing only in Los Angeles County and the San Francisco Bay area. Finally, Proposition 227 required that all public school instruction be in English (subject to waiver opportunities). It passed with 61 percent of the vote.

After the passage of these three ballot initiatives, Republicans regularly lost the presidential vote in California by double digits, failed to win the governorship, save for a fluke recall election in 2003, and were shut out of the Senate delegation.[16] The causal relationship here is rarely questioned. But it is a bad misreading of the California GOP's decline. First, and perhaps most important, the California GOP had been in the minority in the state for a very long time prior to the passage of these ballot initiatives. The state was historically divided in much the same way as the rest of the country. Northern California was settled by Yankees. It favored progressive Republicans, although there was a substantial white ethnic population in the San Francisco area. Southern California was settled, albeit sparsely, by conservative Southern Democrats. During the Great Depression, farmers from heavily Democratic states like Oklahoma flocked to Los Angeles and the Central Valley, while progressives in the North began voting for Democratic candidates. By the end of the 1930s, Democrats had achieved a 20-point registration edge over Republicans. Republicans narrowed this edge during the taxpayer revolt of the 1970s and early 1980s, but the Democrats were able to maintain a fairly steady single-digit lead over Republicans throughout the 1990s. This latter fact is especially salient, as it suggests that there was actually no surge in Democratic registration in the wake of these ballot initiatives, or that if there was, it was balanced out by increased Republican registration.

The years 1954 and 1958 were critical for Democrats in the Golden State. They pulled roughly even with Republicans in the state legislature in 1954, then took control in 1958. They have generally maintained large majorities since then; the Democratic edge in the legislature in the late 1990s was not significantly different from their edge in the 1980s.[17] The GOP's downticket woes began in 1958 as well, rather than in 1996, as Republicans rarely won more than one of the four downballot races, except in GOP landslide years like 1966 and 1994. Discontent among white working-class voters in San Francisco and Los Angeles over the counterculture did help Republicans elect conservative Republican governors, but as was the case with the presidential GOP, these voters were merely borrowed and were never brought completely into the GOP fold. The GOP did have success at the presidential level from 1952 through 1988, but that owes largely to the presence of a California Republican on every GOP ticket except three during that era and the importance of foreign policy issues and the defense industry to California's white working-class voters and suburbanites during the Cold War. Even then, the state never leaned more than a point or two toward the GOP. In 1984 and 1988, it actually leaned toward the Democrats.

The California GOP was in a state of general disrepair well before the ballot propositions of the mid-1990s came along, and it showed no signs of a massive downturn on a variety of measurements after the 2000s. More important, the exit polls show little change in the voting habits of California Latinos from 1988 through 2008 (see table 8.1). Latinos consistently gave Democratic presidential candidates between 66 and 76 percent of the vote, whether the Republican candidate was losing nationally by eight points or winning by eight points. They did so whether the GOP candidate was running in the immediate aftermath of Proposition 187 or as the heir to an administration that had just signed an "amnesty" bill, as George H. W. Bush did in 1988.

We've already seen that Latinos are more heterodox in their voting than we might expect simply by looking at the exit poll numbers. But what if the generalized assumption that immigration is an issue of consummate importance to Latinos is incorrect? What if immigration is not to Latinos as the civil rights agenda was to African Americans in the 1960s? In fact, immigration splits the Latino vote in ways that you would not expect. Consider the exit poll results as reported by Voter News Service (VNS) for Propositions 187 and 209 (see Table 8.2).

The *Los Angeles Times* exit poll found less support for these initiatives among minorities, although it still found nearly one-quarter of Latino voters supported both initiatives. The *Los Angeles Times* poll for Proposition 227—VNS did not poll here—found that around 37 percent of Latino voters supported Proposition

Table 8.1   Two-Party California Presidential Vote by Ethnicity, 1988–2008

	1988		1992		1996		2000		2004		2008	
	R	D	R	D	R	D	R	D	R	D	R	D
White	57%	43%	46%	54%	49%	51%	49%	51%	52%	48%	47%	53%
Hispanic	29%	71%	26%	74%	24%	76%	22%	78%	34%	66%	24%	76%

Table 8.2   Support for Propositions 187 and 209, by Race and Ethnicity

	Proposition 187		Proposition 209	
	Yes	No	Yes	No
White	65%	35%	62%	38%
African American	59%	41%	27%	73%
Latino	31%	69%	30%	70%
Asian	55%	45%	45%	55%

227, along with almost a majority of African Americans.[18] This is consistent with studies by political scientists that have found that there is "significant intra-group variation" on the issue of immigration, and that Latinos do not view the immigration issue solely through an ethnic lens. Moreover, as Latinos experience greater acculturation, they tend to become more supportive of restricting even legal immigration.[19] In other words, immigration seems primed to fade as an issue over time, even within the Latino community.

What ultimately ruined the Republican Party of California were two key trends observed in chapter 3. First, the Latino vote became larger, even if that vote did not shift. In 1988, the California electorate was 82 percent white; by 2008 it was 63 percent white. But just as important, if not more so, is that upper-middle-class suburbanites in California mirrored the national trend away from the GOP. Looking at change in the county-by-county results between 1988 and 2008 and controlling for race, there is a strong, statistically significant relationship between the size of the swing toward the Democrats and both the level of college education[20] and the level of wealth in the county.[21] California followed the pattern evident in the rest of the country; as the Republican Party moved further rightward, especially on social issues, its upper-class suburbs edged toward the Democrats. That is what ultimately spelled doom for the California GOP.

Interestingly, there's not much evidence of Latino backlash against candidates associated with heavily anti-immigrant policies and politics. Table 8.3 gives the GOP share of the Latino vote in several heavily Latino states in various years.

The Republican candidates for governor of Arizona and senator in Nevada both were associated with particularly high-profile incidents in their campaigns involving the illegal immigration issue. In California, the Republican Senate candidate defended Arizona's controversial S.B. 1070, while the Republican

Table 8.3 Republican Vote Shares, Selected 2004, 2008, and 2010 Races

	2004 Pres.	2008 Pres.	2010 Gov.	2010 Sen.
AZ	43%	41%	28%	40%
CA	32%	23%	31%	29%
NV	39%	22%	33%	30%
TX	49%	35%	38%	

gubernatorial candidate's stance on immigration was incoherent, an incoherence that was accentuated by revelations that she may have knowingly employed an illegal immigrant as a housekeeper. Yet the only candidate who appeared to pay a particular price among Latinos was Jan Brewer in Arizona. In California, Nevada, and Texas, every candidate ran ahead of John McCain's percentages. Sharron Angle, who ran an advertisement featuring a white student being assaulted by a gang of Latinos, received about the same share of the Latino votes as gubernatorial candidate Brian Sandoval, who largely avoided the issue. The difference between Angle and Sandoval was that the latter received 62 percent of the non-Hispanic white vote, while the former received only 52 percent. Even Brewer only ran 12 points behind John McCain's 2008 totals and 15 points behind pro-immigration reform George W. Bush's 2004 totals, a fairly shocking result.

The assumption that immigration reform is to the Latino community what the 1960s Civil Rights Acts were to the African American community is overstated. While 69 percent of Latino voters in 2008 described illegal immigration as "very" or "extremely" important to them in exit polls, nearly one-third of those voters voted Republican. On several key ballot issues in California, large portions of the Latino community cast votes that were directly opposed to what is broadly considered their "interest" on immigration issues. The views of Latinos on immigration are simply more heterodox than most observers comprehend.

None of this is to say that Republicans should stop worrying about the Latino vote. There are *no votes* that *either* party should write off in this country. Moreover, even controlling for income and ideology, large portions of the Latino community do not vote as heavily Republican as we would expect vis-à-vis non-Hispanic whites. In other words, even when we control for economic status and ideology, there is still a distinct Latino politics in this country, and one that inures to the Democrats' benefit.[22] That gap is clearly due, at least in part, to Republican positions on immigration and, perhaps more important, the *tone* that certain Republicans take on immigration issues.

Republicans do have a lot to offer Latino voters; they are among the most conservative groups in the country on issues like abortion and defense spending.[23] But if a substantial segment of the Republican Party continues to engage in "immigrant-bashing," and if proposals such as changing the Fourteenth Amendment's definition of citizenship continue to gain popularity, Republicans will probably never reach their full potential in the Latino community and will suffer electorally as a result.

THE END OF THE RAINBOW?

This is an even touchier subject than the assimilation point, but it goes directly to the critical problem with "straight-line analyses" of coalitions. The "permanent majority" thesis essentially posits that Democrats are preparing to put together a "coalition of everyone" that will last a very long time. They envision African Americans, Asians, Latinos, women, upscale whites, and blue-collar whites happily cohabiting the same party for several decades.

We've seen the problem with this before. Electoral coalitions are a lot like water balloons. As you press on one portion, other parts are stretched. As described in chapter 2, FDR learned this the hard way. As African Americans and white ethnics entered the Democratic Party, white Southerners prepared to make their exit. Later, when the Christian Right rose to dominance in the Republican Party and the end of the Cold War severed the bonds between various disparate groups in the Republican coalition, moderate suburbanites fled. At the same time, the rise of economic libertarianism within the party made it more difficult for Republicans to appeal to blue-collar whites. In other words, you cannot simply hold all groups constant, increase the minority population, and expect a stable Democratic majority. Those new groups will insert new issues into the public debate, which will cause new cleavages within and between the parties. This will materialize in unexpected ways. And because the immigration spigot in this country was largely cut off from the 1920s through the 1960s, we've never really seen the way a multi-ethnic citizenry behaves in postindustrial, postmodern America.

But even if we're in somewhat uncharted territory, the history of multi-ethnic coalitions in this country has not been a harmonious one. In the North,

Anglo-Saxon whites were the foundation of the Federalist/Whig/Republican coalition. When the Irish arrived, they joined the Democratic Party. The next group to arrive, the Italians, joined the Republicans (generally). Puerto Ricans became Democratic, and so forth in an even-odd pattern, creating what Michael Barone called a "crazy-quilt pattern of politics, with the two traditional parties characterized by asymmetrical and illogical patterns of support, and few potentially unifying forces."[24] In fairness, Judis and Teixeira do anticipate this argument, but they put as positive a spin on it as one could possibly hope for. They refer to it as a potential "embarrassment of political riches."[25] They note in particular the experience of Mark Green in the 2001 New York mayoral race. Green faced a Latino Democratic primary opponent in a rough-and-tumble primary and won. When he won, Latino voters defected from the Democrats and helped elect Michael Bloomberg mayor. While it is true that Bloomberg was a former Democrat, Latino voters had also played a key role in Rudy Giuliani's victories.

There are many other examples. Bloomberg won a surprisingly close third mayoral term against an African American mayoral candidate largely due to the crossover support he received from Latinos. In Denver, successive races involving minority candidates from 1983 through 1995 resulted in an increased fracturing of the ethnic and racial vote. By 1995, Latino voting patterns in Denver fell roughly halfway between white voting patterns and African American voting patterns.[26]

In 1993, Richard Riordan split the black-brown coalition that had kept Mayor Tom Bradley in power in Los Angeles, defeating an Asian American Democrat.[27] The subsequent 2001 mayoral campaign of Democrat Antonio Villaraigosa against moderate white Democrat James Hahn broke down largely along ethnic lines: in the primary, Villaraigosa and Congressman Xavier Becerra received a combined 79 percent of the Latino vote, while Hahn received 71 percent of the African American vote.[28] Hahn then received 80 percent of the African American vote in the runoff election, despite running to the right of Villaraigosa on many hot-button issues that have been perceived as racialized: in particular, he accused Villaraigosa of being soft on crime. Polling showed that African American attitudes toward immigration played a role, as a majority of African American voters told pollsters that they believed immigration was a bad thing. Interestingly, these polls also showed that 42 percent of the city's Latino population believed that the growing immigrant population was a bad thing.[29] The result was an odd coalition of Latinos and liberal whites against African Americans, Asians, and conservative whites; Hahn won. In the city attorney race, however, Latinos and African Americans joined in support of the moderate Latino candidate and in opposition to liberal whites.[30]

Four years later, Hahn's coalition collapsed, and Villaraigosa was overwhelmingly elected mayor. But even then, African Americans and whites were much more likely to vote for Hahn than for Villaraigosa.[31] This offers a potential preview of what our politics will look like as America becomes increasingly dominated by ethnic minorities. Assuming that the assimilation scenario does not play out, it is more likely that we will see a pastiche of politics as completely unrecognizable to us today as New Deal politics would have been to voters in the 1920s. In some instances, the candidates might not even call themselves "Republicans," but the issue cleavages will nevertheless be real.

Much of the analysis presented so far here has ignored the differences *among* Latino groups as well. It is well known that Cuban voters tend to be more Republican than other groups. This owes in part to the Republican Party's anticommunist heritage. But there are also differences between Latinos from the Caribbean basin and from Mexico. According to the NES, the latter have tended to vote six or seven points more Republican than Puerto Ricans over the past few decades. Political science research reveals that Latinos of Mexican descent tend to feel less of a sense of commonality with African Americans than do those of Puerto Rican or Dominican descent.[32] While 81 percent of Dominican Americans and 71 percent of Cuban Americans say that they have a fair amount or a lot in common with Puerto Ricans, only 45 percent of Mexican Americans responded affirmatively. And Mexican Americans were actually more likely to say that they have a fair amount or a lot in common with whites than with African Americans; they and Cubans were the only Latino groups to give that response.[33]

While black-brown coalitions may prove difficult to maintain, what of black-brown-white ones? Permanent-Democratic-majority theorists predicate Democratic dominance on holding a sufficient portion of the white working class, but what happens if an increasingly ethnic Democratic Party pushes moderate and conservative whites out the door, much as it did with Southerners in the 1930s? While we've seen that the movement in Greater Appalachia against the Democrats in 2008 and 2010 had much to do with the relatively low salience of race in that area of the South, which allowed economic issues to predominate during some of the most racially charged times in American history, it is unlikely that a white Democrat, even a liberal one, would have fared quite as poorly as Obama did. But if the national Democratic Party is increasingly led by ethnic and racial minorities, what will blue-collar whites in places like Minnesota, Wisconsin, Michigan, Ohio, and the like do? They were only tenuously Democratic in 2008 before the financial collapse, in what was already an extremely good Democratic environment. On a more neutral playing field, this poses potentially calamitous issues for the Democratic coalition.

Indeed, even in areas with high Latino populations, it is not clear whom the potential tradeoff between Latinos and non-Hispanic whites benefits. Jan Brewer ran well behind George W. Bush among Latinos and a bit ahead of him among whites. Had she received the same portions of the white and Latino vote as pro-immigrant George W. Bush received in 2004, her 11-point victory would have actually been narrower. It is difficult to attribute direct causation to S.B. 1070 and her increased share of the white vote, but the distinct possibility, at least in the short-to-medium term, is that a "browning" of the Democratic Party would end up a net win for the Republicans. In a state like California, this does not pose a big problem for Democrats because the sizable white liberal populations in the San Francisco area and in Los Angeles ensure that Republicans can almost never win 60 percent of the white vote there. But few states have a San Francisco, much less a Los Angeles.

What of white liberals? They frequently find themselves on the opposite side of important issues from ethnic and racial minorities. As these minorities come to wield majority power in the Democratic Party, it may well move that party rightward. Asian Americans and African Americans supported two of the three controversial California ballot propositions. African American opposition played a critical role in defeating a marriage equality initiative in California and doomed a bill to recognize same-sex marriages in heavily Democratic Maryland.[34] When the Texas House passed a bill requiring women to undergo sonograms before obtaining an abortion, seven Democrats voted "yea," all of whom represented heavily Latino constituencies. Democrats have generally managed these tensions well so far, but there is no guarantee that this will continue.

"Coalitions of everyone" rarely last more than a few elections, especially if there is no overriding issue binding the pieces of the coalition together. There is no reason to believe that the Democrats will be any more successful in building such a coalition than any other party before them. These pieces will inevitably bump up against one another in ways that cause one part of the coalition to exit. This has been the case with every coalition we've studied so far, and there's no reason to suspect the Democrats will avoid this fate.

DO THE EXIT POLLS OVERSAMPLE LATINO REPUBLICANS?

Democrats and political scientists (and Democratic political scientists) argue that the data cited above are largely unreliable because the exit polls oversample Republican Latinos. This argument arose in the 2004 elections,[35] and it reappeared in 2010. In the aftermath of the 2010 elections, a two-part e-mail from the well-regarded firm Latino Decisions was sent to political analysts, purporting to show that Brewer actually won no more than 14 percent of the Latino vote in Arizona, and that Sharron Angle won less than 10 percent of the Latino vote in Nevada.[36] The argument was twofold: that common sense dictated that Angle and Brewer could not have done better among Latinos than John McCain, and that a technique called ecological inference suggested the lower Latino vote for Republicans. As Latino Decisions suggested in a separate publication:

> [T]he exit poll numbers for Sharron Angle in Nevada are mind boggling. Angle, who arguably ran the most offensive campaign against Latino immigrant [sic] is estimated to have won 30% of the Latino vote—an 8 percentage point improvement over John McCain in 2008 who won 22% of the Latino vote in Nevada. It is not possible, nor plausible that Angle improved by 8% among Latinos in 2010 given her attacks on Latinos, and Reid's strong defense of immigration reform....In Arizona, Jan Brewer, the force behind SB1070 who claimed Mexican immigrants were beheading innocent Arizonans in the southern desert is reported to have won 28% of the Latino vote according to the national exit polls. In contrast Latino Decisions found back in May that Brewer was attracting only 12% of the Latino vote, and that in October our tracking poll estimated 13% vote for Republicans in Arizona, and ultimately only 14% vote for Brewer in 2010, a far cry from 28%. In these cases, and across the board in 2010, the NEP Latino exit poll results are laughable.[37]

Two points are relevant here. First, the issues of exit poll bias and Sharron Angle's performance compared to that of John McCain are distinct issues. If there is a fundamental bias in the exit polls, it should occur from year to year. Exit polls that overstated Sharron Angle's share of the Latino vote in 2010 should have also overstated John McCain's share of the Latino vote. This objection should affect very little of the analysis in this chapter, except for the evidence of Latino support for the various California ballot initiatives.

Second, the "ecological inference" technique that they rely upon is problematic. The basic idea behind ecological inference is to take heavily Latino precincts and heavily white precincts and infer from this what the "true" distribution of the Latino portion of the vote was statewide or nationwide. This is the estimation technique used by courts to determine whether there is sufficient racially polarized voting to support a Voting Rights Act challenge. It is not problematic in that context, when courts are simply attempting to determine whether racially polarized voting has occurred, and where it is unimportant whether the actual Latino vote for a candidate is 90 percent or 70 percent. It is not well suited, however, to precise measurements; after all, it is an estimate.

While Latino Decisions suggests that Jan Brewer received around 10 percent of the Latino vote, a brief perusal of the precinct data shows that, even in precincts where Latinos made up almost 100 percent of the Latino vote, Brewer received about 20 percent of the vote. This is less than the exit polls suggest but more than we should see if the Latino Decisions numbers are correct. And we would expect these overwhelmingly Latino precincts to be among Brewer's worst. As we've noted above, as Latinos become wealthier, they become more Republican; this fact forms the basis of the objection to the NEP sample. It is also true that as Latinos move to suburban areas, which tend to be more mixed, they vote more Republican. As Warren Mitofsky noted in a rebuttal to the 2004 study, Latinos who lived in heavily Latino precincts in the NEP gave a much smaller percentage of their vote to Bush than did those who lived in mixed precincts. In addition, the 2004 analysis did not include absentee ballots, which are among the most heavily Republican. It is unclear whether this is a problem for the 2010 study as well.[38] Regardless, by extrapolating from heavily Latino precincts, where Latino voters tend to be more Democratic than those in more heterogeneous precincts, Latino Decisions is likely biasing its results toward finding greater Latino support for Democrats than actually exists.

CHAPTER 9

SUBURBIA VS. THE WHITE WORKING CLASS, AND THE YOUTH VOTE

Suburban residence emphasizes and re-inforces these role patterns and in so doing may produce Republican converts. Unless
the Democrats can meet this threat they may find themselves
defeated by Levittown.

Herbert H. Hyman and Paul B. Sheatsley, 1953[1]

THERE ARE OTHER PIECES to the "permanent-Democratic-majority" thesis. In addition to the traditional Democratic base of liberals and the expanded
"co-base" of minorities, upper-middle-class suburban professionals are expected
to join with the white working class to create a seamless whole that dominates
politics. As chapter 8 showed, the Democrats' claim that they have large growth
potential among minorities is real, but it is also tenuous, and it could actually
lay the basis for continued conservative growth in this country if conservatives
cultivate it properly. Since the publication of *The Emerging Democratic Majority*,
Democrats have additionally posited that a new generation of young, hip, liberal
"millennials" will reinforce the ranks of the Democrats. Democrats became
especially excited about their prospects among young voters after President
Obama won almost 70 percent of these voters in 2008—a shocking number
highlighting the potential demographic time bomb for the GOP we discussed
earlier.[2]

By now, you should be familiar enough with upscale suburbanites and the white working class to see the problem here, especially in the wake of the 2010 midterm elections. It is the classic problem with "coalitions of everybody" that this book has illustrated time and again. The interests of the white working class, the upper middle class, upper-class liberals, and poor minorities simply do not align frequently enough to form a stable coalition. This is not to say that such coalitions will *never* be formed or that we won't see them again. It is just to say that they are difficult to *maintain*, especially if you do not have Bill Clinton's political abilities and a terrified left that is willing to accept compromises.

Because we've already been through much of this, and because the future of the youth vote is so difficult to predict with any accuracy, this book does not dwell on these groups for any length of time. There are, however, some interesting themes worth delving into in more detail than we have done so far.

THE YOUTH VOTE: DEMOGRAPHIC DOOMSDAY FOR REPUBLICANS?

In 2008, Morley Winograd and Michael Hais wrote a book called *Millennial Makeover*. The concept was pretty innovative. They accepted the typical realignment view of political history and the 32-year cycles that come with it. But they tied those cycles to generational tides. In Winograd and Hais's view, realignments coincide with the advent of new technology, accompanied by a new generation with a new worldview to use that technology.[3] They divide American political history into "idealist" realignments and "civic" realignments,[4] with idealist realignments generally ushering in a divisive, combative time in American politics, whereas civic realignments bring with them a commitment to leveling the playing field, embracing one another's individualism, and uniting the country.[5] They posit that the new waves of interconnecting technology that feature prominently in the subtitle of their book—MySpace and YouTube—are ushering in a new civic realignment that will supplant the divisive, conservative, idealist realignment that supposedly emerged in 1968.

Despite its original interpretation of realignment theory, *Millennial Makeover* suffers many of the same faults as the rest of the realignment genre discussed in chapter 11: the view of American political history from fifty thousand feet is malleable enough to project whatever story one wishes onto it. But the book gained currency in the wake of the 2008 elections. President Obama won 66 percent of the under-30 vote—12 points higher than his next-best age group. Bear in mind that Obama also won 30- to 44-year-olds and even 45- to 64-year-olds, and there were only two states where "millennials" provided his margin of victory.[6] This result nevertheless shook the GOP to the core. The danger of running poorly among young voters for an extended period of time is simply attrition: as older, conservative voters die and are replaced by younger, more liberal voters, the country shifts, and the Republicans could be left in the minority. And when combined with the surge in Latino voters, it portends potential electoral doom for Republicans.

But there is a dirty little secret hiding behind this line of argument. And it is a simple one. The surge in the minority vote we saw in 2008 *was* the surge in the youth vote. Figure 9.1 shows the vote swing by age, according to exit poll data. Obviously there is a massive surge among 18- to 24-year-olds and 25- to 29-year-olds that far outstrips Obama's improvement among other age groups. But what happens when nonwhite voters are removed (see figure 9.2)?

Except with respect to 25- to 29-year-olds, the differences among the age groups become much less pronounced. In other words, these groups swung toward Obama largely because these segments of the electorate became much more heavily minority in 2008, as the country continued to "brown" demographically and as Obama turned out marginal minority voters in droves. Now, this is absolutely *not* to suggest that white voters count more. What it does

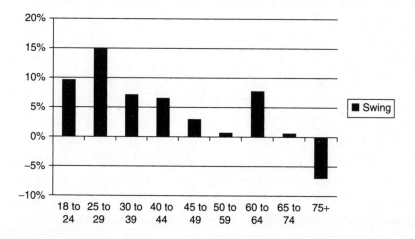

Figure 9.1   Swing, Kerry Vote Share to Obama Vote Share, by Age

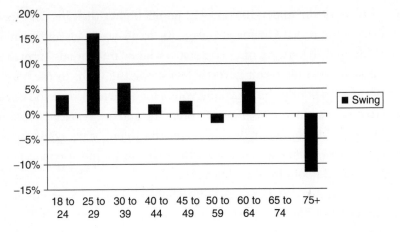

Figure 9.2 Swing, Kerry Vote Share to Obama Vote Share, by Age, Whites Only

suggest is that the GOP does not have both a minority problem *and* a youth problem. It is the same problem, and the extent to which the GOP is able to address the former will determine whether it is able to address the latter.

On a broader level, the song about the youth vote has played many times before. In 1972, in *The Party's Over,* David Broder claimed that the youth vote was the key to a new, emerging progressive coalition.[7] George McGovern and his advisors agreed and tailored their campaign to the supposed "change coalition" that could empower them to claim the presidency. As late as 1975, Ladd and Hadley were convinced that, even though McGovern lost, in the long term these youthful voters would provide the foundation for a new liberal majority.[8]

We now know that this did not happen. McGovern did carry 18- to 24-year-olds and ran ahead of his national average among 25- to 29-year-olds. This left the GOP in roughly the same position it finds itself in today: strongest among the elderly and theoretically vulnerable to a demographic wipeout, especially when one considers the size of the massive baby boom generation. But if we follow these voters as they aged, something very interesting occurs. By 1984, these voters were voting for Reagan at roughly the same rate as every other age group. In 2000, they were Bush's strongest group. In 2008, they gave Barack Obama approximately 41 percent of the vote. Gallup's polling data give us an even broader view of trends by age, and show that partisan lean is hardly an immutable characteristic when it comes to voting (see table 9.1).

Every age group here leans Republican at least once over the years, and every group leans Democrat at least once. There is little evidence that voting patterns

Table 9.1 Democratic Lean, by Year of Birth (Positive # = Democrat Lean, Negative = Republican)

	1940	1944	1948	1952	1956	1960	1964	1968	1972
1905	0.3	−2.4	−2.6	−0.3	−3	4.3	7.9	−6.7	—
1910	−0.7	−2.4	−3.6	−1.3	0	−0.7	7.9	−7.7	−5.5
1915	0.3	4.6	1.4	1.7	7	4.3	3.9	−3.7	−8.5
1920	−0.7	3.6	4.4	1.7	4	10.3	12.9	−1.7	−4.5
1925	—	7.6	2.4	0.7	5	12.3	7.9	−5.7	−7.5

were constants in these voters' lives or that a group that votes Democrat today will not vote Republican 20 years from now. While political science research may suggest that party identification is roughly constant over the course of an individual's lifetime, voting patterns are not.

Finally, party identification is not something that springs up at a single point in time, but rather develops over the course of a voter's young adult life.[9] Republicans are doubtless bearing the burden among youth right now for a successful Clinton presidency (at least in the second term) and a failed Bush presidency. But Obama has not been a particularly successful president, at least so far. If things improve for him, then the Republican travails among the youth will likely continue. If they do not, however, the Republicans will probably enjoy a reversal of fortune among this age cohort.

THE SUBURBS AND THE WHITE WORKING CLASS: COLORADO VERSUS OHIO?

In early 2011, William Galston, a DLC stalwart and former Clinton White House adviser, wrote an intriguing column in the *New Republic* titled "Colorado vs. Ohio."[10] Galston argued that President Obama and his team of 2012 campaign advisers appeared to be poised to make "a mistake of epic proportions." Galston cited two alarming events:

> The first was a Ron Brownstein interview with David Axelrod, who said that he saw Michael Bennet's 2010 senatorial victory in Colorado as "particularly instructive." As Brownstein noted, Bennet prevailed by mobilizing "enough minorities, young people, and socially liberal, well-educated white women to overcome a sharp turn toward the GOP among most of the other white voters in his state." The second event was DNC chair Tim

Kaine's selection of educated, new economy Charlotte, North Carolina, as the site for the 2012 Democratic convention. In the process, he rejected three Midwestern finalists: St. Louis, Minneapolis, and, most notably, Cleveland.

Taken together, these clues suggest that Obama's 2012 campaign will focus more on the Democratic periphery—territory newly won in 2008—than on the heartland, where elections have been won and lost for the past half-century. This could turn out to be a mistake of epic proportions. Why? Because the United States looks a lot more like Ohio than like Colorado.

This echoed earlier criticism from John Judis. Before the 2010 elections, Judis had voiced concerns about the Obama administration's attitude toward the white working class:[11]

> To be sure, there are a number of very specific reasons why Carter and Obama landed in political trouble. Both men contended with rising unemployment—Carter with rampant inflation as well—and voters' approval of a president and his party tend to track closely with changes in the economy. Carter faced friction in his own party and the rise of a powerful business lobby, and Obama has dealt with a Republican Party that has frustrated his dreams of a post-partisan presidency. Yet the most important reason for their difficulties—evident in their inept attempts to brand their programs—has been an inability to develop a politics that resonates with the public.

Judis urged the president to, at the very least, try to frame his programs in populist terms, rather than with the Spock-like, hyperintellectual approach that characterized so much of his presidency.

Both men essentially urged the president to mollify white working-class voters. But there was a problem inherent in that very choice. By moving to shore up his support with white working-class voters, Obama risked pushing away upper-middle-class voters with spending programs. But by trying to improve his support among upper-middle-class voters, he risked pushing away blue-collar voters.

In truth, Obama probably had the right idea trying to rebound among white, college-educated voters. First, they were the source of some of his biggest defections in 2010. That was equally true of Ohio and Colorado, and it is true virtually no matter how you measure "white working class." Consider labor unions. How did they vote? Although there is a dearth of state-by-state exit polling measuring union membership in 2010, we can still get a sense of what happened in the industrial Midwest from 2004 to 2008. Labor's portion of the electorate dropped a point in Michigan, two points in Ohio, and three points in Wisconsin. It stayed the same in Minnesota. At the same time, the Democrats' share of the union vote was essentially flat in every state but Michigan (where it was up five points). In other words, the Obama surge in those states was among nonunion voters; the Democrats' share of the vote among this group went up three points in Minnesota, five points in Ohio, six points in Wisconsin, and seven points in Michigan.

Using the broader definition of the white working class as "whites without college degrees," there is some evidence that Democrats collapsed here from 2008. There were substantial drop-offs in the Democrats' share of the vote in all three states among non-college-educated whites: 12 percent in Wisconsin, 15 percent in Iowa, and 9 percent in Ohio (note that I'm averaging Senate and gubernatorial races that occur in the same state for 2010). We see similar, but typically smaller, drop-offs in the Democratic vote share among whites with college degrees: 6 points, 11 points, and 18 points, respectively.

Finally, an examination of the countywide data in Minnesota, Iowa, Wisconsin, Ohio, Indiana, and Michigan shows that the Democrats took the worst beating among whites *with* college degrees. A simple regression analysis including the vote swing from 2008 to 2010, the racial breakdown of the county, and the level of college education in the county shows that, throughout the upper Midwest, there were big drop-offs among white, college-educated voters. We would expect a county in Wisconsin filled 100 percent with white voters with college degrees to swing 18 points toward the Republicans from 2008 to 2010. An all-white Wisconsin county without any voters with college degrees would swing about 10 points toward the Republicans.

This is where the Democrats' problem keeping these two groups in the same corral becomes apparent. Obama essentially ran an "Ohio strategy" for most of his first term. His stimulus, health-care plan, regulation of Wall Street, and assistance to unionized General Motors and Chrysler all were the exact type of thing that populist Democrats wish for. It produced some benefit among white working-class voters, although this was probably minimized because Obama is not a very convincing populist, personally. But these were the same moves that helped push suburbanites out the door.

Even attempts to run the Ohio strategy in Ohio failed. Governor Ted Strickland was facing off against former congressman John Kasich. Kasich had the misfortune of being a partner at Lehman Brothers around the time of the financial collapse. Strickland ran what you might call the "Ohio strategy on steroids," savaging Kasich for his role in the financial crisis, while running a populist, blue-collar-oriented campaign. In a sense, it worked. Strickland ran only four points behind Obama among whites without college degrees. But the strategy backfired among those with college degrees, where Strickland ran 15 points behind the president's 2008 totals—one of the most severe drops in the country in a competitive race.

The white working class and the upper middle class are two groups that will always be difficult to keep in the same coalition. Their interests are widely divergent, and policies that appeal to one group are likely to push the other group away. The Republicans were able to keep them together during the Eisenhower days because of the unique nature of the times. But now that the Soviet threat has gone and the upper middle class has increasingly embraced liberal cultural values, while the white working class has been slower to do so, their interests are not so clearly aligned. This is a massive problem for any majority that purports to arise from both the white working class and the upper middle class.

CHAPTER 10

IT WASN'T JUST THE ECONOMY, STUPID

We believe that the Republicans will pick up seats in the 1982 election.

Thomas Mann and Norman Ornstein, 1981[1]

JUST AS THERE ARE scholars who attempt to scry the future by extrapolating present demographic trends out for decades, there are also those who argue that it is pointless to engage in such entrail-reading, even in the short term. Some political scientists have built careers arguing that elections are little more than referenda on the state of the economy and claim that all you need to know to understand an election are "structural" considerations, such as the number of seats a party occupies, the number of open seats, and the growth of GDP. From this you can build a model that will explain the election in advance. These political scientists emerged in droves in the run-up to, and the wake of, the 2010 elections, claiming that events such as the BP oil spill and the health-care bill had a minimal impact on the election results.

These scholars are, by and large, sincere. There are also analysts who are merely opportunistic, who argued that Republican governance was to blame for its horrendous showing in the 2006 and 2008 elections, but who attribute the 2010 election cycle to the state of the economy and the high degree of Democratic exposure in vulnerable districts after their surge years of 2006 and 2008. Regardless of motivation, this objection is both serious and important. If elections are exclusively referenda on the state of the economy, then most of the effort that went into this book is for naught. Rather than spending hours poring over election returns and demographic data, analysts should simply wait for second-quarter GDP numbers to come out in an election year, place a large bet on InTrade, and prepare to retire early.

In truth, there is no tension between this objection and the third claim of this book: that realignments do not exist. The trajectory of the economy is probably the number-one contingency that derails apparently strong majorities; economic growth is one of the obvious counternarratives to the "struggle between rich and poor" narrative that dominates realignment theory.[2] No one knows what the Republican coalition of the 1930s would have looked like had the Great Depression not intervened. Perhaps Herbert Hoover's strength in Southern cities would have lasted and his support of "lily white" Republican parties in the South would have been successful, perhaps the white working class energized by Al Smith would have kept Northern cities Democratic, and perhaps we would have skipped the New Deal coalition and moved on to something resembling the Eisenhower coalition in 1932. Had the financial collapse of 2008 struck six months earlier, so that we were at the bottom of a financial free fall on Election Day rather than merely staring over the precipice, perhaps Obama would have enjoyed a smashing 60 percent victory. Similarly, if Democrats are going to be a majority party over the course of a decade, they will run into a recession sooner or later. If they are going to govern for 30 years, they are going to run into a *serious* recession. They will receive the blame for it, and their majority will be damaged.

At the same time, these economic explanations can quickly become far too deterministic. Some true believers in these models seem to suggest that, had the Democrats nominated Dennis Kucinich in 2008, or if the Republicans were to embrace Ron Paul in 2012, then there would be no significant effect on the outcome of the election. Many of them also suggest that the sudden collapse of the economy at the end of the 2008 election had little to do with the ultimate outcome of that election, which in their view was really due to medium-term views of the economy. This view is overly simplistic.

THE ECONOMY, THE 2010 ELECTIONS, AND WHAT IT CAN'T EXPLAIN

There is little doubt that "structural" factors were at work in the 2010 elections. It is likewise clear that these factors did a lot of the heavy lifting for the Republicans. Common sense dictates that when the economy is in recession, people are unhappy. When people are unhappy, they tend to vote out the party in power. Since the onset of the Great Depression, the country has seen ten midterm elections in which the party in power lost more than 10 percent of its seats. Those elections occurred in (in decreasing order of severity and not including 2010): 1974, 1958, 1946, 1938, 1994, 1930, 1942, 1966, 1982, and 2006. Of these elections, six occurred in bad economic times. Looking at this in reverse, of the recessions that have occurred near midterm elections, all but two have resulted in significant losses for the party in power, and those two exceptions (1953–1954 and the early 2000s) involved fairly mild recessions. This trend was apparent even before the Great Depression. Most prominent among this group is the 1894 midterm elections, in which the Democrats lost 57 percent of their House seats. Recessions in years like 1920–1921, 1839–1843, 1873–1979, 1913–1914 have all resulted in bad midterm elections for the party in power. This led some observers to conclude fairly early in the cycle that the Democrats were going to have a rough election in 2010. Unlike FDR, Barack Obama was coming into office at the beginning of a serious recession, rather than at the end of one, so it was unlikely that the beginning of his term would coincide with the beginning of a rebound, as was the case with Roosevelt.[3]

But there are also elections that clearly don't hinge on the economy. The United States had such an event only two years before Obama's election. From 2005 to 2006, real disposable income per capita increased 3 percent.[4] Unemployment was low, and job growth had been restored. Yet the Republicans lost 13 percent of their caucus. A number of noneconomic factors clearly drove these losses: The war in Iraq was taking a turn for the worse, with seemingly no end in sight. President Bush supported a comprehensive immigration reform bill that went nowhere, dividing his base without producing appreciable benefits among Latino voters. And Hurricane Katrina confirmed for many voters that the administration was simply out of its depths when it came to governing.

Other examples abound. In 1994, the economy had picked up steam, which was one reason most pundits never saw that tsunami coming. In 1966, the economy was in the midst of one of the swiftest expansions in history. Yet in the aftermath of the Great Society legislation, a nationwide mid-decade redistricting that enhanced the power of the suburbs, and a Vietnam War that was becoming increasingly unpopular, the Democrats lost 16 percent of their caucus. In 2002, the country was just emerging from recession. Yet perceived Republican success in the War on Terror helped the GOP gain seats in Congress, even as income growth was largely flat. In fact, three of the four midterm elections that occurred immediately before the 2010 midterms are best explained by noneconomic variables. Professor Abramowitz even found compelling data suggesting that the fourth of those midterm elections, 1998, was better predicted by voters' perceptions of the GOP's handling of the Monica Lewinsky scandal than by their views of the state of the economy.[5]

There are problems with using economic data to explain voter behavior at the presidential level as well. The most obvious problem occurs in 1948. That year, the economy grew early on. But by the end of the year, it had begun to soften, especially in the farm belt. When Harry Truman ran his campaign, it was *not* a peace and prosperity campaign—Truman castigated Republicans as the party of Hoover and the Depression, warning that they would remove the safety net that had been set up for various groups, especially farmers.[6] Truman improved over FDR's 1944 showing the most in the farm belt, the region that was suffering from the brunt of the economic downturn. He ran behind FDR in the cities, which were faring well. This is not what we would expect if voters were punishing the "in party" for a bad economy.

Indeed, one of the things that the "economic explanation of everything" cannot account for well is the relative paucity of swing voters in America. African Americans and liberals vote overwhelmingly Democratic, regardless of the state of the economy. Evangelical Christians are reliably Republican. In 2008, when every imaginable factor was working against the Republicans, 46 percent of voters pulled the Republican lever. The economy may drive swing voters, but it does not explain how both parties accumulate such large bases, and why the parties work so hard to cultivate those coalitions.

What of 2010? The interesting thing about 2010 is that the economy was actually not performing that poorly by Election Day. Unemployment was elevated, but it had peaked a year earlier; unlike 1982, it was on a downward track. Inflation was low. And per-capita real disposable income was rising, albeit slowly. Now, the *perception* of an economy in crisis clearly played a role in the 2010 midterms. But it was not the only factor.

DEMOCRATIC EXPOSURE, THE 2010 ELECTIONS, AND WHAT IT CAN'T EXPLAIN

It is also true that, whenever a party occupies a large number of seats in the House, especially when a large percentage of those seats are occupied by freshmen and sophomores, that party is probably going to suffer in the subsequent elections. The reason is simple: as a party picks up more seats, it pushes further into marginal territory. If it picks up a huge number of seats, as Democrats had done in 2006 and 2008, it by definition extends itself into hostile territory. These members are therefore vulnerable, and the party is set up for losses.

Today's Democrats are especially vulnerable to this phenomenon. Due to gerrymandering and Democratic packing of minorities and liberals into a handful of overwhelmingly Democratic districts, the median district in the United States leans toward the Republicans by a few points. Put differently, the most Republican district in the nation leans Republican by 29 points. Democrats have created 25 districts —almost 15 percent of their caucus—that are more heavily Democratic than this. That means that Democrats cannot win a House majority without capturing a substantial number of seats that naturally favor Republicans. In 2010, Democrats occupied 73 seats that leaned toward Republicans. As expected, many of these seats were, in fact, occupied by newly elected members of Congress, who had picked up swing seats in the 2006 and 2008 elections. This is also where Democratic losses were concentrated.

But we should be careful about putting the cart before the horse. Democrats were heavily exposed in 2010 in part because of the coalitional shifts that this book has observed. In the Appalachian districts in particular, exposure was driven by Obama's narrow, deep coalition. Alabama's Fifth District was always expected to be a tough hold for Democrats, as Obama had lost by 23 points there.[7] But that was a relatively recent development, driven in part by Phase Three of the South's Republican shift. In 1992, Bill Clinton had lost the district by only three points; he lost by six points in 1996.[8] Democratic redistricting in 2002 made the district more heavily Democratic.[9]

Similarly, in a trio of districts in Tennessee, Democrats always knew they faced an uphill battle. The open Sixth and Eighth districts leaned Republican by 13 and 6 points, respectively, while conservative Democrat Lincoln Davis represented a district that leaned Republican by 13 points overall.[10] But Clinton had carried the Fourth District by a point in 1996, lost the Sixth District by a point, and carried the Eighth District by seven points.[11] Once again, these districts shifted heavily rightward in the late 2000s, even after Democratic redistricting that was intended to make these districts more Democratic. Immediately after the 2000 redistricting, these districts leaned one point Republican, favored neither party, and leaned one point Democrat, respectively.[12] Indeed, when the Fourth District was open in 2002, a very good GOP year, Davis won his election by six points.

This trend wasn't confined to Southern Greater Appalachia either. Bill Clinton carried West Virginia's First District by 11 points in 1996 and lost Ike Skelton's Fourth District in Missouri by only 5 points.[13] After redistricting, those districts leaned Republican by 6 and 10 points, respectively: Gore did not play so well here.[14] Once again, things deteriorated further by the end of the decade. Obama lost Missouri's Fourth District by 22 points and West Virginia's First by 15 points; they leaned Republican by 9 and 14 points by that point.[15]

To be sure, there were countervailing factors. Democrats were able to hold Virginia's suburban Eleventh District narrowly in 2010 at least in part because it had swung from a district that leaned Republican by four points at the beginning of the decade to one that leaned Democrat by two points in 2010.[16] But nationwide, the shift did not help the Democrats. Going into the 2000 elections, only 191 districts leaned Republican by two or more points. Going into the 2010 elections, 220 districts leaned Republican by two or more points.[17] The increased geographic concentration of the Democratic vote made it much more difficult for the Democrats to hold the House and greatly increased their overall exposure.

THE PROBLEM OF 1982

One way to get a handle on the role of the economy in elections is to compare the 2010 midterms to the 1982 midterms. The latter year was, simply put, a bad year to be a Republican. The party had had a huge surge in the House a few years earlier, and many new Republicans were vulnerable. Worse still, the economy sank into a sharp recession. On Election Day, unemployment was about to peak at 10.8 percent. Disposable income was flat, and GDP was contracting. The substantial verdict from the punditry was that the Republicans were on pace for a bloodbath, and that they would likely be reduced to their post-Watergate numbers. Political science models estimated that the GOP would lose between 40 and 50 seats.[18]

This did not occur. The Republican Party lost only 26 seats, about 13 percent of their caucus. Political scientists may claim that subsequent models have corrected for this and now predict that election correctly.[19] But the secret about that election is that if your model got it right, it actually got it wrong. No extant model accounts for one of the critical factors in GOP losses that year: redistricting. Therefore, unless you believe that overexposure or the economy is somehow driving redistricting, any model that predicted GOP seat loss perfectly also overstated the impact of those two factors.

In 1982, Democrats overwhelmingly controlled redistricting and used it to deadly effect.[20] They also received some lucky breaks, such as a court in Illinois choosing the Democratic map after the legislature deadlocked. Republicans like Paul Findlay of Illinois and Barry Goldwater, Jr., of California almost certainly would have won in their old districts. Findlay won the old parts of his Illinois district by 6 points but lost the heavily Democratic new portions by 16 points, en route to losing by one thousand votes to Richard Durbin.[21] California's 1982 gerrymander was one of the most effective of all time, as Phillip Burton's "contribution to modern art"—Burton's famous description of the contorted districts that he drew for California—contributed to a year in which Democrats won 50 percent of the popular vote for Congress in the state, but 62 percent of the House seats, while enjoying a gain of six seats.[22] Goldwater chose to run for statewide office after his district was merged with another heavily Republican district, even though California was gaining seats.[23] Overall, about half the GOP losses in 1982 were not attributable to the economy, presidential approval, or GOP pickups in the previous cycle. They were due to redistricting, something that no model accounts for.[24] As Judis has observed, the Republican Party probably was saved from a worse defeat by Ronald Reagan's politicking, something that Barack Obama was unable to repeat.[25]

This all reveals a larger shortcoming of these models: they rarely account for critical portions of the narrative that cannot be reduced to numbers on a chart. In 2006, for example, the economic models performed well. But once again, an accurate model most likely overstated the importance of the economy. The GOP suffered from a series of bizarre events that year that accounted for as many as one-third of its losses. The GOP clearly lost the seats of Mark Foley, John Sweeney, Charles Taylor, Bob Ney, Don Sherwood, and Tom DeLay for reasons unrelated to the economy, and it arguably would not have lost the seats of J. D. Hayworth, Richard Pombo, Sue Kelly, and Curt Weldon but for scandals. Most observers thought that Henry Bonilla would easily hold his seat in a December runoff election against Ciro Rodriguez, but he seemed to give up after the November election.[26] No model accounted for these factors, so a model that predicted that Republicans were set to lose 30 seats based on the performance of the economy overstated the importance of whatever economic variables it was relying upon.

There is a similar problem with models that predict presidential elections. For example, most models account for the 1968 election accurately and project that Nixon should have won 50 percent of the two-party vote, as he did. But most observers believe that he almost certainly would have won more than 50 percent of the vote had Wallace not run. A similar problem arises in 1980, when John Anderson probably drew disproportionately from Reagan. Exit polls showed that in 1996, Perot drew disproportionately from Bob Dole, yet the "two-party vote" actually allocates Perot's vote disproportionately to Clinton. Once again, a model that accurately predicts Republican performance in those years is actually inaccurate because the Republican performance was skewed by third-party showings.

At the end of the day, there is simply no substitute for knowing the data and the narrative behind that data. If you start looking at what actually occurred in these races, you see that the economy was an important factor, but that it was not the only factor. Things like candidates, campaigns, contributions, and coalitions play critical, often dominant, roles.

WHAT THE MODELS ACTUALLY SAID ABOUT 2010 . . . AND OTHER ELECTIONS

Shortly before the 2010 elections, Jonathan Chait, senior editor for the *New Republic* and a dedicated proponent of the theory that structural factors drove the election, sought to preempt any suggestion that Obama's agenda was to blame for the midterm losses. He described a model from Princeton's Doug Hibbs, which looked solely at the economy and the number of seats a party had gained in the previous two elections, and which predicted that Democrats would lose 45 House seats. Chait concluded, "If you want to have the 'what did Obama do wrong' argument, you first need to establish what 'wrong' would look like. That's probably a 50 seat-or-more loss."[27]

Of course, a 50-seat-or-more loss is precisely what happened. But the interesting thing is that Hibbs's model was not the only model looking at structural variables. And among this group of models, it was actually on the high end of predicted seat losses for Democrats. The models that did not "cheat" by using generic ballot data as a variable produced the results shown in Table 10.1.

Table 10.1   Errors in Predictive Models Using Structural Variables Only, 2010

Author	Variables Used	Predicted Democratic Loss	Actual Democratic Loss	Error
Lewis-Beck/ Tien[i]	Income, Approval, Midterm	22 seats	63 seats	41 seats
Ansolabehere[ii]	GDP	25–30	63 seats	33–38 seats
Fair[iii]	Inflation, News	–6 percent popular vote	–9 percent popular vote	3 percent popular vote
Masket[iv]	RDI Growth, Approval	40 seats	63 seats	23 seats
Cuzán[v]	Exposure, Pres. Election Results, Midterm, GDP, Inflation	31–36 seats	63 seats	27–32 seats

[i] Michael S. Lewis-Beck and Charles Tien, "The Referendum Model: A 2010 Congressional Forecast," PS: Political Science and Politics (2010): 637-38.

[ii] Stephen Ansolabehere, "State of the Nation," *Boston Review*, September/October 2010, accessed March 31, 2011, http://bostonreview.net/BR35.5/ansolabehere.php.

[iii] "Presidential Vote Equation," accessed February 2, 2011, http://fairmodel.econ.yale.edu/vote2008/index2.htm.

[iv] Stephen J. Dubner, "Predicting the Midterm Elections: A Freakonomics Quorum," October 27, 2010, accessed March 31, 2011, http://www.freakonomics.com/2010/10/27/predicting-the-midterm-elections-a-freakonomics-quorum/.

[v] Alfred G. Cuzán, "Will the Republicans Retake the House in 2010? A Second Look Over the Horizon," September 25, 2010, manuscript in author's possession.

These are not small errors. Even models that allowed for use of the generic ballot underperformed, generally predicting GOP losses in the 50-seat range.[28] In other words, all the models were off in 2010. Not a single major political science model predicted losses in excess of 60 seats. More important, these models were all off in the same direction; this cannot simply be explained away with an error term.

Such spectacular misses are not actually that uncommon—the predictive models also performed horribly in 1992, 1994, 2000, and 2002,[29] to name just a few years. In many of those years, political scientists found that attitudes toward issues played much more important roles than attitudes about the economy in predicting voter behavior.[30] In 2008, economic models systematically overstated the share of the vote that they expected Barack Obama to receive in a year in which every "intangible" suggested the election should be on the "high" end of the error term. The economy and overexposure are clearly important variables to consider when evaluating elections. But they are by no means the only variables. They likely brought only about between one-third and two-thirds of the Democrats' losses in 2010. To explain the rest of the losses, we need to look outside the economy.

WHAT VOTERS WERE SAYING IN 2010

If you looked behind the quantitative numbers in 2010, you would not have been surprised that economic variables understated the extent of the Democrats' losses. Chapter 6 briefly noted that Barack Obama's approval rating did not go upside down on the economy first. Instead, it was the deficit and spending where his approval ratings first saw a big dip—the return to New Deal liberalism was hurting Obama in the midst of an economic downturn. This tendency continued throughout his term. An April 2010 *CBS/New York Times* poll asked respondents: "Who do you think is mostly to blame for the current state of the nation's economy—1. the Bush administration, 2. the Obama administration, 3. Wall Street and financial institutions, 4. Congress, or 5. someone else?"[31] Thirty-two percent of respondents blamed Bush, 22 percent blamed Wall Street, and 10 percent blamed Congress. Four percent blamed Obama. In a subsample of Tea Party supporters, only 10 percent blamed Obama. It seems highly unlikely that when even the vast majority of Tea Partiers refused to lay blame for the state of the economy at the administration's feet that the economy is what dragged the Democrats down.

In July, the Democratic polling firm Democracy Corps allowed respondents who disapproved of the president to give an open-ended response as to why they disapproved of the president and created a word cloud for the responses (figure 10.1).

"Health care" was the overwhelming reason given for disapproving of the president. Issues like "spending," "oil spill," and "everything" were about as common as was "the economy." Later in the survey, fiscal irresponsibility, health care, and the oil spill were the top reasons given for disapproving of the president. More respondents expressed concern that the president was a socialist/communist (8 percent) than were upset about jobs and unemployment (6 percent).[32] Some political scientists would respond that this is just hidden voter psychology coming to the fore; had the economy been performing better, the president would have performed better. But do we really need complex voter psychoanalysis, where we claim to understand voters' feelings on matters better than the voters do? Especially given that economic-based models predicted that the economy would not result in severe Democratic losses, it seems the survey response data could and should be taken at face value.

Figure 10.1   Word Cloud for Disapproval of President Obama, July 2010

The exit poll data also suggest that issues other than the economy dragged the Democrats down. The VNS data demonstrate that 52 percent of voters believed that President Obama's policies would "hurt the country." Eighty-nine percent voted Republican. Fifty-six percent felt that "government was doing too much." Republicans won 77 percent of these voters. Sixty-five percent believed that the stimulus bill either had been a net negative for the economy or had made no difference. Even in the exit poll, only 23 percent of voters blamed Obama for the state of the economy, while 29 percent blamed Bush and 35 percent blamed Wall Street.

Finally, the fact that Democrats lost almost uniformly in conservative-leaning districts suggests that the economy played a more marginal role than many would like to admit (unless, that is, voters in conservative-leaning districts were suffering more from the economic downturn). Rather than being motivated solely by the economy, voters in Democratic districts voted to endorse a fairly aggressive Democratic agenda, while voters in Republican-leaning districts voted to oppose it. That there were so many more Republican-leaning districts than there had been in the past, and that voters in these districts reacted so viscerally to the president's agenda, reflect choices the Democrats made, not the state of the economy.

CHAPTER 11

BEYOND REALIGNMENT

There is a belief in many quarters that the Republican Party is about to disappear.

Review of Reviews, 1893[1]

SO FAR, THIS BOOK has made two broad claims. First, that the 2010 midterm elections were made possible by a Democratic Party that failed to appreciate the fragile nature of its coalition. In 2008, the Democratic Party believed that it had just successfully realigned the country, when in truth it had morphed a reasonably broad, yet tenuous, coalition into a narrow, fragile coalition. It proceeded to govern as though it had the broad coalition—enacting the "mandate" that the press declared it had been given—and hence endured the worst midterm drubbing in recent history. The second claim is that the broad demographic shifts that many Democratic theorists believe are making them invincible are ephemeral and will not bring about their hoped-for realignment.

These claims are critically important. Like so many successors to John of Patmos, permanent-majority theorists on both sides of the aisle prophesy that the end is nigh, that the promised land is just around the corner, and—in some cases—that retribution will soon rain down on their opponents. Sure, there might be times when the opponent will win an election during these new eras, but these will be "deviating" elections, where their enemies cannot hope to get much accomplished, and where anything they did accomplish would be undone when things returned to "normal."

Outbreaks of this eschatological fervor occur among the punditry every 30 years or so. In the late 1960s and early 1970s, books by Kevin Phillips, Ben Wattenberg and Richard Scammon,[2] Lou Harris,[3] and Everett Carll Ladd[4] all argued that we were in a time period when Republicans, Democrats, or some third entity would become dominant. The second recent outbreak occurred, appropriately, around the new millennium, with a horde of Republicans claiming that George W. Bush would lay the groundwork for an invincible Republican majority. A few years later, after the publication of *The Emerging Democratic Majority*, a cottage industry bloomed on the left, arguing that the Democrats were the bright, ascending sun, while the Republicans were the pale, waning moon.

It is not accidental that these books appear in 32-year cycles. All of them inevitably reference Burnham's works (save Phillips, who predates Burnham's seminal works but who seems to have arrived at Burnham's structure of elections independently) and the subsequent realignment theorists. In a sense, realignment theory does the heavy lifting for them. All that they have to do is pinpoint social or political changes occurring around the peak of the cycle, and the theory suggests that these changes will become the dominant ones. Much like the economic determinism discussed in chapter 10, this minimizes the agency of parties and voters and eases the burden of having to deal with voter choice and other complex issues.

This leads to the third claim of this book: realignments do not exist. Parties put together coalitions, and sometimes these coalitions *do* endure for an extended period of time. But just because we accept this latter point does not mean that we have to accept that these coalitions are inevitable, that they will be lasting, or that they come in 32-year cycles. In other words, there is bad news for the prophets of incipient party realignment: the savior ain't coming. Instead, each election cycle presents parties with choices, both in how they approach the election and, if they win, how they govern. Sometimes they choose well, and sometimes they choose poorly. Sometimes they run into "black swan" events that are entirely out of their control. Regardless, after one election, another election is inevitably no more than two years away. And its outcome is unknown.

The distinction is important, and not just in an academic sense. The current administration and the previous one have both governed at times as if we have reached the End of History. The Bush administration frequently seemed unaware that it had not achieved even a popular vote plurality in 2000 and had only a tenuous claim on its Electoral College majority. After winning the narrowest reelection victory for a president since 1916—and accomplishing the unprecedented feat of almost losing during a time of war—Bush's impulse was not to tack to the center or engage in minimalist gestures to broaden the coali-tion. It was to take on Social Security. As for the Obama administration, it is as if it never occurred to them that when the preceding president starts two wars that don't go well, oversees a collapse in the economy unlike any other the country has seen since the late 1920s, and is photographed taking a guitar lesson while a major city is destroyed by a hurricane, his party tends to perform poorly in the subsequent election, and the subsequent president should read a mandate into his election only carefully. Both Obama's and Bush's presidencies were predicated heavily upon contingent events, and yet both presidents seemed convinced that broader forces were at work, guiding them to victory. They were wrong, and it is time to abandon the theory that empowered them.

REALIGNMENT THEORY: WHY NOT 1952 OR 1992?

Over the years, realignment theorists have made a *lot* of claims about what we should expect a realigning election to look like. Professor David Mayhew has summarized 15 such claims collected over the years. Further complicating mat-ters, after it became clear that the realignment that was slated to occur in 1968 would be delayed, political scientists, including to some extent Burnham, began to back off the concept of realignments in favor of a theory called "dealignment," to explain the new era in politics in which neither party seemed to emerge as dominant.[5] But the goal of this book is not to debunk every claim that has ever been made by realignment theorists. Rather, it is simply to examine the *major* claims of realignment theory and see how they hold up in light of the history we have sketched.

A few of these claims should be familiar by now. There is the basic defini-tion of a "critical," or realigning, election as one in which "sharp and durable" changes in the electorate occur.[6] In other words, things look a lot different than they did in the previous election, and these differences have "legs." Added on to that basic definition is the deeper, and more problematic, claim that these crit-ical elections occur every 32 or 36 years or so.[7] Those are the broadest claims, but there are a few other common ones that are important enough to warrant discussion here.

First, Burnham theorized that the 30-ish-year cycle is driven by a desire for change that rumbles under the surface, before reaching a critical intensity.

Other theorists, like E. E. Schattschneider and James Sundquist, subsequently argued that new issues come to the forefront of American politics during realignments as a result of this pent-up desire for change. Thus, in the 1850s, we see slavery arise as a dominant issue. In the 1890s, it is inflation. In the 1930s, it is the New Deal, and so forth.[8] Burnham sees a realignment in 1968, while Judis and Teixeira hypothesize a sort of "half realignment" that is completed in 1980, while others rely on dealignment to explain the postwar experience.[9] These theorists usually posit that we may expect to see high voter turnout, turmoil at the conventions, and a rise of third parties during a realignment.[10] Finally, we expect to see lengthy periods of party control of the House, Senate, and presidency.[11]

There are other claims, but these are the broadest, most commonly accepted ones. The major realignment theorists—Key, Burnham, Schattschneider, and Sundquist—are towering figures in political science, and the concept of party systems is one of the few that has become so broadly accepted that amateur political junkies can recite the basic outlines of the theory. Before launching headlong into an argument about whether realignments exist, let's first examine a smaller, more nuanced claim that was made earlier in the book: to the extent realignments exist, 1952 and 1992 fit the bill much better than 1968 and 2008.

The election of 1952 is commonly categorized as a "deviating" one. These are elections in which a member of the minority party wins the presidency but the underlying alignment is not changed. The idea is that because the issue template did not change much—Ike did not fiddle with the New Deal—we were therefore still in the New Deal coalition, despite the voters having handed Republicans unified control of Congress and the presidency. In much the same way, 1992 is frequently classified as a deviating election in the midst of a conservative Republican ascendancy. In truth, the 1952 and 1992 elections fit the "critical election" definition as well, if not better, than years like 1968 or 2008:

"Sharp and Durable" Voter Changes: This is clearly more applicable to 1952 and 1992 than to 1968 or 2008. While the idea of "sharp and durable" voter changes is overstated—all the voter changes in the canonical critical elections (1800, 1828, 1860, 1896, and 1932) are less "sharp and durable" when you look at them closely—1952 is clearly a breakthrough election for the Republicans in many ways. They carried several Southern states with a generally inoffensive candidate on the Democratic ticket, a tendency that

continues unbroken to this day. Republicans were reborn in the Mountain West. They finally laid solid claim to the white working class, and the suburbs moved to the fore. Similarly, in 1992, Bill Clinton's Democrats artfully modulated their message to appeal to the white working class and suburbs, enjoying an historic Democratic breakthrough in these regions.

The elections of 1968 and 2008 brought few such changes. Nixon won mostly in areas where Eisenhower won, although the scope of his win is, unsurprisingly, scaled down due to the Wallace candidacy. As we've discussed, Obama largely won in the same places that had been in the Democratic column since 2008; if that election was unique, it was more for the areas the *Republicans* added to their coalition than for those the Democrats added.

New Issues Emerge: The 1952 election saw the rise of McCarthyism, the Cold War (both in Korea and Europe), and, most important, prosperity. On the Democratic side there is, at least in one political scientist's measurement, a lasting shift in rhetoric from "populism" to "universalism."[12] The same can be said of 1992, when America shifted from debating how (or whether) to win the Cold War to what to do about the peace, when "New Democrats" changed the Democratic message, and when crime and other issues began to fade into the background. A case here can be made for 1968 as well, as the Vietnam War, the counterculture, urban unrest, crime, and other issues first made their appearance at the presidential level. Similarly, in 2008, the economy replaced the War on Terror as the dominant issue. It is probably worth noting, however, that major new issues emerge in several other elections during this time period as well: 1964, 1976, 1980, and 2004, to name just a few.

Spiking Voter Turnout: Figure 11.1 shows the change in turnout from election to election, from 1904 through 2008. In other words, when the line is above the midpoint, turnout has increased from the previous presidential election. When it is below the midpoint, turnout has decreased.[13]

The election of 1952 actually has the sharpest spike in turnout of any election in this time period. A significant spike emerges in 1992 as well. In 1968, the turnout rate fell. Interestingly, despite the excitement of the 2008 campaign, turnout increased at a higher rate in 2004.

Two other interesting observations emerge from this chart. First, there is no spike in 1932. The largest turnout spike comes instead in 1928. This is consistent with the earlier observation that the 1932 election is in many ways

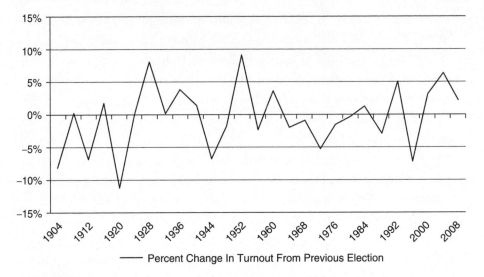

— Percent Change In Turnout From Previous Election

Figure 11.1 Percent Change in Turnout From Previous Election

a continuation of the 1928 election, in a worse economic environment and with a less divisive Democratic nominee. Second, there are miniature spikes in 1908 and 1916, elections that are rarely considered realigning.

Turmoil at Conventions: This has become something of a moot point in the age when most intraparty disagreements are settled in primaries. But 1952 was the last time that a convention took multiple ballots, and the convention was beset with charges that Eisenhower had stolen the nomination. He was met with boos from the conservative Taft delegates, and Everett Dirksen bellowed at the Eisenhower-friendly Dewey delegates from the podium: "We followed you before. And you took us down the road to defeat…don't do this to us."[14] Nevertheless, the 1968 Democratic convention was disastrous, while the 1992 Republican convention featured the drama of Pat Buchanan's speech and the prominent display of social conservatism's rise in the Republican Party. The most harmonious of these years was 2008, although the Obama-Clinton primary campaign is probably the closest analogy we have in the modern era to a turbulent convention. The only other conventions that could even roughly be described as turbulent were the 1976 GOP convention and the 1980 Democratic convention.

Strong Third-Party Showing: This is true of 1952, as Strom Thurmond's Dixiecrats had bolted from the Democratic Party four years before. The election of 1968 occurred in the midst of the Wallace bolt, while 1992

Table 11.1   Characteristics of Realignment, 1952, 1968, 1992, 2008 (Yes, No, Maybe)

	Durable Change	New Issues	Turnout Spike	Convention Turmoil	Third Party
1952	Y	Y	Y	M	Y
1968	N	Y	N	Y	Y
1992	Y	Y	Y	M	Y
2008	N	M	N	M	N

saw Perot attain the strongest showing of any third-party candidate since Teddy Roosevelt in 1912. There was no third-party effort in 2004 or 2008.

None of these elections was followed by an extended period of one-party control of Congress. Putting this all together in a table, we see the results in Table 11.1.

Of all these elections, the strongest case can be made for 1952 as realigning. This is followed by 1992, 1968, and then 2008. In fact, 2008 had very few indicators of a realigning election. Why, then, do analysts insist on positing the two weakest cases as the most likely realigning elections? First, because they fit the doctrinal 32-year cycle. Second, and perhaps most important, because they fit the popular narrative of conflict between economic royalism and populism. Neither the Clinton era nor the Eisenhower era was a great time for those with the strongest ideological commitments to either party, and hence with the most invested in the realignment cause. However, 1968 and 2008 fit nicely into the tale of the epic struggle for dominance between liberalism and conservatism. That, however, is not grounds to declare a realignment.

WHY NOT —?: REALIGNMENT THEORY'S FATAL FLAW

This illustrates the critical problem with realignment theory. It is ultimately far too subjective to be useful. Earlier, this book analogized it to finding an image of Jesus in a grilled-cheese sandwich. You can almost always make the case that it exists, if you look hard enough. Just in the brief discussion above, indicia of realignments appear in 1952 (change, issues, turnout, third party), 1960 (turnout, third party), 1968 (issues, convention, third party), 1980 (issues, turnout, third party), 1992 (issues, change, turnout, third party), 2000 (issues, third party), 2004 (issues, turnout), and 2008 (issues).

This difficulty extends even further backward in time as well. Tables 11.2 and 11.3 demonstrate the difficulty that scholars have in identifying critical elections, using different techniques and definitions.

Table 11.2   Years in Which Scholars Have Detected Evidence of Critical Elections

	1828	32	36	40	44	48	52	56	60	64	68	72	76	80	84	88	92	96
Key																		X
Burnham	X							X										X
Gerring[i]	X																	X
CFZ[ii]			X			X					X		X					X
Bartels[iii]	—	—	—	—	—	—	—	—					X	X				X

[i] Gerring, *Party Ideologies in America*: 1828–1996.
[ii] Clubb, Flanigan, and Zingale, *Partisan Realignment*, table 3.1a.
[iii] Larry M. Bartels, "Electoral Continuity and Change, 1868–1896," *Electoral Studies* 17 (1998), 315.

Table 11.3   Years in Which Scholars Have Detected Evidence of Critical Elections

	1900	04	08	12	16	20	24	28	32	36	40	44	48
Key								X					
Burnham									X				
Gerring[i]								X					
CFZ[ii]						X			X				X
Bartels[iii]			X			X			X	X			

[i] Gerring, *Party Ideologies in America*: 1828–1996.
[ii] Clubb, Flanigan, and Zingale, *Partisan Realignment*, table 3.1a.
[iii] Larry M. Bartels, "Electoral Continuity and Change, 1868–1896," *Electoral Studies* 17 (1998), 315.

The only election for which there seems to be unanimous agreement that a realignment occurred was 1896. But even this misses important nuances. In many of these studies, the evidence for 1896 as a realignment is quite weak. In the Clubb, Flanigan, and Zingale study, 1848, 1868, 1920, and 1948 all show stronger indicia of realignment than 1896. In the Bartels study, 1876, 1880, 1912, 1920, 1936, and 1972 all show stronger realigning tendencies than 1896. Other scholars dispute the primacy of 1828, making the case for 1824, 1836, and 1840 as critical elections.[15] Eighteen-ninety-six is actually something of a freakish election; the wholesale abandonment of the Republicans by the West is never repeated until 1912. The changes were certainly sharp. But they were not durable.

Mayhew in particular makes the case for 1876 as the quintessential realigning election. Burnham observed the strength of 1874 as a potential realigning election, but, after assuring the reader that he is not "attempting to explain away inconvenient data," attempts to explain away the inconvenient data by attributing the change to the peculiarities of the Civil War. In reality, it is more than that.[16] In 1872, a third party, the Liberal Republicans, was so strong that it essentially took over the Democratic Party. Two years later, the country saw the onset of a massive depression that brought one of the sharpest turnabouts in congressional history, as Democrats (who had largely been on the wrong side of the Civil War only a few years earlier) took control of Congress. In 1876, Rutherford B. Hayes and Samuel J. Tilden fought a nasty election in which turnout spiked, and that was ultimately decided by presidential commission. It resulted in the end of Union military rule of the South. The South proceeded on its path toward becoming solidly Democrat, the Civil War issue receded, and economic issues grew in importance.[17]

More important, there was an actual shift in voting. The notion that Lincoln Republicans were the majority party from 1860 through 1896, when they became the *dominant* party, is a bit too neat. Lincoln's issues died in 1876 and would not be resurrected until the 1950s. Republicans won large presidential victories from 1860 through 1872, but lost the popular vote all but one time from 1876 through 1892 (and that one time, 1880, they won by a razor-close nine thousand votes). Republicans rarely controlled the House during this time, after a lengthy period of party control from 1860 through 1972. Surely 1876 is an election of as lasting importance as 1896, especially when one considers that the map of 1900 bears as much resemblance to that of 1888 as that of 1896.

So why not 1876? Why not 1880, 1912, 1920? The answer is simple: those elections don't fit neatly into cycles. And those elections emphasize narratives other than our traditional conservative/liberal economic conflict. But there's no reason to favor this struggle; indeed, if foreign policy were our interest, we might claim to see 32/36-year cycles that peak in 1920 (rise of isolationism), 1952 (Cold War consensus), 1988 (end of Cold War), and so forth. Even then, you would have to make room for important elections in 1940 and 1972. This ultimately is a thin reed on which to hang a political science theory, and it is an even weaker foundation for electoral strategies. There simply is no 32-year cycle to critical elections. It is probably more accurate to say that every 8 to 12 years, an election that features some important shift in the issue matrix and that poses a threat to the dominant coalition occurs. That is interesting but not awe-inspiring. When 14 elections over a 31-election period have shown signs of being "critical," the concept has lost its meaning. As Mayhew concludes: "To recapitulate, neither statistics nor stories bear out the canonical realignment calendar of 1860, 1896, and 1932. Something like faith seems to be needed to keep it in place."[18] Realignment theory, especially in its coarsest, most deterministic form, has about as much analytical support as numerology.

BRINGING BACK KEY: CONTINGENCY AND ROADS NOT TAKEN

Mayhew's book is subtitled "a critique of an American genre," not "a development of an alternative." There is nothing wrong with this; attempting to tear down a major political science theory is an ambitious enough project for one book. But it does leave the reader a bit perplexed. After all, it is clear that *something* changed in 1932. Were someone to arrive at your doorstep with a time machine and say that they were traveling back to the 1920s to begin a political career and wanted to know which party they should join to have the best chance of winning the election, you would say "Republican" without missing a beat. If, however, that person announced that they were headed back to the 1930s, you would likely say "Democrat." Similarly, it was undeniably better to be a Democrat in the 1910s and to be a Republican in the 1900s, all other things being equal. Accepting this doesn't require accepting a deterministic view of political cycles, it just requires a basic knowledge of political history.

For an alternative, it is probably best to go back to the beginning of this morass and see what V. O. Key actually meant when he inadvertently brought realignment theory into the world of political science. Key examined only two elections. His goal was not to inject historical determinism into American politics. In fact, it was the opposite: to advance the "understanding of the democratic governing process."[19] In Key's view, the choices of the voters and how they affected politics was what was interesting, not the other way around: the voter retains agency; our politics are not driven by outside forces. We drive them, through our choices.

Mayhew hints, albeit briefly, at an alternative view of elections based on this perspective. In looking at the 1896 election, he discusses the losing Bryanite cause as important because it "is a member of a large universe of not easily analyzable 'roads not taken.'"[20] This, combined with the concept of contingency, is the key to understanding elections and electoral coalitions. Every election presents a party, the country, and the candidates with choices. The party must decide whom to nominate. The American people must choose whom to elect—and while they do so as individuals, there are clearly clustered coalitions that form around these choices. The candidate and his party must then choose how to run and, if they win, how to govern. Each of these choices also leaves behind a road not taken, an alternate course of action that would bring potentially different results. The health of majority coalitions is always contingent on both skillful choices at various forks in the road and, of course, the good luck of a random event not intruding. The economic determinists of chapter 10 emphasize one form of random event—the course of the economy—while proponents of permanent majorities deemphasize both. But in truth, all manner of contingencies are important, as we saw in Part I of this book.

The period from 1888 through 1932 is a good illustration of the interaction of these variables. In 1888, the Republican Party nominated Benjamin Harrison, grandson of the former president and a senator from Indiana. Republicans won the House and the Senate. Harrison's win was extremely tenuous—he actually lost the popular vote by roughly a hundred thousand votes. The House majority was only 27 seats. The Republicans, however, did not see it this way. They had just defeated a Democratic incumbent and had won the most decisive Electoral College win since Ulysses S. Grant's second term.

If a successful Congress is defined as one in which you show the country you can "govern," regardless of whether it believes that you are governing "well," then 1889 through 1890 was a decisive victory for Republicans. Congress passed the Dependent Pension Act (an attempt to keep Civil War veterans in the Republican camp), the Sherman Antitrust Act, the Sherman Silver Purchase Act, and the McKinley Tariff. It spent a billion dollars in the process, an eye-popping sum of money at the time, earning the nickname "the Billion Dollar Congress." At the state level, Republicans were likewise ambitious. They passed mandatory schooling laws in Illinois and Wisconsin and mandated the teaching of English.[21] In the spirit of the Republican slogan of the 1880s—"a schoolhouse on every hill, and no saloon in the valley"—state Republicans passed prohibition laws.[22]

The results were disastrous. In a time of relative prosperity—the recession arising from the Panic of 1890 was shallow and brief—Republicans lost 93 seats, over half their caucus. Two years later Harrison was defeated by Cleveland. Now it was Republicans' turn to fret. The Democrats held the "trifecta" and used their majorities to remove the final federal protections for African Americans, weakening Republicans in the South. In the North, Germans and Irish abandoned Republicans over prohibition and the English-only laws. One Wisconsin politician worried that without German support, Republicans might never win the state again. Woodrow Wilson, observing the returns, crowed that "the Republican Party is going...to pieces."[23]

If you were Grover Cleveland in 1892, you would look at the last election, note that Republicans had been held to their lowest share of the popular vote since Lincoln's four-way race in 1860, see massive congressional majorities, and rest easy, secure in the knowledge that you had just assembled a permanent Democratic majority, or at least a lasting one. And, had events not intervened, 1892 might well have been a canonical realigning year (it is, after all, close enough to the 32- to 36-year cycle). But a few weeks into Cleveland's term, the economy collapsed. Unemployment hit an estimated 15 percent, as bread lines grew and strikes proliferated across the country.[24] Making matters worse, Cleveland had to disappear from the public eye to recover from surgery on his jaw; his condition was kept secret from the American people. In the 1894 elections, Democrats lost 125 seats. In 1896, the Republicans really did break the deadlock between the parties. Their nativism and opposition to alcohol was quickly forgiven; in the heavily ethnic Midwestern cities where Cleveland had won a 162,000-vote plurality in 1892, McKinley scored a 464,000-vote win.[25] Republicans were actually lucky to have lost in 1892, as it enabled them to win handily, especially when Democrats nominated a candidate, William Jennings Bryan, who completely alienated the Northeast.

By 1900 unemployment was back to 5 percent, and the public was in no mood to throw the Republicans out. This begins the so-called System of 1896. But to accept the existence of this system, you then have to explain the massive dip in Republican performance from 1910 through 1916. The Bull Moose/Republican split of 1912 is frequently blamed, but Democrats had captured the House in 1910, before the split erupted, and they were able to retain control of the House after the 1914 midterms and the 1916 elections, when the breach was largely healed. As detailed in chapter 1, Wilson had actually assembled a broad coalition of Southerners and Western Progressives in his 1916 run that offered some potential for continued successful governance. Had Wilson made different choices in his second term, he might have been able to hold that coalition together, and we would probably observe the spike in turnout in 1916 and conclude that 1916 was a realigning year. Instead, Wilson took the United States into a war that the two most tenuous members of his coalition—ethnics and Progressives—opposed, and then insisted stubbornly on peace terms that they loathed. Other events over which he had little control interrupted: the bombings, the recession, the flu pandemic, and his stroke.

The subsequent landslides of Harding, Coolidge, and Hoover are lumped together with those of McKinley, Roosevelt, and Taft, but this is dubious analysis at best. First, the later wins were much bigger than the McKinley/Roosevelt/Taft wins, and two of them extended into the South. Moreover, the wins of Roosevelt, and to a lesser extent of McKinley, represented the high tide of Progressivism in the country. Harding and Coolidge, and to a lesser extent Hoover, represented its nadir: it was almost as though two different Republican parties were governing. Consider this: In 1912, two candidates who competed for the mantle of Progressivism combined for almost 70 percent of the vote. In 1924, the two conservative candidates shared over 80 percent of the vote. This is glossed over in attempts to neatly periodize American history. But the distinctions are real. This whole System of 1896 that Burnham hypothesized is nothing more than a collection of good and bad choices by parties, mixed with a bit of luck.

The bottom line is that permanent majorities are neither predetermined nor inevitable. Here's a series of thought experiments to illustrate this: What if the Populists had been stronger and Benjamin Harrison had been reelected in 1892 and presided over the Panic of 1893? What if Populists had been weaker and William Jennings Bryan hadn't been the Democrats' nominee in 1896, 1900, and 1908? What if TR had won at the Republican convention in 1912 and had led a reluctant America into World War I? What if Warren Harding hadn't died, had stood for reelection and lost in 1924, and a Democrat had been reelected in 1928? What if Herbert Hoover, widely viewed as an unbeatable nominee for either party, had decided he was a Democrat after winning the 1920 New Hampshire primary (without actually running in it)? Every one of these roads not taken represents a choice that, had it been made differently, would have altered our understanding of politics and probably caused us to pronounce the forthcoming realignments "inevitable."

The 1930s only raise more questions. What if Roosevelt had not survived his polio or had lost his excruciatingly close 1928 gubernatorial race? Democrats' bench had been wiped out in the 1920s. Would "Cactus Jack" Garner or "Alfalfa Bill" Murray really have appealed to white ethnics? If Smith had been renominated, would he have carried the South? Even if they had won the nomination, the Democrats would have remained a conservative party, perhaps unable to deal with the Depression. Could Roosevelt have enacted the New Deal in 1932 if the Democrats had not nominated a Catholic in 1928, who mobilized massive numbers of voters? What if Hitler had waited a year to invade Poland? Such evidence as we have indicates that a Republican probably would have won in 1940; Roosevelt had no apparent New Deal heir, and the Democrats might well have concluded that "New Dealing" was a failure and reverted to their Jacksonian roots.

Obviously, you can't unmake the past. Yet none of these questions is an idle one. Each represents a concrete decision that, had it been made differently, would have changed the course of political history. Many of these decisions were close ones that easily could have gone the other way. This illustrates why the Democrats failed after the 2008 elections (and why Republicans failed after 2004). Democrats won a reasonably close election under historically favorable circumstances in 2008 and, egged on by journalists and academics who believed that a realignment was nigh, thought they had won the mandate to end all mandates. They were drawn to a narrative about a lasting New Deal majority that was, in fact, never created. Even worse, they believed their own press releases about their historic mission. It isn't a unique story either; Republicans had been in a similar spot only two years earlier, and other parties have made the same mistake time and again, including FDR himself in 1937. Against this background, it becomes readily apparent why talks of realignments, much less *permanent* realignments, are so wrong-headed and dangerous.

WHERE WE'RE HEADED: OPEN-FIELD POLITICS

This book offers no sexy prediction about what will happen next in American politics. It doesn't declare an inevitable winner or loser. Instead, it offers up something far more intriguing. Michael Barone has written about the era of open-field politics that we entered in 2006, when the parties finally broke out of the trench warfare that had characterized a decade of presidential and congressional elections. Of course, as noted in chapter 3, we actually broke out of trench warfare in the 1990s. Although the overall Republican and Democratic caucuses in the House remained the same size, they swapped around 90 seats from 1996 through 2006; when you add the seats that switched hands in 1992, 1994, 2008, and 2010, each party has held about three hundred of the House seats at least once in the past two decades. This is a key development, and it is astonishing how little attention it has received.

This is the result of two key trends discussed in this book: the breakdown of sectional parties and the breakup of the Eisenhower coalition. As noted in chapter 1, during the 1920s we had strongly sectional parties. How sectional were they? We can see exactly how much in figure 11.2. The Republicans almost never managed to win races in the South or in the Jacksonian areas: west Tennessee, south and west Kentucky, southern Indiana, northern Missouri, and Oklahoma. The Democrats rarely won seats in the North, except in New York City. There were some indications that this might break down during the late 1920s, but then the Great Depression intervened.

The Democratic breakthrough during the New Deal period is apparent in our map of the 1930s (figure 11.3). The Republicans are even more constrained to the North, while Democrats are basically able to win everywhere. The sectional walls were breaking down.

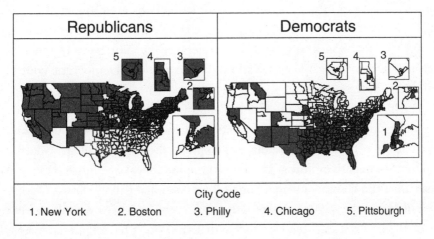

Figure 11.2   House Districts the Parties Won *At Least* Once, 1922–1928

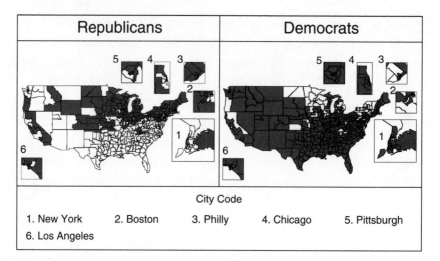

Figure 11.3   House Districts the Parties Won *At Least* Once, 1932–1940

When the GOP regained its footing in 1938, the battles for control of Congress began to oscillate wildly. With the exception of 1940, every congressional election from 1938 through 1952 saw 20 seats or more switch hands between the parties. In the midst of the so-called New Deal era, Congress was going through the most unstable period of the twentieth century. Things settled down in 1952, of course, due to a series of unusual events. As this book has demonstrated, the odd confluence of issues and the position of the parties during the Cold War and in the post–New Deal period conspired to give the GOP a relative lock on the Electoral College, while the slow breakdown of Democratic strength in the South and continued tolerance by Northern Democrats of Southern Democratic apostasies allowed for continued Democratic control of the House, at least in name.

During the 1980s, as the Cold War wound down, as Democrats became less approving of Southern Democratic dalliances with conservatism, and as Republicans continued to organize and spread their appeal in the South, the Republicans began to show a broader geographic appeal (see figure 11.4). At the same time, the Democrats maintained their "national party" status.

Finally, in the 1990s, we see both parties achieve what we could safely call national party status. This isn't to say that they don't have regional strengths

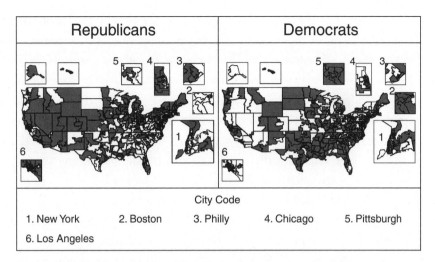

Figure 11.4   House Districts the Parties Won *At Least* Once, 1982–1990

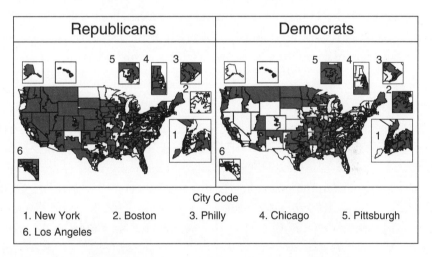

Figure 11.5   House Districts the Parties Won *At Least* Once, 1992–2000

and weaknesses, but overall, there is no region they are automatically shut out of (see figure 11.5).

The map of House competition in the 2000s is virtually indistinguishable from the 1990s map, suggesting that we are still at a point in our history when both parties can compete across the entire country. In other words, we now have two parties that are able to win nationally. Democrats did not win the House in 2006 because they were achieving permanent majority status. They won because the contingencies lined up correctly. Republican wins in the 1990s and 2000s were never overwhelming, and with a large number of seats trading hands, it was inevitable that things would come together for the Democrats in the near term. Although the Democrats have made choices over the past few election cycles that have alienated Jacksonians up and down the ticket, that doesn't make them automatically unable to win in the South, any more than the losses in 2008 and 2010 meant that the GOP would be unable to win in the North. Overwhelming GOP control of redistricting may mean that in the short term there are not enough swing seats for the Democrats to gain control of Congress, but aggressive redistricting schemes always go awry sooner or later (usually sooner), as Georgia Democrats and Pennsylvania Republicans learned in the 2000s.

This is the way it has typically been in this country. From 1824 to 1894, party control of the House changed hands 12 times: about once every three elections. If we look at congressional maps as late as the 1880s, we see two political parties that are competing across the country (figure 11.6).

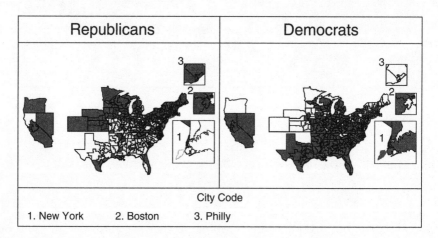

Figure 11.6 House Districts the Parties Won *At Least* Once, 1882–1890

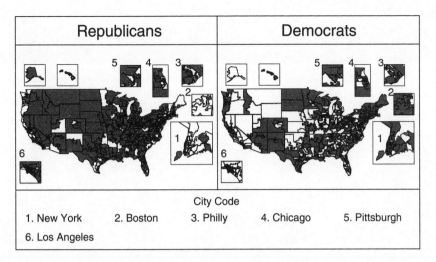

Republicans	Democrats

City Code

1. New York   2. Boston   3. Philly   4. Chicago   5. Pittsburgh

6. Los Angeles

Figure 11.7   House Districts the Parties Won *At Least* Once, 2002–2010

This picture is not quite like the map of the 1990s—the GOP was already uncompetitive in the Deep South, but there are important similarities. The Democrats compete everywhere, while the Republicans win everywhere but the Deep South (and even win there a few times). This is what the world looks like when parties compete, and this is "typical" American history. The oscillations of the past few election cycles are not flukes; they are normal. It is the period between 1950 and 1980 that is the fluke.

CONCLUSION

2012 AND BEYOND

SO FAR IN THIS book, I've discussed the distant past and the recent past and then skipped ahead to the medium-to-long-term future of American elections. I've steadfastly avoided commentary on the 2012 elections. Having started each chapter with a quote from a prognostication gone awry, I'm especially cognizant of the risk that, a hundred years hence, some upstart elections analyst might pluck a paragraph from this book and use it as an example of how foolish psephologists can be. Additionally, the theme of this book is that electoral coalitions are heavily influenced by contingencies and are always shifting. It follows, then, that we can't really *know* what will happen one year hence because the various contingencies that will determine that election have not yet been resolved. Remember, at this point in 2007, most people were pretty sure the 2008 elections would center on Iraq, not the economy.

With that in mind, let's undertake a cautious examination of the 2012 playing field and perhaps even peer a bit further into the future. As of this writing, in May 2011, Obama is considered by many commentators to be the overwhelming favorite for reelection.[1] The Intrade online futures markets give the Democrats a 60 percent chance of holding the White House, only a few points worse than their assessment during the heady first days of Obama's presidency. To many, Obama is still the avatar of hope and change that he was in late 2008, the Republicans are too marginalized to win, and the Democrats have a powerful, dominant majority in the offing.

Needless to say, these analysts are living in the past. As we've seen, it is not 2008 anymore. Obama's coalition—borrowed from Bill Clinton—is in deep trouble. As president, Obama has done very little to expand his appeal past the voters who cast ballots for him in 2008; the transformational president who hoped for a new, broad majority has instead seen the Democratic coalition narrow. His approval ratings have been mired between 45 percent and 51 percent—they have fallen between those numbers on 95 percent of the days Gallup has polled since the beginning of 2010.

Even these tepid ratings demonstrate the depth and narrowness of his coalition. His approval rating for March 2011 was 47 percent. But it was a paltry 39 percent among whites.[2] To put this in perspective, when Bill Clinton hit a similar 34 percent approval rating among whites in June 1993, his overall approval rating was 37 percent. The difference is that Obama maintains an 85 percent approval rating among African Americans, while Clinton's approval among that group had fallen to 61 percent in 1993.[3] Again, this is not to say that black votes don't count equally. It is just to observe that Obama's approval rating owes to his unusual strength among core Democratic groups, rather than to his broad appeal.

This presents a problem for the president going into 2012. A 51 percent approval rating—the high end of Obama's range—is typically enough to get a president reelected. But it does not leave much room for error. And the concentration of pro-Obama voters among core Democratic constituencies poses a unique set of problems. Minority voters tend to be concentrated in a few congressional districts and even in particular states. Many of these states, such as Mississippi, have heavily racialized voting patterns, where even unanimous approval ratings among African Americans would not be enough for Obama to overcome white opposition. To put it differently, 14 states have larger minority populations than the United States as a whole, and only three of these could really be considered "swing states": New Mexico, Nevada, and Florida. In other words, if you could challenge state lines under the Voting Rights Act, there would be one heck of a vote dilution claim.

More important, the Midwest is the key swing region in American politics. Over the past five cycles, the Democrats have carried Minnesota, Iowa, Wisconsin, Ohio, Pennsylvania, and Michigan in a majority of the elections, but their PVIs have been only slightly off center. These states combine for 80 electoral votes, and they are heavily white: all are at least 75 percent non-Hispanic white; Iowa is more than 90 percent white.[4] The president's weakness among white voters—especially those without graduate degrees—will create a huge electoral problem for him if it continues into next fall.

This says nothing about other problems bedeviling the president. The economy continues a sluggish recovery, one that is so gradual that Americans are having trouble perceiving it. Aside from killing Osama bin Laden, almost all of his accomplishments remain, as of this writing, politically divisive. And Republicans remain enthusiastic about voting, depriving him of the enthusiasm gap that helped drive his 2008 win.

Some Democrats have argued that we're now seeing the development of a dual electorate, one that inures to Democrats' benefit in presidential years. Presidential elections do tend to bring marginal voters to the polls, and because those marginal voters are more likely to be minority voters, the presidential electorate will tend to be more Democratic than off-year elections. Jonathan Chait explains that "[m]idterm elections tend to be low-turnout affairs with disproportionately old voters. This fact had little partisan significance until very recently, when age suddenly became a highly predictive factor. The whites who showed up in 2010 were far older than the whites who voted in 2008."[5]

There is no doubt that the 2012 electorate will be both younger and less white than that of the 2010 elections. But we've already observed one problem with this argument: the youth vote was more Democratic in large part because it also tended to be more heavily minority. When we talk about more young voters, minority voters, and Democratic voters entering the electorate, we're talking about the same thing—hence, we're triple-counting. We also have to bear in mind that Republican voting was depressed in 2008 and is unlikely to remain so for 2012. In other words, we'll probably have an electorate that is somewhere between the 2008 and 2010 electorates. Finally, a significant number of voters abandoned their historic party preferences to participate in the history-making election of the nation's first African American president. Even more turned out for the first time just to make such history. Whether reelecting the first African American president generates the same enthusiasm, and causes voters to abandon their base party preference at similar rates, remains to be seen.

This is critical because slight changes in the 2008 electorate can have far-reaching consequences. For example, African American voters constituted 13 percent of the electorate in 2008, an all-time high. Assume the African American share of the electorate drops to 11 percent—traditional African American turnout. Also, assume that African American Republicans don't cast votes for a Democrat this time, and that Republicans therefore claim 8 percent of the African American vote, tying their pre-2008 worst showing. Holding everything else constant, Obama's 7.5 percent margin from 2008 would shrink to 4.5 percent. Similarly, if we see the same racial breakdown in 2012 that we saw in 2008, but Republicans perform as well among whites as they did in 2010, Obama would lose by 2 points.[6]

Finally, the growing Latino population is unlikely to help Obama in the short term. As I noted earlier this year, "for all the recent hype about the growing Latino vote, it has actually grown quite slowly."[7] It has constituted 8 or 9 percent of the electorate for almost a decade now. Even if it grows again in 2012—and remember, 2008 saw historic registration drives and get-out-the-vote efforts—it would not be enough to transform a state like Texas into a swing state...yet.

This is not to say that everything is rosy for the Republicans. Republican pundits seem to be relying heavily on the "it's the economy, stupid" argument. As we saw in chapter 10, this argument gets you only so far. Voters will process a number of factors. The economy is an important one, but it is not the only one. Do I think Obama will have a tough time being reelected with 8 percent unemployment? Yes. At the same time, though, voters still don't blame him for the tough economy, and I can see plenty of ways that he can pull off the feat. In particular, the upcoming budget battles—and the developing GOP stance on Medicare cuts—gives the president a chance to define the GOP and run a "Harry Truman" campaign, where a president wins despite a flagging economy by making the opposition seem unacceptable. Obama's acts have not been able to win over working-class whites. But the economic collapse of 2008 did, at least temporarily. Growing Republican economic libertarianism may have a similar effect.

More important, the Republican field, as of right now, does not induce a feeling of awe. The fact that Donald Trump was able to rocket to the top of the Republican primary polls shortly after he suggested that he might enter the race speaks volumes to the weakness of the Republican field. There are a number of reasons for this, but one stands out as critically important. Republicans have traditionally selected their candidates from one of two sources: constitutional officeholders (counting Senate majority leader as the modern version of the constitutional office of president of the Senate) and governors of large states. Since 1940, all but three nominees have fallen into one of those two categories and one of those three exceptions, Dwight Eisenhower, was as close as you can get to a constitutional officeholder.

George W. Bush chose a vice president who realistically could not run for president, and no one sees the other recent Republican constitutional office-holders—Dennis Hastert, Trent Lott, and Bill Frist—as presidential material. At the same time, a variety of factors have conspired to deprive the GOP of its farm team among big-state governors. In the 20 gubernatorial elections held in the ten most populous states in 2002 and 2006, Republican candidates won nine. But a closer examination reveals problems for all of these winners. Ohio governor Bob Taft II finished his term by pleading "no contest" to four criminal misdemeanors stemming from undisclosed gifts. George Pataki of New York is too liberal. I am fairly convinced that one of the two Florida governors elected during these years would be a prohibitive favorite but for unique circumstances: Jeb Bush's surname is Bush, and Charlie Crist left the Republican Party. If Texas Governor Rick Perry enters he could be a formidable candidate, although his comments regarding possible secession efforts and his ties to George W. Bush could create problems for him. That leaves Arnold Schwarzenegger . . . and we'll be kind and simply note that he's constitutionally disqualified since he is a naturalized citizen.

So the Republicans are left with a fairly decent crop of "B-list" candidates and potential candidates: Jon Huntsman of Utah, Mitt Romney of Massachusetts, Tim Pawlenty of Minnesota, and Representative Michele Bachmann of Minnesota. But from a *coalitional* standpoint, these B-list candidates have some real strengths. First, setting aside Bachmann, their status as governors sets them apart from the congressional Republicans. They will cast zero votes over the next two years. Critically, they won't *have* to weigh in on the upcoming budget battles, although primary politics might force them to do so.

Second, and more important, none of them is a Southerner. One of the quiet themes of this book is that our nation's politics are deeply rooted in culture. All other things being equal, a Northern nominee from either party will cause the North to lean his party's direction. A Southern nominee will have a similar effect. At the beginning of George W. Bush's presidency, the yet-unfinished Southern shift advantaged a Southern-accented GOP nominee. But with Phase Three of that shift largely completed over the past decade, the GOP doesn't really have to worry about the South in the short run. And with the Obama administration alienating many Northern suburbanites and working-class voters whom Bill Clinton had brought into the Democratic tent, a Northern/

Midwestern/Western Republican would probably be best positioned to win over those voters.

Of course, this advantage would not apply to a Perry candidacy, which is why Perry probably has the least potential to expand the GOP coalition beyond what President George W. Bush was able to accomplish. At the same time, though, Perry is possessed of some interesting strengths. Like Bush, he demonstrated some crossover appeal to Latino voters; in 2006, the two Republican candidates for governor (in a four-way race) combined for 49 percent of the Latino vote. While Perry could underperform among suburbanites, his stylistic contrast with Obama could enhance the GOP's appeal to working-class whites. In other words, in a Perry–Obama race, we could see a substantial shift in the country's party coalitions, with the GOP taking an even more populist tone. And let's not forget, in 2009, socially conservative Republicans won in Northern suburbs like Westchester and Nassau counties in New York. If the conditions deteriorate enough, a Perry or Bachmann could put together broad coalitions. Smart strategists wrote off FDR and Reagan, and it was an epic mistake.

We've already explored some of the factors that will play a key role in the general election, but there are three other factors we have overlooked. They are Susana Martinez, Brian Sandoval, and Marco Rubio, the newly elected governor of New Mexico, the governor of Nevada, and the junior senator from Florida, respectively. None of these three is likely to run for president. But as a vice presidential selection, they could potentially turn the politics of 2012 upside down. For one thing, all three hail from swing states; if they remain popular, they could take key states off the map entirely. More important, their Latino heritage could do for Republicans what Al Smith did for Democrats and cause this historically, although not overwhelmingly, Democratic group to look strongly at the Republicans.

We should be careful here. Remember, pan-Latino identity is weaker than many commentators assume. Lumping Mexican Americans, Cuban Americans, and Puerto Ricans (to say nothing of voters from South America and the Caribbean Basin) in the same group makes about as much sense as lumping together voters from Italy, Ireland, and Germany as "European immigrants." In particular, the selection of Rubio might not advantage the GOP as much as the selection of Martinez or Sandoval, as Cuban Americans already lean Republican. However, Florida has more electoral votes, so nailing that state down may be more important than appealing to Mexican American voters. And, of course, all three politicians may prove inept at their jobs or not ready for prime time; that is a more important consideration than anything else. Finally, a more Latino-friendly GOP could cause problems among other pieces of the Republican coalition, particularly economic populists. These voters could flirt with the Democrats or a third party if the GOP is perceived as becoming too pro-immigrant.

In short, 2012 offers the GOP the same type of opportunity as 2010, and it stems from the same factors. The president did not transform American politics in 2008. To the contrary, during the presidential campaign, he largely lost the remnants of the traditional Democratic base in the South. In 2009 and 2010, his desire to accomplish big things, and his supporters' and advisors' belief that he could create a realignment, caused him to drift away from the successful formula that had brought suburbanites and blue-collar voters into the Democratic coalition. The party paid the price in 2010 and continues to pay the price. Whether the GOP can take advantage of this opening remains to be seen. Obama may have lost his majority in 2010, but it is far from certain that he will be unable to get some variant of it back in 2012.

Beyond 2012, the picture quickly becomes even murkier. If the GOP wins in 2012, it will be confronted with a sluggish economy that hasn't yet responded to the traditional economic remedies. If it wins, it will still have to govern a party that is split between Christian conservatives, economic libertarians, blue-collar voters (assuming it wins), and, if it is to survive, minority groups. This presents the GOP with challenges similar to those that have proved so difficult for President Obama and his Democratic coalition. As I've stated, both parties are now at rough parity, and even a massive win over Obama, which is not out of the question if the economy continues to struggle, will not mean that the game is over. The GOP will still have to face the voters in 2014, and if it hasn't delivered, those voters will quickly return to the Democrats.

Similarly, if the GOP loses, it still has a promising future. The GOP elected a slate of strong potential candidates across the West and Midwest in 2010, most of whom will be favored to win in the 2014 midterms if there is a Democratic president, and all of whom will be in their primes during the 2016 elections. There isn't a logical successor in the Democratic Party because Joe Biden will be 73 on Election Day 2016, while Hillary Clinton will be 69. Andrew Cuomo may be the closest thing for the Democrats right now, but he has a long road ahead in governing New York. Of course, events may conspire to elect yet another Democratic president in 2016, giving the Democrats popular vote wins in six of seven presidential elections since 1992. Even then, it won't be because there's a permanent Democratic majority, just as Republican wins in those years wouldn't mean that the Obama election of 2008 was a fluke. Wins by either party in those years and beyond, even big ones, are entirely possible in the new electoral landscape. But sooner or later, and probably sooner, whatever majority coalition that emerges in 2012 will be lost once again.

NOTES

INTRODUCTION

1. Ronald Brownstein, "Southern Exposure," *National Journal*, May 23, 2009, accessed April 3, 2011, http://www.magnetmail.net/images/clients/NJG_EVENTS/attach /NJ_Southern_Exposure_090523.pdf.
2. Susan Page, "In Congress, a Democratic Wave," *USA Today*, November 5, 2008, accessed March 6, 2011, http://www.usatoday.com/news/politics/election2008/2008–11 -05–1a-cover_N.htm.
3. Andy Barr, "Dems Talk of 'Permanent Progressive Majority'," *Politico*, November 7, 2008, accessed March 7, 2011, http://www.politico.com/news/stories/1108/15407.html.
4. Michael Lind, "Obama and the Dawn of the Fourth Republic," *Salon*, November 7, 2008, accessed March 7, 2011, http://www.salon.com/news/opinion/feature/2008/11/07 /fourth_republic.
5. Richard Wolffe, *Renegade: The Making of a President* (New York: Three Rivers Press, 2010), 102.
6. Paul Krugman, "Franklin Delano Obama?" *New York Times*, November 10, 2008, accessed March 7, 2011, http://www.nytimes.com/2008/11/10/opinion/10krugman .html.
7. Brad Wilmouth, "Olbermann Links GOP & Tea Party to Racism and 'Incitement to Violence' in 'Special Comment'," *NewsBusters*, March 23, 2010, accessed July 2, 2011, http://newsbusters.org/blogs/brad-wilmouth/2010/03/23/olbermann-links-gop-tea-party -racism-and-incitement-violence-special-.
8. Ronald Brownstein and Richard Rainey, "GOP Plants Flag on New Voting Frontier," *Los Angeles Times*, November 22, 2004, accessed April 3, 2011, http://articles.latimes .com/2004/nov/22/nation/na-fast22.
9. John Micklethwait and Adrian Wooldridge, *The Right Nation: Conservative Power in America* (New York: Penguin Books, 2005).
10. Burnham's works are voluminous, but his most well-known writings in the subject of realignments are Walter Dean Burnham, "The Changing Shape of the American Political Universe," *American Political Science Review* 56 (1965): 7–28; Walter Dean Burnham, "Party Systems and the Political Process," in William Nisbet Chambers and Burnham, eds., *The American Party Systems: Stages of Political Development* (New York: Oxford University Press, 1967), 289–304; and Walter Dean Burnham, *Critical Elections and the Mainsprings of American Politics* (New York: W. W. Norton & Company, 1971).
11. David R. Mayhew, *Electoral Realignments: A Critique of an American Genre* (New Haven, CT: Yale University Press, 2002).
12. For a more thorough examination of this, see Joel Garreau, *The Nine Nations of North America* (Boston: Houghton Mifflin, 1981).

13. In 1972 (for Richard Nixon), 1984 (for Ronald Reagan), 1988 (for George H. W. Bush), and 1992 (for Bill Clinton).

14. William E. Leuchtenburg, *The White House Looks South* (Baton Rouge: Louisiana State University Press, 2005), 22.

15. V. O. Key, Jr., *Southern Politics* (New York: Vintage Books, 1949).

16. Emile B. Ader, "Why the Dixiecrats Failed," *Journal of Politics* 15 (1953): 360.

17. J. B. Shannon, "Presidential Politics in the South—1938, II," *Journal of Politics* 1 (1939): 297.

18. For a more thorough explication of the politics of the Southern Hills, see H. C. Nixon, "Politics of the Hills," *Journal of Politics* 8 (1946): 123–33.

19. David Hackett Fischer, *Albion's Seed: Four British Folkways in America* (New York: Oxford University Press, 1989), 787.

20. Larry Hoefling, *Chasing the Frontier: Scots-Irish in Early America* (New York: iUniverse, Inc., 2005), 23.

21. William G. Carleton, "The Second Reconstruction: An Analysis from the Deep South," *Antioch Review* 18 (1958): 180.

22. Fischer, *Albion's Seed*, 688.

23. Walter Russell Mead, "The Jacksonian Tradition," *National Interest*, Winter 1999/2000, accessed March 13, 2011, http://www.denbeste.nu/external/Mead01.html.

24. Gerald R. Webster, "Demise of the Solid South," *Geographical Review* 82 (1992): 50. One should not go too far with the idea of Southern liberalism. Strom Thurmond hailed from the populist wing of the party—he was attacked as having CIO backing—but that meant that he favored spending money on things like schools and roads. V. O. Key, Jr., *Southern Politics* (New York: Vintage Books, 1949), 142–51.

25. Walter Dean Burnham, *Voting in American Elections: The Shaping of the American Political Universe Since 1788* (Palo Alto, CA: Academia Press, 2010), 103.

26. Jay Cost, "Breaking Down the Tax Vote," *Weekly Standard*, December 17, 2010, accessed March 6, 2011, http://www.weeklystandard.com/blogs/breaking-down-tax -vote_523501.html.

27. There is a "common space" score that theoretically allows comparisons of all congressmen. I find it highly problematic for reasons that are well beyond the scope of this endnote. "Common space" scores are not used.

CHAPTER 1   THE EMERGING DEMOCRATIC MAJORITY

1. "The Dissolution of the Solid South," *Sewanee Review* IV (1896): 493.

2. Susan Dunn, *Roosevelt's Purge* (Cambridge, MA: The Belknap Press of Harvard University Press, 2010), 55.

3. George Brown Tindall, *The Disruption of the Solid South* (Athens: University of Georgia Press, 1972), 25.

4. Earl Black and Merle Black, *The Rise of Southern Republicans* (Cambridge, MA: The Belknap Press of Harvard University Press, 2002), 13–14.

5. Kevin Phillips, *William McKinley* (New York: Times Books, 2003), 79.

6. Walter Dean Burnham, *Presidential Ballots: 1836–1892* (Baltimore: The Johns Hopkins University Press, 1955), 638–39; Edgar Eugene Robinson, *The Presidential Vote: 1896–1932* (Palo Alto, CA: Stanford University Press, 1934), 277.

7. David Sarasohn, "The Election of 1916: Realigning the Rockies," *Western Historical Quarterly* 11 (1980): 296.

8. As David Hackett Fischer put it, "The emotional violence of its rhetoric, the intensity of its agrarian reforms and the flamboyant individuality of its leaders brought success in one region and failure in another." David Hackett Fischer, *Albion's Seed: Four British Folkways in America* (New York: Oxford University Press, 1989), 867.

9. Sarasohn, "The Election of 1916: Realigning the Rockies," 287, 304–05.

10. David Pietrusza, *The Year of the Six Presidents* (New York: Avalon Publishing Group, Inc., 2007), 142.

11. Ibid., 145.

12. Beverly Gage, *The Day Wall Street Exploded: A Story of America in Its First Age of Terror* (New York: Oxford University Press, 2009), 160–61.

13. Michael J. Dubin, *Party Affiliations in the State Legislatures: A Year by Year Summary, 1796–2006* (Jefferson, NC: McFarland & Company, Inc., 2007).

14. Kevin Phillips, *The Emerging Republican Majority* (New Rochelle, NY: Arlington House, 1969), 149.

15. Burnham, *Presidential Ballots*, 638–39; Robinson, *Presidential Vote*, 277.

16. Michael J. Dubin, *United States Congressional Elections, 1788–1997: The Official Results of the Elections of the 1st through 105th Congress* (Jefferson, NC: McFarland & Company, Inc., 1998), 430–40.

17. Sarasohn, "Realigning the Rockies," 290.

18. Garland S. Tucker, *The High Tide of American Conservatism: Davis, Coolidge and the 1924 Election* (Austin, TX: Emerald Book Co. 2010), 237–38.

19. Ibid., 251.

20. Supporters even ran him in the 1920 New Hampshire Democratic primary, where he came in first ("unpledged" technically won).

21. Michael Barone, *Our Country: The Shaping of America From Roosevelt to Reagan* (New York: The Free Press, 1992), 20.

22. Samuel Lubell, *The Future of American Politics* (Garden City, NY: Doubleday Anchor Books, 1956), 29.

23. Phillips, *Emerging Republican Majority*, 336.

24. Ibid., 57–58.

25. Kristi Anderson, *The Creation of a Democratic Majority, 1928–1936* (Chicago: The University of Chicago Press, 1979), 51.

26. Ibid., 40–41.

27. CQ Press, *Guide to U.S. Elections*, 5th ed., vol. 2 (Washington, DC: CQ Press, 2005), 1517.

28. Phillips, *Emerging Republican Majority*, 149.

29. James R. Sweeney, "Rum, Romanism, and Virginia Democrats: The Party Leaders and the Campaign of 1928," *Virginia Magazine of History and Biography* 90 (1982): 404.

30. In Virginia, for example, Hoover carried 17 of Virginia's 23 cities. Sweeney, "Rum, Romanism, and Virginia Democrats," 425.

31. Dubin, *United States Congressional Elections*, 470–77.

32. Dubin, *Party Affiliations in the State Legislatures*, 141.

33. Barone, *Our Country*, 47, n. 16 & 17.

34. Dubin, *United States Congressional Elections*, 470–77, 487; Kenneth C. Martis, *The Historical Atlas of United States Congressional Districts, 1789–1983* (New York: The Free Press: A Division of Macmillan Publishing Co., Inc., 1982), 165, 240.

35. Dubin, *United States Congressional Elections*, 487.

36. Dubin, *United States Congressional Elections*, 487; Martis, *Historical Atlas*, 165, 246.

37. This was Roosevelt's own assessment after the 1928 elections. See, e.g., Earland I. Carlson, "Franklin D. Roosevelt's Post-Mortem of the 1928 Election," *Midwest Journal of Political Science* 8 (1964): 298–308.

38. CQ Press, *Guide to U.S. Elections*, 1517.

39. William E. Leuchtenburg, *The White House Looks South* (Baton Rogue: Louisiana State University Press, 2005), 32–35.

40. Ibid., 56.

41. William G. Thiemann, "President Hoover's Efforts on Behalf of FDR's 1932 Nomination," *Presidential Studies Quarterly* 24 (1994): 87–88.

42. Harold F. Gosnell and Norman N. Gill, "An Analysis of the 1932 Presidential Vote in Chicago," *American Political Science Review* 6 (1935): 967–84.

43. David Burner, *The Politics of Provincialism: The Democratic Party in Transition, 1918–1932* (New York: Alfred A. Knopf, 1970), 234–41; John M. Allswang, *A House for All Peoples: Ethnic Politics in Chicago: 1890–1936* (Lexington: University Press of Kentucky, 1971).

44. Clyde P. Weed, *The Nemesis of Reform, The Republican Party During the New Deal* (New York: Columbia University Press, 1994).

45. Ibid., 44.

46. Ibid., 75–76.

47. "The Literary Digest Poll Gives Coolidge Big Majority," *Middlesboro Daily News*, October 31, 1924; "Final Returns of Literary Digest Poll Shows Mr. Hoover holding the Lead in 42 States," *St. Petersburg Independent*, November 2, 1928; "Roosevelt Favored: Literary Digest Poll Shows Slight Gain for Hoover," *Montreal Gazette*, November 4, 1932; Archibald M. Crossley, "Straw Polls in 1936," *Public Opinion Quarterly* 1 (1937): 24–35.

48. Anderson, *The Creation of a Democratic Majority*, 31. For a criticism of Anderson's work, and an argument (which I find fairly unpersuasive) that the Democratic gains from 1924 to 1936 were due to conversion of Republican voters, rather than mobilization of non-voters, see Robert S. Erikson and Kent L. Tedin, "1928–1936 Partisan Realignment: The Case for the Conversion Hypothesis," *American Political Science Review* 75 (1981): 951–62.

49. Anderson, *The Creation of a Democratic Majority*, 35.

50. Ibid., 37.

51. Kevin J. McMahon, *Reconsidering Roosevelt on Race: How the Presidency Paved the Road to Brown* (Chicago: University of Chicago Press, 2004), 32.

52. Jean Edward Smith, *FDR* (New York: Random House, 2007), 372–73.

53. Arthur S. Link, "The Negro as a Factor in the Campaign of 1912," *Journal of Negro History* 32 (1947): 86, 93; Seth M. Scheiner, "President Theodore Roosevelt and the Negro, 1901–1908," *Journal of Negro History* 47 (1962): 181.

54. Weiss, *Farewell*, 105–106.

55. Leuchtenburg, *The White House Looks South*, 65.

56. Weiss, *Farewell*, 52–54.

57. Ibid., 189.

58. Ibid., 196–97.

CHAPTER 2   THREE WEDDINGS AND A WAKE

1. Quoted in Clyde P. Weed, *The Nemesis of Reform: The Republican Party During the New Deal* (New York: Columbia University Press, 1994), 115.

2. Susan Dunn, *Roosevelt's Purge* (Cambridge, MA: The Belknap Press of Harvard University Press, 2010), 236.

3. Elmo Roper, "The Politics of Three Decades," *Public Opinion Quarterly* 29 (1965): 370–71.

4. Steve Kornacki, "The GOP's New Fake Racial History," September 2, 2010, accessed February 6, 2011, http://www.salon.com/news/politics/war_room/2010/09/02 /haley_barbour_race_history. See also Steve Benen, *Washington Monthly*, September 2, 2010, accessed February 17, 2011, http://www.washingtonmonthly.com/archives /individual/2010_09/025497.php.

5. Thomas F. Schaller, *Whistling Past Dixie: How Democrats Can Win Without the South* (New York: Simon & Schuster Paperbacks, 2006), 23.

6. Ibid., 17.

7. Vincent P. de Santis, "Republican Efforts to 'Crack' the Democratic South," *Review of Politics* 14 (1952): 247.

8. Ibid., 251.

9. See Gilbert Thomas Stephenson, "Racial Distinctions in Southern Law," *American Political Science Review* 1 (1906): 44.

10. R. Hal Williams, *Realigning America: McKinley, Bryan and the Remarkable Election of 1896* (Lawrence: University Press of Kansas, 2010), 56.

11. Richard E. Welch, Jr., "The Federal Elections Bill of 1890: Post-scripts and Prelude," *Journal of American History* 52 (1965): 511–26.

12. Seth M. Scheiner, "Theodore Roosevelt and the Negro, 1901–1908," *Journal of Negro History* 47 (1962): 170, 178.

13. Ibid., 181.

14. George Brown Tindall, *The Disruption of the Solid South* (Athens: University of Georgia Press, 1972), 19.

15. Ibid., 47.

16. Dunn, *Roosevelt's Purge*, 46.

17. Paul H. Douglas, "The Prospects for a New Political Alignment," *American Political Science Review* 25 (1931): 907.

18. James T. Patterson, *Congressional Conservatism & the New Deal: The Growth of the Conservative Coalition in Congress, 1933–39* (Lexington: University of Kentucky Press, 1967), 13.

19. William E. Leuchtenburg, *The White House Looks South* (Baton Rouge: Louisiana State University Press, 2005), 49, 65; Dewey W. Grantham, Jr., "The South and the Reconstruction of American Politics," *Journal of American History* 2 (1966): 228.

20. William E. Leuchtenburg, *The White House Looks South*, 79.

21. Patterson, *Congressional Conservatism*, 70–71.

22. Ibid., 94.

23. J. B. Shannon, "Presidential Politics in the South: 1938, I," *Journal of Politics* 1 (1939): 149–50.

24. Dunn, *Roosevelt's Purge*, 72.

25. Leuchtenburg, *The White House Looks South*, 49.

26. P. Orman Ray, "The November Elections," *American Political Science Review* 13 (1919): 78–85. Like Roosevelt, Wilson disparaged the South's tendency to stand in the way of the liberalization of the Democratic Party, although he tended to keep his views quieter. Howard L. Reiter, "The Building of a Bifactional Structure: The Democrats in the 1940s," *Political Science Quarterly* 116 (2001): 110.

27. Dunn, *Roosevelt's Purge*, 23.

28. Ibid., 79.

29. DW-NOMINATE is discussed more fully in the Indroduction.

30. Dunn, 250.
31. Marian D. Irish, "The Proletarian South," *Journal of Politics* 2 (1940): 233.
32. Wilbur J. Cash, "Jehovah of the Tar Heels," *American Mercury* 17 (1929): 318.
33. Byron E. Shafer and Richard Johnston, *The End of Southern Exceptionalism: Class, Race, and Partisan Change in the Postwar South* (Cambridge, MA: Harvard University Press, 2006), 33–34.
34. Bernard Cosman, "Presidential Republicanism in the South, 1960," *Journal of Politics* 24 (1962): 305.
35. Shafer and Johnston, *End of Southern Exceptionalism*, 12.
36. Tindall, *Disruption of the Solid South*, 56.
37. Arthur N. Holcombe, "The Changing Outlook for a Realignment of Parties," *Public Opinion Quarterly* 10 (1946–1947): 466.
38. Tindall, *Disruption of the Solid South*, 56.
39. The process here is relatively simple: The GOP vote share for each year in the roughly 1,100 Southern counties is used as the dependent variable, and the Eisenhower vote share in those counties is used as an independent variable. This results in a linear equation, where the intercept represents the GOP share of the Stevenson vote, and where the GOP share of the Eisenhower vote can be deduced by setting the appropriate variable to 100 percent in the regression equation. The relationships are statistically significant in every year except for the 1964 election. The relationship carries further back into presidential history; in the interest of time, my study was discontinued in 1916.

    Post-1968, an additional independent variable is introduced for percentage of African Americans, based on estimates taken from http://www.census.gov/popest/archives/. This is because African Americans were not voting in large numbers in 1952 and hence are separate from the Eisenhower/Stevenson vote. Incidentally, the results suggest that the GOP did very poorly among African American voters in every year save 1976, which is consistent with what exit polls and experience would suggest.
40. Joseph A. Aistrup, "Republican Contestation of U.S. State Senate Elections in the South," *Legislative Studies Quarterly* 15 (1990): 227; Holcombe, "The Changing Outlook," 466; Alexander Heard, *A Two-Party South?* (Chapel Hill: University of North Carolina Press, 1952); Donald S. Strong, *Urban Republicanism in the South* (Tuscaloosa: University of Alabama, 1960); V. O. Key, Jr., *Politics, Parties and Pressure Groups*, 4th ed. (New York: Thomas Y. Crowell, 1964), 238–52.
41. Tindall, *Disruption of the Solid South*, 24.
42. Had Kennedy's Catholicism played a central role, we would expect to see wild shifts at the county level when we compare the 1956 and 1960 maps, much like what the country witnessed from 1924 to 1928. We do not see this. We have to exclude Mississippi, Louisiana, and South Carolina from our analysis because of "unpledged" slates of electors, but in the remaining eight states, Kennedy's share of the vote was within 20 points of Stevenson's in 97.4 percent of counties, within 5 percent in 49 percent of counties, and within 2 percent in one out of five Southern counties. This is roughly the same level of stability we see comparing 1952 to 1956, and that was with identical candidates from both parties on the ticket in both elections. From 1952 to 1956, Stevenson's 1956 vote share had varied less than 20 points from his 1952 share in 98.5 percent of counties, less than 5 points in 58.7 percent of counties, and less than 2 points in 27.2 percent of counties.

43. Herbert Brownell, "Eisenhower's Civil Rights Program: A Personal Assessment," *Presidential Studies Quarterly* 21 (1991): 235–37.

44. The following chart is the result of the author's calculations based on county-by-county data made available on uselectionatlas.org.

		Percentage of Times Republican Candidates Carried Southern Counties, 1964–1988							
		0	1	2	3	4	5	6	7
%	0 (n=588)	46%	30%	16%	6%	2%	0%	0%	0%
Times Ike/	1 (n=126)	26%	14%	21%	17%	16%	6%	0%	0%
Nixon Carried Southern	2 (n=160)	3%	8%	10%	27%	26%	21%	4%	0%
Counties, 1952–'60	3 (n=234)	0%	0%	2%	3%	6%	24%	28%	36%

45. Aistrup, "Republican Contestation," 228.

46. Frank B. Atkinson, *The Dynamic Dominion: Realignment and the Rise of Two-Party Competition in Virginia* (Lanham, MD: Rowman & Littlefield Publishers, Inc., 2006), 62–63.

47. Ibid., 89.

48. Tindall, *Disruption of the Solid South*, 59.

49. Burnham also notes that the Republican ran the strongest in the three urban centers (Mobile, Montgomery, and Birmingham), as well as in the traditionally Republican areas of the state. Walter Dean Burnham, "The Alabama Senatorial Election of 1962: Return of Inter-Party Competition," *Journal of Politics* 26 (1964): 799, 805.

50. Russell Merritt, "The Senatorial Election of 1962 and the Rise of Two-Party Politics in South Carolina," *South Carolina Historical Magazine* 98 (1997): 283.

51. Tindall, *Disruption of the Solid South*, 60.

52. Grantham, "The South and the Reconstruction of American Politics," 240.

53. Aistrup, "Republican Contestation," 232.

54. Senator Josiah Bailey of North Carolina put it best by railing against "new deacons" who have "come into the house which was built by others and intend to take possession and drive the builders out." Dunn, *Roosevelt's Purge*, 86.

55. Martin P. Wattenberg, "The Building of a Republican Regional Base in the South: The Elephant Crosses the Mason-Dixon Line," *Public Opinion Quarterly* 55 (1991): 427.

56. Hugh Davis Graham, "Richard Nixon and Civil Rights: Explaining an Enigma," *Presidential Studies Quarterly* 26 (1996): 93–95.

57. Wattenberg, "The Building of a Republican Regional Base," 426. The precise numbers are as follows:

Year	1952	1956	1960	1964	1968	1972	1976	1980	1984	1988
Percent Republican	18.3%	23.6%	22.9%	24%	27.3%	31.5%	30.4%	33.3%	45.9%	51%

58. Michael Barone and Grant Ujifusa, *The Almanac of American Politics, 1984* (Washington, DC: National Journal, 1983), 794.

59. Fred I. Greenstein and Raymond E. Wolfinger, "The Suburbs and Shifting Party Loyalties," *Public Opinion Quarterly* 22 (1958–1959): 473.
60. William H. Whyte, "The Transients," in Llewellyn Miller, ed., *Prize Articles of 1954* (New York: Ballantine Books, 1954); Louis B. Harris, *Is There a Republican Majority?* (New York: Harper, 1954), 122.
61. Scott Greer, "Catholic Voters and the Democratic Party," *Public Opinion Quarterly* 25 (1961): 624.
62. Angus Campbell and Homer C. Cooper, *Group Differences in Attitudes and Votes* (Ann Arbor: Survey Research Center, University of Michigan, 1956), 48.
63. In the South, it becomes difficult to tease out suburbs from city because city and suburb frequently occupy the same county. In the North and West, the county and city are frequently separate. Note that this is not meant to be an exhaustive list, just a fairly representative sample. The "key" counties examined are: CA—Orange, Riverside; CO—Adams, Jefferson; IL—DuPage, Lake; KS—Johnson; MD—Baltimore, Montgomery; MI—Macomb, Oakland; MO—Jefferson, St. Louis; NJ—Bergen, Morris; NY—Nassau, Suffolk, Westchester; PA—Bucks, Chester, Montgomery; VA—Arlington, Fairfax, Henrico; WI—Waukeesha.
64. Samuel Lubell, *Revolt of the Moderates* (New York: Harper, 1956), 112–14.
65. Samuel Lubell, *The Future of American Politics*, 2nd ed. (Garden City, NY: Doubleday Anchor Books, 1956), 83.
66. Michael Barone, *Our Country: The Shaping of America From Roosevelt to Reagan* (New York: The Free Press, 1992), 122.
67. "Life on the Newsfronts of the World," *Life*, October 3, 1938.
68. Dubin, *United States Congressional Elections*, 532.
69. Kevin Phillips, *The Emerging Republican Majority* (New Rochelle, NY: Arlington House, 1969), 152.
70. Charles Peters, *Five Days in Philadelphia: 1940, Wendell Willkie, and the Political Convention that Freed FDR to Win World War II* (New York: PublicAffairs, 2005), 45.
71. Phillips, *The Emerging Republican Majority*, 373.
72. Lubell, *The Future of American Politics*, 55.
73. David Pietrusza, *1960: LBJ vs. JFK vs. Nixon* (New York: Union Square Press, 2008), 12.
74. Ibid., 11–12.
75. Ibid., 63.
76. Ibid., 38, 49–50.
77. Charles J. Pach, Jr., and Elmo Richardson, *The Presidency of Dwight D. Eisenhower* (Lawrence: University Press of Kansas, 1991), 62–63.
78. Vincent P. deSantis, "The Presidential Election of 1952," 148–49.
79. Phillips, *The Emerging Republican Majority*, 69.
80. Pietrusza, *1960*, 50; Phillips, *The Emerging Republican Majority*, 72.
81. Phillips, *The Emerging Republican Majority*, 167.
82. Ibid., 77.
83. Ibid., 108.
84. Ibid., 343.
85. Gordon Tullock, "Nixon, Like Gore, Also Won Popular Vote, But Lost Election," *PS: Political Science and Politics* 37 (2004): 1–2; Brian J. Gaines, "Popular Myths about Popular Vote–Electoral College Splits," *PS: Political Science and Politics* 34 (2001): 71.
86. Harold I. Gullan, *The Upset That Wasn't: Harry S. Truman and the Crucial Election of 1948* (Lanham, MD: Ivan R. Dee, 1998), 60.

87. Lubell, *The Future of American Politics*, viii, 1.
88. Richard M. Scammon and Ben J. Wattenberg, *The Real Majority* (New York: Coward-McCann, 1970), 33.
89. DeSantis, "The Presidential Election of 1952," 136–37.
90. "Gallup and Fortune Polls," *Public Opinion Quarterly* 4 (1940): 83. Early editions of *Public Opinion Quarterly* reprinted all of Gallup's and Fortune's polling. These polls are all taken from early *Public Opinion Quarterly* issues.
91. Roper, "Politics of Three Decades," 370.
92. Michael Barone and Richard E. Cohen, *The Almanac of American Politics 2008: The Senators, the Representatives and the Governors: Their Records and Election Results, Their States and Districts* (Washington, DC: National Journal Group, 2007), 21.
93. Peters, *Five Days in Philadelphia*, 123.
94. "Gallup and Fortune Polls," *Public Opinion Quarterly* 5 (1941): 143.
95. Ibid., 139.
96. Gullan, *The Upset That Wasn't*, 160.
97. DeSantis, "The Presidential Election of 1952," 143.
98. Gullan, *The Upset That Wasn't*, 178.
99. DeSantis, "The Presidential Election of 1952," 149; Gullan, *The Upset That Wasn't*, 151; Barone, *Our Country*, 215. Polling revealed that voters preferred a Democrat to a Republican, 51 percent to 30 percent, "if hard times returned." This election may be the only one in the postwar era in which a faltering economy worked to the incumbent party's advantage.
100. Tom Wicker, *Dwight D. Eisenhower* (New York: Times Books, 2002), 3.
101. John Judis and Ruy Teixeira, *The Emerging Democratic Majority* (New York: Scribner, 2002), 25.
102. Everett Carll Ladd, Jr., et al., "The Polls: Taxing and Spending," *Public Opinion Quarterly* 43 (1979): 129.
103. Hazel Gaudet Erskine, "Polls: Some Gauges of Conservatism," *Public Opinion Quarterly* 28 (1964): 161.
104. Ladd et al., "Taxing and Spending," 127.
105. Keith T. Poole and Howard Rosenthal, *Congress: A Political-Economic History of Roll Call Voting* (New York: Oxford University Press, 1997), 62, 63, 83.
106. J. B. Shannon, "Presidential Politics in the South," *Journal of Politics* 3 (1948): 478.
107. Barone, *Our Country*, 165.
108. Gullan, *The Upset That Wasn't*, 4.
109. J. B. Shannon, "Presidential Politics in the South," 487.
110. Barone, *Our Country*, 185.
111. Gullan, *The Upset That Wasn't*, 205.

CHAPTER 3   THE RISE OF THE CLINTON COALITION

1. Arthur M. Schlesinger, Jr., "How McGovern Will Win," *New York Times Magazine*, July 30, 1972.
2. Gary C. Jacobson, "Explaining Divided Government: Why Can't the Republicans Win the House?" *PS: Political Science and Politics* 24 (1991): 640–43; Joel Lieske, "Cultural Issues and Images in the 1988 Presidential Campaign: Why the Democrats Lost. Again!" *PS: Political Science and Politics* 24 (1991): 180–87; David J. Smyth and Susan Washburn Taylor, "Why Do the Republicans Win the White House More

Often than the Democrats?" *Presidential Studies Quarterly* 22 (1992): 481–91; I. M. Destler, "The Myth of the 'Electoral Lock'," *PS: Political Science and Politics* 29 (1996): 491–94.

3. Frank B. Atkinson, *The Dynamic Dominion: Realignment and the Rise of Two-Party Competition in Virginia* (Lanham, MD: Rowman & Littlefield Publishers, Inc., 2006), 189–91.

4. Michael Barone, Grant Ujifusa, and Douglas Matthews, *The Almanac of American Politics: The Senators, the Representatives—Their Records, States and Districts. 1974* (Boston: Gambit, 1973), 926.

5. Michael Barone, Grant Ujifusa, and Douglas Matthews, *The Almanac of American Politics 1976: The Senators, the Representatives, the Governors—Their Records, States and Districts* (New York: E. P. Dutton & Co., Inc., 1975), 338–39.

6. David W. Rohde, *Parties and Leaders in the Postreform House* (Chicago: University of Chicago Press, 1991), 7–8.

7. Ibid., 22.

8. Ibid., 25.

9. Ibid., 23.

10. Ibid., 46.

11. Ibid., 59–60.

12. Dennis R. Hoover, et al., "Evangelicalism Meets the Continental Divide: Moral and Economic Conservatism in the United States and Canada," *Political Research Quarterly*, 55 (2002): 367.

13. Lou Dubose, Jan Reid, and Carl M. Cannon, *Boy Genius: Karl Rove, the Brains behind the Remarkable Political Triumph of George W. Bush* (New York: PublicAffairs, 2003), 157.

14. Corwin E. Smidt and James M. Penning, "A Party Divided? A Comparison of Robertson & Bush Delegates to the 1988 Michigan Republican State Convention," *Polity* 23 (1990): 131.

15. Ibid., 129, 131.

16. Rohde, *Parties and Leaders*, 47.

17. "The South Rises Again in Congress," *Time*, May 18, 1981, accessed January 28, 2011, http://www.time.com/time/magazine/article/0,9171,951659,00.html.

18. Jon F. Hale, "The Making of the New Democrats," *Political Science Quarterly* 110 (1995): 211.

19. John Judis and Ruy Teixeira, *The Emerging Democratic Majority* (New York: Scribner, 2002), 29.

20. Michael Takiff, *A Complicated Man: The Life of Bill Clinton as Told by Those Who Know Him* (New Haven, CT: Yale University Press, 2010), 93.

21. William Galston and Elaine C. Kamarck, *The Politics of Evasion: Democrats and the Presidency* (Washington, DC: Progressive Policy Institute, 1989), accessed February 14, 2011, http://www.ppionline.org/documents/Politics_of_Evasion.pdf, 18–19.

22. Ibid., 17.

23. Ibid.

24. Joe Klein, *The Natural: The Misunderstood Presidency of Bill Clinton* (New York: Broadway Books, 2002), 35.

25. Ibid., 35.

26. Judis and Teixeira, *Emerging Democratic Majority*, 131.

27. Seymour Martin Lipset, "The Significance of the 1992 Election," *PS: Political Science and Politics* 26 (1993): 13.

28. Klein, *The Natural*, 39.

29. Martin P. Wattenberg, "The Hollow Realignment Partisan Change in a Candidate-Centered Era," *Public Opinion Quarterly* 51 (1987): 14.

30. Ibid., 17.

31. Takieff, *A Complicated Man*, 138.

32. 1992 Democratic Party Platform, accessed March 23, 2011, http://www.udel.edu/htr/American/Texts/demoplat.html.

33. Wattenberg, "The Hollow Realignment," 41.

34. Ibid., 28.

35. Judis and Teixeira, *Emerging Democratic Majority*, 29.

36. Everett Carll Ladd, "The 1992 Vote for President Clinton: Another Brittle Mandate?" *Political Science Quarterly* 108 (1993): 3.

37. Walter Dean Burnham, *Voting in American Elections: The Shaping of the American Political Universe Since 1788* (Palo Alto, CA: Academia Press, 2010), 194.

38. Judis and Teixeira, *Emerging Democratic Majority*, 29.

39. Wattenberg, "The Hollow Realignment," 128–29.

40. George Gallup, Jr., *The Gallup Poll: Public Opinion 1993* (Wilmington, DE: Scholarly Resources, Inc., 1994), 153.

41. Dick Morris, *Power Plays: Win or Lose—How History's Great Political Leaders Play the Game* (New York: HarperCollins Publishers, 2002), 118.

42. Everett Carll Ladd, "The 1994 Congressional Elections: The Postindustrial Realignment Continues," *Political Science Quarterly* 110 (1995): 10; Jeffrey M. Stonecash and Mack D. Mariani, "Republican Gains in the House in the 1994 Elections: Class Polarization in American Politics," *Political Science Quarterly* 115 (2000): 102.

43. Gerald M. Pomper, "The Presidential Election," in *The Election of 1996*, ed. Gerald M. Pomper (Chatham, NJ: Chatham House Publishers, 1996), 197.

44. For a more thorough exploration of this thesis, see William G. Mayer, "The 1992 Elections & the Future of American Politics," *Polity* 25 (1993): 469.

45. Walter Dean Burnham, "Bill Clinton: Riding the Tiger," in *The Election of 1996*, ed. Pomper, 12.

46. Exit Polls, Election Results, *New York Times*, http://elections.nytimes.com/2008/results/president/exit-polls.html, accessed March 5, 2011.

47. Klein, *The Natural*, 16.

48. Congressional Quarterly Political Staff, *Politics in America 2000: The 106th Congress*, eds. Philip D. Duncan and Brian Nuttin (Washington, DC: CQ Press, 1999), 141.

49. Judis and Teixeira, *Emerging Democratic Majority*, 90.

50. Ibid., 1.

CHAPTER 4   THE LEFT STRIKES BACK!

1. John B. Judis and Ruy Teixeira, *The Emerging Democratic Majority* (New York: Scribner, 2002), 117.

2. Judis and Teixeira, *Emerging Democratic Majority*, 11.

3. Samuel Lubell, *The Future of American Politics* (Garden City, NY: Doubleday Anchor Books, 1956), 200.

4. V. O. Key, Jr., "A Theory of Critical Elections," *Journal of Politics* 1 (1955): 4.

5. V. O. Key, Jr., "Secular Realignment and the Party System," *Journal of Politics* 21 (1959): 198–210.

6. Evertt Carll Ladd, Jr., with Charles D. Hadley, *Transformations of the American Party System: Political Coalitions from The New Deal to the 1970s*, 2nd ed. (New York: W. W. Norton & Company, Inc., 1978), 24.
7. Judis and Teixeira, *Emerging Democratic Majority*, 12–17.
8. Ibid., 16–17.
9. For Judis and Teixeira, an ideopolis represents those metropolises where the cities and suburbs are increasingly interconnected and disproportionately inhabited by professionals. Fairfax County, Virginia, is the classic ideopoli—a suburb that is largely indistinguishable from the central city in many regards. Judis and Teixeira also include many college towns in their definition, such as Dane County, Wisconsin.
10. Judis and Teixeira, *Emerging Democratic Majority*, 5.
11. Ibid., 134.
12. Jeremy C. Pope and Jonathan Woon, "Measuring Changes in American Party Reputations, 1939–2004," *Political Research Quarterly* 62 (2009): 655–56.
13. Judis and Teixeira, *Emerging Democratic Majority*, 106.
14. Nader had actually challenged Clinton in 1996, receiving less than 1 percent of the vote.
15. Michael Kinsley, "The Art of Finger-Pointing: Why Wait Until Next Week? Let's Start Now," *Slate*, October 31, 2000, accessed March 1, 2001, http://www.slate.com/id/92290/.
16. Jacob Weisberg, "Why Gore (Probably) Lost," *Slate*, November 8, 2000, accessed March 1, 2011, http://www.slate.com/id/1006450/.
17. Judis and Teixeira, *Emerging Democratic Majority*, 141.
18. Ibid., 141.
19. "Exit Polls—Election Results 2008," accessed March 26, 2011, http://elections.nytimes.com/2008/results/president/exit-polls.html.
20. Ibid.
21. Ibid.
22. The later data points are derived from exit poll data, which have larger sample sizes and are probably more accurate than the NES.
23. For a reminder of how convoluted Kerry's war stance was, see William Saletan, "Would Kerry Vote Today for the Iraq War?" *Slate*, August 12, 2004, accessed March 26, 2011, http://www.slate.com/id/2105096/.
24. Kate Kenski, Bruce W. Hardy, and Kathleen Hall Jamieson, *The Obama Victory: How Media, Money, and Message Shaped the 2008 Election* (New York: Oxford University Press, 2010), 43–44.
25. Frank Newport et al., *Winning the White House, 2008: The Gallup Poll, Public Opinion, and the Presidency* (New York: Infobase Publishing, 2009), 193.
26. Hannah Goble and Peter M. Holm, "Breaking Bonds? The Iraq War and the Loss of Republican Dominance in National Security," *Political Research Quarterly* 62 (2009): 218.
27. John Heilemann and Mark Halperin, *Game Change: Obama and the Clintons, McCain and Palin, and the Race of a Lifetime* (New York: HarperCollins Publishers, 2010), 86.
28. Ibid., 46, 57.
29. Ibid., 42–43.
30. Ibid., 51.
31. Ibid., 35–37.
32. Ibid., 137–38.
33. Steve Chapman, "Democrats Make a Bad Trade," *Reason*, December 3, 2007, accessed February 15, 2011, http://reason.com/archives/2007/12/03/democrats-make-a-bad-trade.

34. Scott Moss, "Clinton: More Liberal?" *Politico*, February 18, 2008, accessed February 1, 2011, http://www.politico.com/news/stories/0208/8573.html.

35. David Greenberg, "Memo to Obama Fans: Clinton's Presidency Was Not a Failure," *Slate*, February 12, 2008, accessed February 11, 2011, http://www.slate.com/id/2183941/.

36. Ryan Lizza, "The Legacy Problem: Hillary and Her Rivals Take on the Clinton Administration," *New Yorker*, September 17, 2007, accessed January 5, 2011, http://www.newyorker.com/reporting/2007/09/17/070917fa_fact_lizza#ixzz1Hk0rrNdt.

37. Matt Bai, "The Clinton Referendum," *New York Times*, December 23, 2007, accessed March 15, 2001, http://www.nytimes.com/2007/12/23/magazine/23clintonism-t.html?ref=politics.

38. Ibid.

39. Markos Moulitsas, "The Calm before the Storm," *Daily Kos*, August 22, 2005, accessed February 8, 2011, http://www.dailykos.com/story/2005/08/22/140273/-The-calm-before-the-storm.

40. Lizza, "The Legacy Problem."

41. Heilemann and Halperin, *Game Change*, 151.

42. John Dickerson, "It's Your Party Now: Obama and the Death of Clintonism," *Slate*, June 3, 2008, accessed February 11, 2011, http://www.slate.com/id/2192825/.

43. Lizza, "The Legacy Problem."

44. Newport et al., *Winning the White House*, 198.

45. Ibid., 199.

46. Roger Simon, "Hillary the Unstoppable," *Politico*, September 13, 2007, accessed February 19, 2011, http://www.politico.com/news/stories/0907/5809.html. Jay Cost was one of the few pundits at the time to accurately note: "It's called a campaign. It has not yet begun. The real one, at least, has not yet begun....I am not arguing that Obama is going to win this battle. My point is simply that it is going to be one *hell* of a battle." Jay Cost, "Clinton Expands Her Lead," *RealClearPolitics.com*, October 3, 2007, accessed March 27, 2011, http://www.realclearpolitics.com/horseraceblog/2007/10/clinton_expands_her_lead.html.

47. Newport et al., *Winning the White House*, 219.

48. Dan Balz, "Clinton Provides an Opening in Debate," *Washington Post*, October 31, 2007, accessed March 15, 2007, http://voices.washingtonpost.com/44/2007/10/post-z66.html; Dan Balz, "No Done Deal: The Once 'Inevitable' Candidate Find Herself in a Tight Race," *Washington Post*, December 9, 2007.

49. "Exit Polls," accessed March 26, 2011, http://www.cnn.com/ELECTION/2008/primaries/results/epolls/#IADEM.

50. Inside the South, the Democratic primary was heavily polarized along racial and educational lines. Those two variables alone explain 80 percent of the variance in the county-wide votes for Clinton and Obama in the South.

51. John B. Judis, "The Next McGovern?" *New Republic*, April 23, 2008, accessed May 12, 2011, http://www.tnr.com/article/politics/the-next-mcgovern.

CHAPTER 5   MR. JACKSON VOTES FOR MR. CLAY

1. Evertt Carll Ladd, Jr., with Charles D. Hadley, *Transformations of the American Party System: Political Coalitions from the New Deal to the 1970s*, 2nd ed. (New York: W. W. Norton & Company, Inc., 1976), 293.

2. Kate Kenski, Bruce W. Hardy, and Kathleen Hall Jamieson, *The Obama Victory: How Media, Money, and Message Shaped the 2008 Election* (New York: Oxford University Press, 2010), 115.

3. David Axelrod, "Campaign Organization and Strategy," in *Electing the President 2008: The Annenberg Election Debriefing*, ed. Kathleen Hall Jamieson (Philadelphia: University of Pennsylvania Press, 2009), 71.

4. Lydia Saad, "Gallup Daily: No Bounce for Obama in Post-Biden Tracking, McCain Creeps Ahead, 46% to 44%," Gallup.com, August 26, 2008, accessed March 15, 2011, http://www.gallup.com/poll/109834/Gallup-Daily-Bounce-Obama-Post-Biden -Tracking.aspx.

5. Frank Newport et al., *Winning the White House, 2008: The Gallup Poll, Public Opinion, and the Presidency* (New York: Infobase Publishing, 2009), 423.

6. John Heilemann and Mark Halperin, *Game Change: Obama and the Clintons, McCain and Palin, and the Race of a Lifetime* (New York: HarperCollins Publishers, 2010), 240, 251.

7. "Candidate Support by Education among Whites," accessed March 15, 2011, http: //www.gallup.com/poll/108046/Candidate-Support-Education-Among-Whites.aspx.

8. Frank Newport et al., *Winning the White House, 2008*, 493.

9. Ibid., 497.

10. Ibid., 502.

11. "Candidate Support by Education among Whites."

12. Jeffrey M. Jones, "Republicans Still Face Enthusiasm Gap to Democrats: Slight Increase in Enthusiasm in Past Week," September 2, 2008, accessed March 15, 2011, http://www .gallup.com/poll/109966/republicans-still-face-enthusiasm-gap-democrats.aspx.

13. Frank Newport et al., *Winning the White House*, 492.

14. Peter Wallsten and Janet Hook, "Palin Bounce Has Democrats Off Balance: Some Fear Obama's More Aggressive Tone Could Enhance Her Appeal Among White, Blue-Collar Voters," *Los Angeles Times*, September 10, 2008, accessed March 15, 2011, http: //articles.latimes.com/2008/sep/10/nation/na-palineffect10.

15. Matt Stoller, "The Obama Campaign Is Out of Our Hands," *OpenLeft*, September 8, 2007, accessed March 15, 2011, http://www.openleft.com/diary/8043/.

16. Chris Bowers, "Maybe We Aren't Taking McCain Seriously Enough," *OpenLeft*, September 7, 2008, accessed March 15, 2011, http://www.openleft.com /diary/8037/.

17. Chris Bowers, "Average of Today's Polls," *OpenLeft*, September 8, 2008, accessed March 15, 2011, http://www.openleft.com/diary/8071/.

18. Jerome Armstrong, "I'm Feed [sic] Up With It.... Enough," *MyDD*, September 11, 2008, accessed March 15, 2011, http://mydd.com/2008/9/11/quotim-feed-up-with-it -enoughquot.

19. Frank Newport, "Democrats' Election Enthusiasm Far Outweighs Republicans': Different Pattern than Occurred in 2004," October 13, 2008, accessed March 15, 2011, http://www.gallup.com/poll/111115/democrats-election-enthusiasm-far-outweighs -republicans.aspx.

20. Kenski et al., *The Obama Victory*, 121.

21. Heilemann and Halperin, *Game Change*, 381.

22. Kenski et al., *The Obama Victory*, 190–91.

23. Ibid., 182.

24. Bill McInturff, "The Role of Polling," in *Electing the President 2008: The Annenberg Election Debriefing*, ed. Kathleen Hall Jamieson (Philadelphia: University of Pennsylvania Press, 2009), 89.

25. Ibid., 17.
26. John Woolley and Gerhard Peters, "The American Presidency Project," accessed March 15, 2011, http://www.presidency.ucsb.edu/data/popularity.php?pres=43&sort=time&dir ect=DESC&Submit=DISPLAY.
27. There is a time delay; because polls are typically conducted over several days, it can take a while for them to begin to reflect reality after a catastrophic event.
28. "In Face of Stiff Opposition, Dole Holds Her Ground, Adds to Modest Lead," *SurveyUSA*, September 8, 2008, accessed March 15, 2011, http://www.surveyusa.com /client/PollReport.aspx?g=4fd3b4f0–7649-4982–99df-fb2a2eb9c455.
29. Heilemann and Halperin, *Game Change*, 327.
30. E.g., Jackie Calmes and Megan Thee, "Voter Polls Find Obama Built a Broad Coalition," *New York Times*, November 4, 2008, accessed March 16, 2011, http://www.nytimes. com/2008/11/05/us/politics/05poll.html.
31. Andy Barr, "Dems Talk of 'Permanent Progressive Majority,'" *Politico*, November 7, 2008, accessed March 15, 2011, http://www.politico.com/news/stories/1108/15407. html.
32. Sam Tanenhaus, *The Death of Conservatism* (New York: Random House, Inc., 2009), 8, 114.
33. Dylan Loewe, *Permanently Blue: How Democrats Can End the Republican Party and Rule the Next Generation* (New York: Random House, Inc., 2010), 9, 54.
34. Jay Cost and Sean Trende, "Election Review, Part 1," *RealClearPolitics*, January 7, 2009, accessed March 15, 2009, http://www.realclearpolitics.com/articles/2009/01/election _review_part_1_1.html#1–1-6.
35. Ibid.
36. Ibid.
37. Kerry carried only four counties in this region that Clinton had not; Obama won these counties with 60 percent of the vote.
38. Jay Cost and Sean Trende, "Election Review, Part 2: The South Atlantic," *RealClearPolitics*, January 12, 2009, accessed March 15, 2011, http://www.realclear politics.com/articles/2009/01/election_review_part_ii_the_so.html.
39. Donald R. Deskins, Jr., Hanes Watson, Jr., and Sherman C. Puckett, *Presidential Elections, 1789–2008: County, State, and National Mapping of Election Data* (Ann Arbor: The University of Michigan Press, 2010).

CHAPTER 6   STORM CLOUDS

1. Harold I. Gullen, *The Upset That Wasn't: Harry S. Truman and the Crucial Election of 1948* (Lanham, MD: Ivan R. Dee, 1998), 223.
2. Richard Wolffe, *Revival: The Struggle for Survival Inside the Obama White House* (New York: Crown Publishers, 2010), 60–62.
3. Dan Balz and Haynes Johnson, *The Battle for America 2008: The Story of an Extraordinary Election* (New York: Penguin Group, 2009), 160.
4. Kate Kenski, Bruce W. Hardy, and Kathleen Hall Jamieson, *The Obama Victory: How Media, Money, and Message Shaped the 2008 Election* (New York: Oxford University Press, 2010), 20.
5. "Trends in Political Values and Core Attitudes, 1987–2007: Political Landscape More Favorable to Democrats," March 22, 2007, accessed March 17, 2011, http://people-press .org/reports/pdf/312.pdf.

6. Ibid.
7. Frank Newport et al., *Winning the White House, 2008: The Gallup Poll, Public Opinion, and the Presidency* (New York: Infobase Publishing, 2009), 513.
8. Kenski et al., *The Obama Victory*, 146.
9. Barack Obama, *The Audacity of Hope* (New York: Crown Publishers, 2006), 11.
10. Kenski et al., *The Obama Victory*, 244.
11. Ibid., 44, 244.
12. Frank Newport, ed., *The Gallup Poll: Public Opinion 2009* (Lanham, MD: Rowman & Littlefield Publishers, Inc., 2010), 60.
13. Ibid., 68–69.
14. Ibid., 72–73.
15. "President Obama Job Approval," *RealClearPolitics*, accessed March 21, 2011, http://real clearpolitics.com/epolls/other/president_obama_job_approval-1044.html.
16. Newport, *The Gallup Poll: Public Opinion 2009*, 200.
17. Ibid., 205.
18. Ibid., 200.
19. Ibid., 208, 227.
20. Ibid., 244.
21. Ibid., 253.
22. Ibid., 340.
23. Ibid., 353.
24. Ibid., 397, 405.
25. Even Harry Byrd admitted that John Dalton was "as good as elected" until he made a speech expressing some openness to taking on debt. Frank B. Atkinson, *The Dynamic Dominion: Realignment and the Rise of Two-Party Competition in Virginia* (Lanham, MD: Rowman & Littlefield Publishers, Inc., 2006), 76.
26. The strange career of Mills Godwin epitomizes the dances these shifts forced Democrats to perform. In the 1950s, he was an architect of the state's "massive resistance" response to segregation. In the 1960s, he reached out to African Americans and the AFL-CIO and received their endorsement; they provided his victory margin against Mountain Republican Linwood Holton. And in the 1970s, when Democrats nominated a very liberal candidate in Henry Howell, Godwin switched parties and was elected as the state's second Republican governor.
27. Amy Gardner, "'89 Thesis a Different Side of McDonnell: Va. GOP Candidate Wrote on Women, Marriage and Gays," *Washington Post*, August 30, 2009, accessed March 15, 2011, http://www.washingtonpost.com/wp-dyn/content/article/2009/08/29 /AR2009082902434_pf.html.
28. "Deeds on the Ropes on Taxes," http://www.youtube.com/watch?v=vE6d36a2gso& feature=player_embedded.
29. Sean Trende, "Can the Clinton Coalition Survive Obama?" *RealClearPolitics*, November 13, 2009, accessed January 15, 2011, http://www.realclearpolitics.com/articles/2009/11/13 /can_the_clinton_coalition_survive_the_age_of_obama_99046.html.
30. Patrick Murray, "Gov. Corzine and the Toll Hike, Take 2," *Monmouth University/ Gannett New Jersey Poll*, September 21, 2008, accessed March 12, 2011, http://www .monmouth.edu/polling/admin/polls/MUP18_3.pdf.
31. Patrick Murray, "Christie Builds Lead over Corzine," *Monmouth University/Gannett New Jersey Poll*, August 4, 2009, accessed March 12, 2011, http://www.monmouth.edu /polling/admin/polls/MUP27_1.pdf.
32. Claire Heininger and Josh Margolin, "Chris Christie Promises Change to a 'Broken' State in Campaign Kickoff," *NJ.com*, February 4, 2009, accessed March 17, 2011, http: //www.nj.com/news/index.ssf/2009/02/chris_christie_promises_change.html.

33. Michael Respoli, "GOP Gov. Candidate Chris Christie Condemns N.J. Public Schools as Gov. Corzine Heralds System," *NJ.com*, June 22, 2009, accessed March 25, 2011, http://www.nj.com/news/index.ssf/2009/06/gop_gov_candidate_chris_christ.html.

34. Independent Chris Daggett received about 6 percent of the vote statewide, so we have to allocate his vote to perform an apples-to-apples comparison.

35. Sean Trende, "Party Switchers Have Short Lifespans," *RealClearPolitics*, December 22, 2009, accessed March 1, 2011, http://realclearpolitics.blogs.time.com/2009/12/22/party-switchers-have-short-lifespans/.

36. Michael Barone and Richard E. Cohen, *The Almanac of American Politics 2010: The Senators, the Representatives, and the Governors: Their Records and Election Results, Their States and Districts* (Washington, DC: National Journal, 2009), 723.

37. "President Obama Job Approval," *RealClearPolitics*, accessed March 28, 2011, http://real clearpolitics.com/epolls/other/president_obama_job_approval-1044.html.

38. Wolffe, *Revival*, 52.

39. Ibid., 53.

CHAPTER 7   HURRICANE

1. Chuck Todd and Sheldon Gawiser, *How Barack Obama Won* (New York: Vintage Books, 2009), 132.

2. Stuart Rothenberg, "April Madness: Can GOP Win Back the House in 2010?" *RealClearPolitics*, April 24, 2009, accessed March 23, 2011, http://www.realclear politics.com/articles/2009/04/24/april_madness_can_gop_win_back_the_house_in_2010_96149.html.

3. Charlie Cook, "Obama's Midterm Exam," *Cook Political Report*, May 2, 2009, accessed March 23, 2011, http://www.cookpolitical.com/node/4237.

4. Chris Cillizza, "Immigration as an Emerging Electoral Issue," *Washington Post*, May 13, 2010, accessed March 23, 2011, http://voices.washingtonpost.com/thefix/morning-fix/1pa-senate-2-with-just.html.

5. Ronald Brownstein, "Southern Exposure," *National Journal*, May 23, 2009, accessed March 20, 2011, http://www.magnetmail.net/images/clients/NJG_EVENTS/attach/NJ_Southern_Exposure_090523.pdf.

6. Ibid.

7. Judis and Teixeira, *Emerging Democratic Majority*, 5.

8. "Partisan Voting Index: Districts of the 111th Congress, Arranged by PVI Value, Most Republican to Most Democratic," *Cook Political Report*, accessed March 20, 2011, http://www.cookpolitical.com/sites/default/files/pvivalue.pdf.

9. Stuart Rothenberg, "Can Democrats Get Re-Elected by Voting Against Obama?" *RealClearPolitics*, July 10, 2009, accessed March 20, 2011, http://www.realclear politics.com/articles/2009/07/10/can_democrats_get_re-elected_by_voting_against_obama_97380.html.

10. Todd and Gawiser, *How Barack Obama Won*, 36.

11. 2010 National House Exit Poll, accessed March 20, 2011, http://www.cnn.com/ELECTION/2010/results/polls/#USH00p1.

12. Todd and Gawiser, *How Barack Obama Won*, 35; 2010 National House Exit Poll, accessed March 20, 2011, http://www.cnn.com/ELECTION/2010/results/polls/#USH00p1.

13. Todd and Gawiser, *How Barack Obama Won*, 33; 2010 National House Exit Poll, accessed March 20, 2011, http://www.cnn.com/ELECTION/2010/results/polls/#USH00p1.

14. 2010 National House Exit Poll, accessed March 20, 2011, http://www.cnn.com/ELECTION/2010/results/polls/#USH00p1.

15. Todd and Gawiser, *How Barack Obama Won*, 29.

16. Todd and Gawiser, *How Barack Obama Won*, 34; 2010 National House Exit Poll, accessed March 20, 2011, http://www.cnn.com/ELECTION/2010/results/polls/#USH00p1.

17. 2010 National House Exit Poll, accessed March 20, 2011, http://www.cnn.com /ELECTION/2010/results/polls/#USH00p1.

18. Given the wave elections of 2006 and 2008, this probably gives us a pretty good look at the districts that are at least "open" to electing a Democrat: this is a comprehensive look at "swing" and "Democratic" districts.

19. Michael Baker, "Oklahoma Elections: Republican Shocker in Little Dixie," *NewsOK*, November 4, 2010, accessed April 22, 2010, http://newsok.com/oklahoma-elections -republican-shocker-in-little-dixie/article/3510961.

20. Trende, "Assessing the Obama Coalition," 2011, http://www.realclearpolitics.com /articles/2010/11/16/assessing_the_obama_coalition_107969.html.

21. All numbers here are taken from StateVote, "2011 State and Legislative Partisan Composition," accessed March 15, 2011, http://www.ncsl.org/documents /statevote/2010_Legis_and_State_post.pdf; StateVote, "2010 State and Legislative Partisan Composition Prior to the Election," http://www.ncsl.org/documents /statevote/2010_Legis_and_State_pre.pdf.

22. Michael J. Dubin, *Party Affiliations in the State Legislatures: A Year by Year Summary, 1796–2006* (Jefferson, NC: McFarland & Company, Inc., 2007), 16–17, 141.

23. Ibid., 122–23.

24. Ibid., 82–83.

CHAPTER 8   THE GOP AND THE LATINO VOTE

1. *New York Times*, November 9, 1934.

2. Aaron Gould Sheinin, "Updated: Two Black Democrats Bolt Party for GOP," *Atlanta Journal-Constitution*, December 9, 2010, accessed March 30, 2011, http://blogs.ajc.com /georgia_elections_news/2010/12/09/black-county-commissioner-switches-parties- joins-gop/.

3. Kevin Phillips, *The Emerging Republican Majority* (New Rochelle, NY: Arlington House, 1969), 283–85.

4. David L. Leal et al., "The Latino Vote in the 2004 Election," *PSOnline*, accessed March 24, 2011, http://faculty.washington.edu/mbarreto/papers/2004vote.pdf.

5. "We asked…You told us: Hispanic Origin," October 1992, accessed March 7, 2011, http://www.census.gov/apsd/cqc/cqc7.pdf.

6. "U.S. Summary 2000," July 2002, accessed March 28, 2011, http://www.census.gov /prod/2002pubs/c2kprof00-us.pdf.

7. John Judis and Ruy Teixeria, *The Emerging Democratic Majority* (New York: Scribner, 2002), 38.

8. Alan I. Abramowitz, "Deja Vu All Over Again? Why a Repeat of 1994 Is Highly Unlikely," accessed March 31, 2011, http://www.centerforpolitics.org/crystalball/articles /aia2009092402/.

9. A special thanks to Jay Cost for sharing this observation.

10. In 2008, about 37 percent of whites self-identified as conservative, versus 29 percent of Latinos and 20 percent of African Americans. About 20 percent of whites self- identified as liberal, compared to 26 percent of Latinos and 28 percent of African Americans.

11. Noel Ignatiev, *How the Irish Became White* (New York: Routledge Classics, 1995). Regardless of the merits of Ignatiev's argument of *how* the Irish became white, his argument that they were once not considered white is intriguing and fairly compelling.

12. *Rollins v. State*, 18 Ala. App. 354, 92 So. 35 (1922). For a more thorough documentation of American attitudes toward turn-of-the-century immigrants, see David R. Roediger, *Working Toward Whiteness: The Strange Journey from Ellis Island to the Suburbs* (New York: Basic Books, 2005).

13. Richard D. Alba, *Italian Americans: Into the Twilight of Ethnicity* (New York: Prentice Hall, 1985).

14. Karen M. Kaufmann, "Black and Latino Voters in Denver: Responses to Each Other's Political Leadership," *Political Science Quarterly* 118 (2003): 110.

15. Albert R. Hunt, "Republicans Ignore Past Anti-Immigrant Debacles," *Bloomberg Businessweek*, May 23, 2010, accessed March 29, 2011, http://www.businessweek.com /news/2010–05-23/republicans-ignore-past-anti-immigrant-debacles-albert-r-hunt .html; Judis and Texieira, *Emerging Democratic Majority*, 83–85.

16. Markos Moulitsas, "Immigration Law Is Definitely Arizona's Prop 187," *Daily Kos*, April 27, 2010, accessed March 2, 2011, http://www.dailykos.com/story/2010/4/27/861239 /-Immigration-law-is-definitely-Arizonas-Prop-187.

17. Michael J. Dubin, *Party Affiliations in the State Legislatures: A Year by Year Summary, 1796–2006* (Jefferson, NC: McFarland & Company, Inc., 2007), 28.

18. "Ballot Propositions 187, 209, and 227: California's Ongoing Experiment with Direct Democracy, Propositions 187, 209, and 227," *JRank.org*, http://www.jrank.org/cultures /pages/3625/Ballot-Propositions-187–209-227.html.

19. M. V. Hood III, Irwin L. Morris, and Kurt A. Shirkey, " '¡Quedate o Vente!': Uncovering the Determinants of Hispanic Public Opinion toward Immigration," *Political Research Quarterly* 50 (1997): 640.

20. $p=2.70246 \times 10^{-13}$.

21. Because wealth and education correlate so heavily, it was necessary to run the regressions separately.

22. Ryan L. Classen, "Political Opinion and Distinctiveness: The Case of Hispanic Ethnicity," *Political Research Quarterly* 57 (2004): 609.

23. Classen, "Political Opinion and Distinctiveness," 616.

24. Michael Barone, *Our Country: The Shaping of America from Roosevelt to Reagan* (New York: The Free Press, 1990), 27.

25. Judis and Teixeira, *Emerging Democratic Majority*, 61.

26. Kaufmann, "Black and Latino Voters in Denver," 115.

27. Raphael J. Sonenshein and Susan H. Pinkus, "The Dynamics of Latino Political Incorporation: The 2001 Los Angeles Mayoral Election as Seen in 'Los Angeles Times' Exit Polls," *PS: Political Science and Politics* 35 (2002): 68.

28. Sonenshein and Pinkus, "The Dynamics of Latino Political Incorporation," 69.

29. Ibid., 70.

30. Ibid., 73.

31. Raphael J. Sonenshein and Susan H. Pinkus, "Latino Incorporation Reaches the Urban Summit: How Antonio Villaraigosa Won the 2005 Los Angeles Mayor's Race," in *PS: Political Science and Politics* 4 (2005): 718–19.

32. Karen M. Kaufmann, "Cracks in the Rainbow: Group Commonality as a Basis for Latino and African-American Political Coalitions," *Political Research Quarterly* 56 (2003): 205–06. This controls for potential racial differences between members of groups.

33. Ibid., 581–82.
34. John Wagner, *Washington Post*, March 11, 2011, accessed March 29, 2011, http://voices .washingtonpost.com/local-breaking-news/maryland/md-house-kills-same-sex-marria .html.
35. David L. Leal et al., "The Latino Vote in the 2004 Election," *PS: Political Science and Politics* 38 (2005): 41.
36. Matt Barreto, "Proving the Exit Polls Wrong—Harry Reid Did Win Over 90% of the Latino Vote," *Latino Decisions*, November 15, 2010, accessed March 29, 2011, http://latino decisions.wordpress.com/2010/11/15/proving-the-exit-polls-wrong-harry-reid-did-win-over-90-of-the-latino-vote/; Matt Barreto, "Proving the Exit Polls Wrong 2: Jan Brewer Did Not Win 28% of the Latino Vote," November 29, 2010, accessed March 29, 2011, http://latinodecisions.wordpress.com/2010/11/29/proving-the-exit-polls-wrong -2-jan-brewer-did-not-win-28-of-the-latino-vote/.
37. Gary Segura and Matt Barreto, "How the National Exit Poll Badly Missed the Latino Vote in 2010," *Latino Decisions*, November 4, 2010, accessed March 29, 2011, http: //latinodecisions.wordpress.com/2010/11/04/how-the-national-exit-poll-badly-missed -the-latino-vote-in-2010/.
38. Warren J. Mitofsky and Gordon Tullock, "The Latino Vote in 2004," *PS: Political Science and Politics* 38 (2005): 187–88.

CHAPTER 9   SUBURBIA VS. THE WHITE WORKING CLASS, AND THE YOUTH VOTE

1. Herbert H. Hyman and Paul B. Sheatsley, "The Political Appeal of President Eisenhower," *Public Opinion Quarterly* 17 (Winter, 1953–1954): 482.
2. Carl M. Cannon, "Youth Vote: Dems' Secret Weapon 40 Years in the Making?" *RealClearPolitics*, March 25, 2011, accessed March 31, 2011, http://www.realclearpolitics .com/articles/2011/03/25/youth_vote_dems_delayed_time_release_capsule.html.
3. Morley Winograd and Michael D. Hais, *Millennial Makeover: MySpace, YouTube & the Future of American Politics* (New Brunswick, NJ: Rutgers University Press, 2008), 23–24.
4. Ibid., 31.
5. Ibid., ch. 2.
6. Chuck Todd and Sheldon Gawiser, *How Barack Obama Won* (New York: Vintage Books, 2009), 31.
7. David S. Broder, *The Party's Over: The Failure of Politics in America* (New York: Harper & Row, 1971), 204–08.
8. Everett Carll Ladd, Jr., *Transformations of the American Party System: Political Coalitions from the New Deal to the 1970s*, 2nd ed. (New York: W. W. Norton & Company, Inc., 1978), 7.
9. Publius, "Party ID," *TheNextRight*, May 22, 2009, accessed March 1, 2011, http://www .thenextright.com/publius/party-id.
10. William Galston, "Colorado vs. Ohio: Two Possible Reelection Strategies for Obama, Only One of Which Can Succeed," *New Republic*, February 23, 2011, accessed March 31, 2011, http://www.tnr.com/article/the-vital-center/83993/obama-2012-reelection -colorado-ohio.
11. John B. Judis, "The Unnecessary Fall: A Counter-History of the Obama Presidency," *New Republic*, August 12, 2010, accessed January 26, 2011, http://www.tnr.com/article /politics/magazine/76972/obama-failure-polls-populism-recession-health-care.

CHAPTER 10   IT WASN'T JUST THE ECONOMY, STUPID

1. Quoted in Michael Lewis-Beck and Tom W. Rice, "Forecasting U.S. House Elections," *Legislative Studies Quarterly* 9 (1984): 481–83; Mann and Ornstein, "The 1982 Election: What Will It Mean?" *Public Opinion* (June/July 1981): 48.

2. David R. Mayhew, *Electoral Realignments: A Critique of an American Genre* (New Haven, CT: Yale University Press, 2002), 154–59.

3. Sean Trende, "Is a 2010 Republican Comeback Really Impossible?" *RealClearPolitics*, May 12, 2009, accessed February 11, 2011, http://www.realclearpolitics.com /articles/2009/05/12/is_a_2010_republican_comeback_really_impossible_96455.html; Paul Bedard and Nikki Schwab, "Nate Silver Sees Major Gains for GOP in 2010," *U.S. News & World Report*, August 13, 2009, accessed February 11, 2011, http://www.usnews .com/news/blogs/washington-whispers/2009/08/13/nate-silver-sees-major-gains-for -gop-in-2010.

4. United States Bureau of Economic Analysis, accessed March 12, 2011, http://www.bea .gov/national/nipaweb/TableView.asp?SelectedTable=58&ViewSeries=NO&Java=no& Request3Place=N&3Place=N&FromView=YES&Freq=Qtr&FirstYear=2004&LastYea r=2010&3Place=N&Update=Update&JavaBox=no#Mid.

5. Alan I. Abramowitz, "It's Monica, Stupid: The Impeachment Controversy and the 1996 Midterm Election," *Legislative Studies Quarterly* 26 (2001): 211–26.

6. Harold I. Gullan, *The Upset That Wasn't: Harry S. Truman and the Crucial Election of 1948* (Lanham, MD: Ivan R. Dee, 1998), 151.

7. Michael Barone and Richard E. Cohen, *The Almanac of American Politics 2010: The Senators, the Representatives, and the Governors: Their Records and Election Results, Their States and Districts* (Washington, DC: National Journal, 2009), 55.

8. Philip D. Duncan and Christine C. Lawrence, *Politics in America 1998: The 105th Congress* (Washington, DC: CQ Press, 1997), 20.

9. Michael Barone and Richard E. Cohen, *The Almanac of American Politics 2004: The Senators, the Representatives, and the Governors: Their Records and Election Results, Their States and Districts* (Washington, DC: National Journal, 2003), 71.

10. Barone and Cohen, *The Almanac of American Politics 2010*, 1388, 1392, 1396.

11. Duncan and Lawrence, *Politics in America 1998*, 1344, 1350, 1356.

12. Barone and Cohen, *The Almanac of American Politics 2010*, 1491, 1495, 1499.

13. Duncan and Lawrence, *Politics in America 1998*, 1557, 830.

14. Barone and Cohen, *The Almanac of American Politics 2004*, 1720, 934.

15. Barone and Cohen, *The Almanac of American Politics 2010*, 1601, 880.

16. Barone and Cohen, *The Almanac of American Politics 2004*, 1668; Barone and Cohen, *The Almanac of American Politics 2010*, 1553.

17. *The Cook Political Report's Partisan Voting Index (PVI)*, April 9, 2009, accessed February 5, 2011, http://www.cookpolitical.com/sites/default/files/2008pvisummary.pdf.

18. Lewis-Beck and Rice, "Forecasting U.S. House Elections," 24; Randall J. Jones and Alfred G. Cuzán, "A Retrospective on Forecasting Midterm Elections to the U.S. House of Representatives," *Foresight*, Fall 2006, accessed March 31, 2011, http://uwf .edu/govt/documents/FS.Issue5.Jones.Cuzan.pdf.

19. Brendan Nyhan, "Judis vs. Judis on Presidents and the Economy," August 13, 2010, accessed March 6, 2011, http://www.brendan-nyhan.com/blog/2010/08/judis-vs-judis -on-presidents-and-the-economy.html.

20. Alan I. Abramowitz, "Partisan Redistricting and the 1982 Congressional Elections," *Journal of Politics* 45 (1983): 767–70.

21. Michael Barone and Grant Ujifusa, *The Almanac of American Politics 1984: The President, the Senators, the Representatives, the Governors: Their Records and Election Results, Their States and Districts* (Washington, DC: National Journal, 1983), 372.

22. Michael Barone, *Our Country: The Shaping of America From Roosevelt to Reagan* (New York: The Free Press, 1992), 625.

23. Michael Barone and Grant Ujifusa, *The Almanac of American Politics 1982: The President, the Senators, the Representatives, the Governors: Their Records and Election Results, Their States and Districts* (Washington, DC: Barone & Company, 1981), 114; Barone and Ujifusa, *Almanac of American Politics 1984*, 128.

24. Barone, *Our Country*, 625, 758, n. 7.

25. John Judis, "Defending 'The Unnecessary Fall of Barack Obama': Was I Too Harsh on the President?" *New Republic*, August 25, 2010, accessed January 15, 2011, http://www .tnr.com/article/politics/77204/unnecessary-fall-barack-obama-response.

26. *Rothenberg Political Report*, November 29, 2006, 3–4.

27. Jonathan Chait, "How to Tell If Obama Blew the Election, Or If It Was Blown At All," *New Republic*, October 29, 2010, accessed March 13, 2011, http://www.tnr.com/blog /jonathan-chait/78761/how-tell-if-obama-blew-the-election-or-if-it-was-blown-all.

28. *Democratic Strategist*, accessed March 15, 2011, http://www.thedemocraticstrategist .org/psrw/2010/11/political_science_research_wat_3.php.

29. Jay P. Greene, "Forewarned before Forecast: Presidential Election Forecasting Models and the 1992 Election," *PS: Political Science and Politics* 26 (1993): 17–21; James E. Campbell, "The Referendum That Didn't Happen: The Forecasts of the 2000 Presidential Election," *PS: Political Science and Politics* 34 (2001): 33–38; Randall J. Jones and Alfred G. Cuzán, "A Retrospective on Forecasting Midterm Elections to the U.S. House of Representatives," *Foresight*, Fall 2006, accessed March 31, 2011, http://uwf .edu/govt/documents/FS.Issue5.Jones.Cuzan.pdf.

30. Alan I. Abramowitz and Jeffrey A. Segal, "Beyond Willie Horton and the Pledge of Allegiance: National Issues in the 1988 Elections," *Legislative Studies Quarterly* 15 (1990): 565–80; Alan I. Abramowitz, "It's Monica, Stupid: Voting Behavior in the 1998 Midterm Election," *Legislative Studies Quarterly* 28 (2001): 211–26.

31. *CBS/NY Times Poll*, "National Survey of Tea Party Supporters," April 5–12, 2010, accessed March 31, 2011, http://s3.amazonaws.com/nytdocs/docs/312/312.pdf.

32. Democracy Corps, "Grim Stability Will Require Race-by-Race Fight," July 8, 2010, accessed February 3, 2011, http://www.democracycorps.com/wp-content/files /DC1006292010.political.FINAL_.pdf.

CHAPTER 11   BEYOND REALIGNMENT

1. Quoted in R. Hal Williams, *Realigning America: McKinley, Bryan and the Remarkable Election of 1896* (Lawrence: University Press of Kansas, 2010), 24.

2. Richard M. Scammon and Ben J. Wattenberg, *The Real Majority: An Extraordinary Examination of the American Electorate* (New York: Coward McCann & Geoghegan, 1971).

3. Lou Harris, *The Anguish of Change* (New York: W. W. Norton, 1973).

4. Everett Carll Ladd, Jr., *Transformations of the American Party System: Political Coalitions from the New Deal to the 1970s*, 2nd ed. (New York: W. W. Norton & Company, Inc., 1978). The book was initially published in 1975.

5. Martin P. Wattenberg, *The Decline of American Political Parties, 1952–1996* (Cambridge, MA: Harvard University Press, 1998).
6. V. O. Key, Jr., "A Theory of Critical Elections," *Journal of Politics* 1 (1955): 11; Walter Dean Burnham, *Critical Elections and the Mainsprings of American Politics* (New York: W. W. Norton & Company, 1971), 4–5.
7. Burnham, *Critical Elections*, 256.
8. Burnham, *Critical Elections*, 27; James L. Sundquist, *Dynamics of the Party System: Alignment and Realignment of Political Parties in the United States* (Washington, DC: Brookings Institution Press, 1983), 93, 298–99.
9. David R. Mayhew, *Electoral Realignments: A Critique of an American Genre* (New Haven, CT: Yale University Press, 2002), 37; John Judis and Ruy Teixeira, *The Emerging Democratic Majority* (New York: Scribner, 2002), 14.
10. Mayhew, *Electoral Realignments*, 20–21.
11. Jerome M. Clubb, William H. Flanigan, and Nancy Zingale, *Partisan Realignment: Voters, Parties, and Government in American History* (Beverly Hills, CA: Safe, 1980), 162, cited in Mayhew, *Electoral Realignments*, 27.
12. John Gerring, *Party Ideologies in America: 1828–1996* (Cambridge, UK: Cambridge University Press, 1998), ch. 7.
13. Walter Dean Burnham, *Voting in American Elections: The Shaping of the American Political Universe Since 1788* (Palo Alto, CA: Academia Press, 2010), 86–110. The potential electorate from 2008 is estimated based upon a fairly constant trend in the size of the potential electorate over the past several elections.
14. "1952: A War Hero Leads GOP to Victory," *NPR*, accessed March 22, 2011, http://www.npr.org/news/national/election2000/conventions/past.eisenhower.html.
15. Mayhew, *Electoral Realignments*, 60–61.
16. Burnham, *Critical Elections*, 15.
17. Mayhew, *Electoral Realignments*, 55–59.
18. Ibid., 59.
19. Key, "A Theory of Critical Elections," 317.
20. Mayhew, *Electoral Realignments*, 161.
21. Ibid., 12.
22. Ibid., 14.
23. Ibid., 24.
24. Ibid., 24.
25. Ibid., 152.

CONCLUSION   2012 AND BEYOND

1. Roger Simon, "Obama Faces Problem On Left, Not Right," *Politico*, April 12, 2011, accessed May 16, 2011, http://dyn.politico.com/printstory.cfm?uuid=937F283E-37D4–46DC-BA8E-73C99C198227.
2. Jeffrey M. Jones, "Obama Approval Slips Among Blacks, Hispanics in March," *Gallup*, April 7, 2011, accessed May 16, 2011, http://www.gallup.com/poll/146981/Obama-Approval-Slips-Among-Blacks-Hispanics-March.aspx.
3. George Gallup, Jr., *The Gallup Poll: Public Opinion 1993* (Wilmington, DE: Scholarly Resources, Inc., 1994), 107.
4. http://www.census.gov/compendia/statab/rankings.html.

5. Jonathan Chait, "Handicapping Obama In 2012," *New Republic*, February 15, 2011, accessed May 16, 2011, http://www.tnr.com/blog/jonathan-chait/83499/handicapping-obama-in-2012.
6. Sean Trende, "Getting Real About Obama's Chances, Part II," *RealClearPolitics*, April 22, 2011, accessed March 16, 2011, http://www.realclearpolitics.com/articles/2011/04/22/getting_real_about_obamas_chances_part_ii_109630.html.
7. Ibid.

INDEX